# Rites of Passage:
# How Today's Jews Celebrate, Commemorate, and Commiserate

## Studies in Jewish Civilization
## Volume 21

Proceedings of the
Twenty-First Annual Symposium
of the Klutznick Chair in Jewish Civilization-
Harris Center for Judaic Studies

October 26-27, 2008

# Rites of Passage: How Today's Jews Celebrate, Commemorate, and Commiserate

## Studies in Jewish Civilization
## Volume 21

### Editor:
### Leonard J. Greenspoon

The Klutznick Chair in Jewish Civilization-
Harris Center for Judaic Studies
The Kripke Center for the Study of Religion and Society

Purdue University Press
West Lafayette, Indiana

Library of Congress Cataloging-in-Publication Data

Rites of passage : how today's Jews celebrate, commemorate, and commiserate /
editor, Leonard J. Greenspoon.
    p. cm. -- (Studies in Jewish civilization ; v. 21)
Includes bibliographical references.
ISBN 978-1-55753-577-1
1. Judaism--Customs and practices. 2. Life cycle, Human--Religious aspects--
Judaism. 3. Life change events--Religious aspects--Judaism. 4. Jewish way of life.
I. Greenspoon, Leonard J. (Leonard Jay)
BM700.R45 2010
296.4'4--dc22
                                              2010021856

# Table of Contents

Acknowledgements ............................................................ vii

Editor's Introduction ....................................................... ix

Contributors ................................................................ xvii

"What Makes a Bat Mitzvah Blossom": Pre-Bat Mitzvah Rituals for
    Daughters and Mothers ................................................ 1
*Penina Adelman*

More Bar Than Mitzvah: Anxieties over Bar Mitzvah Receptions in
    Postwar America ..................................................... 9
*Rachel Kranson*

Becoming Orthodox Women: Rites of Passage in the Orthodox
    Community ............................................................ 25
*Leslie Ginsparg Klein*

Talking about the Jewish Wedding Ritual: Issues of Gender, Power,
    and Social Control ................................................. 33
*Irit Koren*

The Making of a Rabbi: *Semichah* Ordination from Moses to Grosses .............. 57
*Jonathan Gross*

Perspectives on Evaluating New Jewish Rituals ........................... 63
*Vanessa Ochs*

Memory, Questions and Definitions: Images of Old and
    New Rites of Passage ............................................... 71
*Ori Z. Soltes*

A Need for New Rituals? American Judaism and
    the Holocaust ...................................................... 127
*Oliver Leaman*

Karaism: An Alternate Form of Jewish Celebration ...................... 141
*Daniel J. Lasker*

Without a *Minyan*: Creating a Jewish Life in a Small Midwestern
Town ....................................................................................... 155
*Daniel Mandell, Barbara Smith-Mandell, and Jerrold Hirsch*

Raising the Bar, Maximizing the Mitzvah: Jewish Rites of
Passage for Children with Autism ......................................... 187
*Steven Puzarne*

# Acknowledgements

The Twenty-First Annual Klutznick-Harris Symposium took place in Omaha, Nebraska, on October 26 and 27, 2008. Like this volume, it was titled "Rites of Passage: How Today's Jews Celebrate, Commemorate, and Commiserate."

The first Symposium that I organized and oversaw was held in October 1996. That may have been my rite of passage as holder of the Klutznick Chair in Jewish Civilization at Creighton University. By the time we began planning our twenty-first Symposium, we had developed—and continued to perfect— our own set of rituals, from deciding on a topic and formulating our Call for Papers, through evaluating proposals and determining travel schedules, to reserving hotel rooms, arranging for shuttles, and ordering food.

It is not a task for the faint of heart or those averse to detail. And it is most decidedly not a task for one person. For several years, I have been blessed with the most accommodating and understanding colleagues in the entire world (within or outside of academia): Dr. Jean Cahan, director of the Harris Center for Judaic Studies at the University of Nebraska-Lincoln; Dr. Ronald Simkins, director of the Kripke Center for the Study of Religion and Society at Creighton; and Mrs. Fran Minear, who works with both Ron and me. Additionally, Mary Sue Grossman, director of operations and programming for the Omaha Jewish Federation's Center for Jewish Education, insures that everything runs smoothly at the Jewish Community Center, where our presentations take place on Sunday. A committed group of individuals works with us on Monday for an equally smooth series of events on the Creighton campus.

This volume marks the beginning of a new collaboration with the Purdue University Press, whose director Charles Watkinson has extended every possible professional and personal courtesy to make us feel at home among the growing number of Jewish Studies publications of his Press. Special thanks also go to our colleague Zev Garber, who, acting in the best tradition of "matchmaking," brought together our Series and the Purdue University Press. May this new venture by mutually beneficial and satisfying!

In addition to the Harris Center, the Kripke Center, and the Jewish Federation of Omaha, this Symposium was nourished and supported by the continuing generosity of the following:

> The Ike and Roz Friedman Foundation
> The Riekes Family
> The Creighton College of Arts and Sciences

Creighton University Committee on Lectures, Films, and Concerts
The Gary Javitch Family Foundation
The Center for Jewish Education
The Henry Monsky Lodge of B'nai B'rith
The Dr. Bruce S. Bloom Memorial Endowment
and Others

Leonard J. Greenspoon
Omaha, Nebraska
May 2010
ljgrn@creighton.edu

# Editor's Introduction

It is characteristic of religions that they develop and maintain rituals through which the community celebrates or commemorates significant events. Typically, individuals or family units within the community also make use of rituals to mark important milestones in their lives. The communal celebrations or commemorations are generally laid out on the calendar in an annual cycle; naturally, most individual or family occasions are intended as once-in-a-lifetime events.

Thus, for someone actively involved in a religious community, the calendar is regularly filled with a series of activities that add meaning and bring a sense of belonging that extends from the individual to the family to the local—and often the national and international—community, and vice versa. Nowhere is this "rhythm" of life more richly experienced or minutely observed than in the Jewish community.

Our focus in this volume is on what scholars tend to call "rites of passage." Most people speak of them simply as life cycle events or milestones. Jews like to speak of *simchas*, when there's something—birth, Bar or Bat Mitzvah, or wedding, for example—to celebrate. Whatever we call them, such rituals have the power to connect us with generations past as well as with our contemporaries. In this respect, rites of passage may be viewed as both conservative and dynamic. In fact, it is the interplay between these two impulses (if you will) that forms the unifying thread among the articles contained in this collection.

In the process of describing and analyzing a wide variety of data, each author also comes to grips, some more explicitly than others, with basic questions such as: How do rituals originate and develop? Why do some rituals become successful and long lasting, while others fall to the wayside? What happens to a ritual when its religious community (or parts of that community), in response to either outside or inside influences, changes to such a degree that the ritual risks losing its relevance? Of course, there are many more questions and permutations of questions that can be, and are, asked, but these three can suffice to make the point: the study and the practice of rites of passage, bringing together as they do many disciplines and many emotions, are multifaceted, important, and prone to surprise both researcher and practitioner alike.

We begin with **Penina Adelman**, "'What Makes a Bat Mitzvah Blossom': Pre-Bat Mitzvah Rituals for Daughters and Mothers." Her article is a reflection on rituals for the youngest group extensively discussed in this volume, pre-Bat Mitzvah girls:

The Bat Mitzvah ceremony, the coming of age ritual for Jewish girls, is quite recent. In over 5,000 years of Jewish history, the first evidence of a Bat Mitzvah rite may have occurred in nineteenth century Baghdad.

As with many new rituals for girls and women today, there is wide latitude in the creation of new ones and innovations in traditional ones. This is due to the blank slate that is often the starting point for rituals for Jewish females. Jewish women who came of age in the 50s, 60s, and 70s now have daughters who are reaping the benefits of their struggles to be seen and heard in the synagogue.

As a folklorist, the author of this study describes the creation and development of programs for pre-Bat Mitzvah girls and their mothers. Within this context, she raises questions about the significance of these new rituals for Jewish women and girls and for the Jewish community as a whole.

**Rachel Kranson** follows, with "More Bar Than Mitzvah: Anxieties over Bar Mitzvah Receptions in Postwar America." As the title of her article indicates, she discusses celebrations surrounding the Bar Mitzvah:

"The way things are going, the inauguration of the first Jewish president of the United States is going to be a let-down for the man," joked a member of Great Neck, New York's Temple Beth El in 1961. "The ceremony probably won't be able to stand comparison with his Bar Mitzvah." This lighthearted jab at Bar Mitzvah parties was just one example of a general current of anxiety surrounding the increased extravagance of Jewish lifecycle celebrations in the years after World War II. Throughout the postwar period, Jewish clergy, intellectuals, performers, and writers derided receptions that "stressed the 'bar' more than the 'mitzvah.'"

This article analyzes the uneasy discourse surrounding the ways that Jews celebrated their Bar Mitzvahs in the postwar years. Critiques and concerns ranged from humorous digs to serious condemnation by clergy-members and intellectuals, who feared that the conspicuous consumption exhibited at these affairs degraded American Jews' religious and cultural life.

Anxiety over the rapid accumulation of wealth experienced by many American Jews during the postwar years underlay the critique of Bar Mitzvahs. In the imagination of postwar critics of American Jewish life, extravagant lifecycle events represented a tragic outcome of the Jewish encounter with American affluence. The debate over Bar Mitzvahs, then, provides us with a window into how American Jews grappled with upward mobility in the years after World War II.

Next is **Leslie Ginsparg Klein**, "Becoming Orthodox Women: Rites of Passage in the Orthodox Community." The age under discussion in this article encompasses young Orthodox women of high school age:

Throughout the twentieth century, Jewish communities developed rites of passage for their daughters that celebrated the entrance into adulthood, such as the Bat Mitzvah and confirmation ceremonies. The growth of the feminist movement and egalitarianism in Judaism affected conceptions of what constituted coming of age for Jewish girls.

However, the Orthodox community, the most traditional branch of Judaism, eschewed both feminism and egalitarianism. How then did Orthodox girls become Orthodox women? How did Orthodox education prepare girls to come of age? What life choices were celebrated and discouraged for girls entering into adulthood? How did the changes in an increasingly liberal and feminist-influenced American society and greater Jewish community affect conceptions within Orthodoxy?

This article addresses these questions by looking at Orthodox girls' high schools, a strongly female space where discussions of becoming Jewish women were constantly taking place. It investigates changing conceptions of how the entrance into adulthood was defined and commemorated, and what those evolving rites of passage indicate about what the Jewish community valued and celebrated.

**Irit Koren** provides an analysis of "Talking about the Jewish Wedding Ritual: Issues of Gender, Power, and Social Control." Brides are at the center of this article, which also includes grooms, parents, and rabbis:

This chapter is based on a sociological study of the ways in which women who identify as Orthodox feminists challenge, resist, and adapt the traditional wedding ritual. These women sought to modify the ritual; doing this required them to negotiate extensively with their husbands, mothers, fathers, and the officiating rabbis.

The relevant data was collected through in-depth narrative interviews with thirty women—all of whom live in Jerusalem and are highly Jewishly literature—and with a subset of their husbands, parents, and rabbis. The study's aims are threefold: to examine the discourse produced by each of the groups that was interviewed; to demonstrate how the theme of each group's discourse reflects the group's relative position along three hierarchiceal axes: gender, authority, and religious knowledge; and to delve into the societal significance of these discourses and their power to shape reality.

The results demonstrate the direct connection between the discourse a group produces in discussing the ritual and that group's dominant or subordinate position along the axes and explains the significance of each one of these discourses in terms of social power and gender relations.

**Jonathan Gross** is an Orthodox rabbi in Omaha. He reflects on "The Making of a Rabbi: *Semichah* Ordination from Moses to Grosses": After mastering a difficult Haftarah for a bar mitzvah, it is hard to imagine that there is anything left for a Jewish boy to learn. What makes a person a rabbi? What does the title mean? What knowledge and skills are required?

This essay journeys through the ages from the very first rabbi, Moses, all the way to current *semichah* programs and curricula. Biblical references to rabbinic leadership, curricula listed in the Talmud, the loss of the first *semichah* tradition, and the fifteenth century controversy over reinstating it are all discussed.

This article compares the modern training of a rabbi to the modern rabbi's role and analyzes whether or not they are in sync. The paper also includes some personal reminiscences illustrating the familial traditions that are often involved in deciding to become a rabbi.

In "Perspectives on Evaluating New Jewish Rituals," **Vanessa Ochs** opens the second section of articles, which look beyond a single age group or rite of passage:

The author of this article, which originated as the Symposium keynote address, has conducted wide research on emerging Jewish rituals and their adaption in America. She has observed that when people initially encounter a new ritual practice, they typically ask three questions: Is it authentic? Is it permissible? And: Will it endure?

In investigating the answers to these questions, the author devises and presents a checklist of the characteristic hallmarks of stronger new rituals, that is, those that have the greatest likelihood of enduring. As she observes, new rituals need community ritual organizers, as it were, to plead for their cause. They need to persuade first time participants in the new ritual that shocking innovations ought to become tomorrow's hallowed traditions.

The next article is **Ori Soltes**, "Memory, Questions and Definitions: Images of Old and New Rites of Passage." His particular interest is art and artifacts:

This study begins with the observation that Jewish identity is rife with questions regarding the definition of categories—what is "Jewish"? What is art as opposed to craft?—and that Jewish rites of passage reflect this truth and the truth that part of the answer to such questions articulates an interweave between the individual and the community, as between memory and futurity. Art and artifacts, particularly within the past generation, reflect a growing address of this complication. A child enters the community with a *Brit Milah*—and in many cases, where the physiology of gender prohibits a *Brit*, a baby naming. Garments and accoutrements reflect this bi-genderal expansion.

With the increased pairing of Bat with Bar Mitzvah, gender-specific symbols of individualized enfranchisement in the community, by way of a new vocabulary of *tallitot* and *kippot*, have spread, and with that spread a further blurring of the traditional line between art and craft. That blur may also be seen not only in works of art for wedding ceremonies, but even in those that serve for the commemoration of loved ones in the form of *Yartseit* candle holders.

These, in turn, intersect the proliferation of objects reflecting on the Shoah and the commemoration of its anonymous dead. A relatively recent holiday interweaves the individual and the community, with a new vocabulary of artistic word, sound, and image, as its paired counterpart, *Yom Ha'Atzma'ut*, celebrating the rebirth and birthday of a communal land, has also yielded art that, coming full circle, interweaves memory with questions.

**Oliver Leaman** explores "A Need for New Rituals? American Judaism and the Holocaust." In so doing, he also raises questions about the nature and efficacy of ritual:

The Holocaust has had a huge impact on Jewish life, and yet it has not noticeably affected the religion. There have been some attempts at incorporating the Holocaust into rites of passage such as Bar/Bat Mitzvah, weddings, and funerals, and into the liturgy itself, but these have had a limited success and tend to be part of alternative services that are rarely employed. This is in many ways puzzling, since if there is anything on which the Jewish world agrees, it is on the significance of the Holocaust for Judaism.

To try to understand why rites of passage do not on the whole directly respond to the Holocaust, it is useful to examine various theories of how rituals in religion, and in Judaism in particular, operate, and why some are successful and others are not. An examination is made of attempted changes to rites of passage incorporating new material linked to the Holocaust, and an account provided of which ceremonies look more plausible than others, and why. The larger issue of why the Holocaust has not in general been used in rites of passage is raised and linked to its proximity in time to us today.

Almost without exception, we think of Jewish rites of passage within the rabbinic tradition. **Daniel J. Lasker**, with "Karaism: An Alternate Form of Jewish Celebration," invites us to go beyond these familiar parameters:

Karaism has been an alternate form of Judaism for at least 1100 years, basing its observances on a close reading of the Hebrew Bible in place of acceptance of rabbinic tradition. As a result, Karaite practices differ from Rabbanite ones in a number of central rituals, including dietary laws, Sabbath and holiday observance, marriage laws, and liturgy. Despite their minority status through the centuries, Karaites have managed to survive and, in many cases, to thrive intellectually and culturally. Furthermore, with a few exceptions, Karaites have been recognized by the greater Jewish community as part of the same body politic, despite their different Jewish way of life.

There are perhaps between 30,000 and 40,000 Karaites in the world today, most notably in Israel and also in the Bay Area of the United States. Despite their minority status and the inroads of secularization and assimilation to the majority Rabbanite culture or to their non-Jewish surroundings, many Karaites continue to maintain their unique practices with their own synagogues, rabbis, and other ritual functionaries.

This overview of contemporary Karaite Jewish celebrations serves not only as a presentation of an alternate Jewish way of life, but also as a means of evaluating the limits of Jewish pluralism and tolerance of minority interpretations of Judaism.

**Daniel Mandell**, **Barbara Smith-Mandell**, and **Jerrold Hirsch** all live and practice Judaism outside of a metropolitan area. Their experiences are chronicled and evaluated in "Without a *Minyan*: Creating a Jewish Life in a Small Midwestern Town":

In 1999, the Mandell family moved to Kirksville, a small town (17,000) in northeastern Missouri, where they became one of just a few Jewish families, and the only one with children observing holidays and keeping kosher. Their adjustment has been difficult and empowering.

They left behind a vibrant congregation and, from necessity, have learned how to organize and lead Seders and other celebrations where before they had been primarily participants. With the closest synagogue ninety miles away, they cannot attend regularly and have had to adjust how they celebrate holidays and *simchas*. While they often feel isolated, they have become what friends call "the Jewish community center of Kirksville": they invite others (Jewish or not) to holiday celebrations and deal with the opportunities and burdens of being "on display" as the most public Jews in town.

Their sons, David and Joshua, are each the only Jew in their school; they often feel isolated and are sometimes treated badly by other children. They discuss their experiences with oral historian Jerrold Hirsch; their parents, Daniel and Barbara, analyze their experiences, separately and together, and consider how those experiences reflect or contrast with trends in American Jewish life.

As a practicing cantor, **Steven Puzarne** has practical experience within the context of the synagogue. He shares some of this experience in "Raising the Bar, Maximizing the Mitzvah: Jewish Rites of Passage for Children with Autism":

A learned Rebbe once observed that in both Hebrew and Yiddish, the words to learn and to teach are virtually the same, suggesting that according to Jewish tradition, teaching is simply a more intensive form of learning. Over the past few years, the author of this article has had the honor and privilege of intensively learning with, and from, a special group of young people—children with autism—as they prepared to become *B'nei Mitzvah.*

Working in both group and one-on-one settings, the author has had the opportunity to observe several important trends and make several revelatory discoveries, all of which hold great promise for these young people and the Jewish community of which they are a rightful part:

• An increased Jewish communal awareness of the burgeoning number of special needs children within our midst.

• A concomitant sense of obligation to offer these children and their families equal opportunities for Jewish enrichment.

• The remarkable and seemingly innate love of Jewish ritual and spirituality that these young people possess.

• The profound transformative affect that becoming B'nei Mitzvah has on special needs children, producing benefits that are both far-reaching and long lasting.

While this Jewish rite of passage is ancient, the participation of special needs children is more recent. To date, the author and his colleagues have supported six special needs children in ascending to the Torah, and they have reciprocated by reminding us of a simpler time when transformation superseded celebration as the order of the day.

Leonard J. Greenspoon

# Contributors

Penina Adelman

Newtonville, MA
jasmine@brandeis.edu

Leslie Ginsparg Klein

New York University
ginsparg@comcast.net

Jonathan Gross

Rabbi
Beth Israel
12604 Pacific Street
Omaha, NE 68154
rabbigross@orthodoxomaha.org

Jerrold Hirsch

Truman State University
Department of History
100 E. Normal
Kirksville, MO 63501
jhirsch@truman.edu

Rachel Kranson

New York University
rachel.kranson@gmail.com

Irit Koren

Yeshiva University
korenirit@gmail.com

Daniel J. Lasker

Ben-Gurion University of the Negev
Department of Jewish Thought
P.O. Box 653
Beer Sheva, Israel
lasker@bgumail.bgu.ac.il

Oliver Leaman

University of Kentucky
Judaic Studies
1429 Patterson Office, Twr 0027
Lexington, KY 40506
Oliver.Leaman@uky.edu

Barbara Smith-Mandrell

Truman State University Press
100 East Normal Avenue
Kirksville, MO 63501-4221
bsm@truman.edu

David Mandell

Truman State University
Department of History
100 E. Normal
Kirksville, MO 63501
dmandell@truman.edu

Vanessa L. Ochs

University of Virginia
Department of Religious Studies
P.O. Box 400126
Charlottesville, VA 22904-4126
Vlo4n@virginia.edu

Steven Purzarne

Cantor
Executive Director
Vision of Wholeness
California
visionofwholeness@gmail.com

Ori Z. Soltes

Georgetown University
Theology Department
P.O. Box 571135
New North 120
Washington, DC 20057-1135
solteso@georgetown.edu

# What Makes a Bat Mitzvah Blossom: Pre-Bat Mitzvah Rituals for Daughters and Mothers

## Penina Adelman

The Bat Mitzvah ceremony, the coming of age ritual for Jewish females, is actually quite recent. In over 5,000 years of Jewish history, the first evidence of a Bat Mitzvah rite may have occurred in nineteenth century Baghdad. Rabbi Joseph al-Hakam observed that if a twelve-year-old girl received a dress as a gift and made the appropriate blessing for wearing a new garment, she automatically became a Bat Mitzvah.[1] That is, she performed a mitzvah at the age of Jewish female majority and thus became a Jewish adult in the eyes of her community.

As with so many rituals for Jewish girls and women today, there is wide latitude in the creation of new rituals and innovation in traditional ones. This is due to the blank slate that is most often the starting point for rituals for Jewish females. Those women who came of age in the 1950s, 1960s, and 1970s now have daughters[2] who are reaping the benefits of their struggles to be seen and heard in the synagogue, the home, and other arenas of Jewish life. For three decades, I have been observing and documenting many of these extraordinary rituals performed by Jewish women and girls along the entire spectrum of the life cycle and year cycle.[3]

The blank slate in regard to rituals for Jewish women and girls has worked to their benefit. Necessity being the mother of invention, as women in the mid-twentieth century were faced with life-transforming situations with nothing traditional to mark them, they took up the gauntlet and devised their own rituals and ceremonies. One example of such created ceremonies is the girl's baby naming, sometimes called *Simchat Bat* or *Zeved HaBat*, which was unheard of before the 1980s.[4] When women who had grown up between 1945 and 1960 experienced pregnancy or pregnancy loss, infertility, or the onset of labor, these momentous events demanded ritual.

Then came ritual practices based on old traditions or the remnant of a tradition, such as *Ushpizot*, *Rosh Hodesh*, or *Miriam's Cup*. In the case of *Ushpizot*, the medieval practice of inviting guests into the Sukkah, women noticed the absence of female guests and began inviting the matriarchs or other biblical women, historical women, female ancestors, and women who just could not attend the meal in the Sukkah on that particular night. These were the *Ushpizot*, the feminine version of *Ushpizin*, or male guests. *Rosh Hodesh*, the monthly New Moon celebration, was originally given to women as a reward for not having contributed any of their gold to the making of the Golden Calf at the foot of Mount Sinai.[5] As recently as the nineteenth and early twentieth centuries, *Rosh Hodesh* was marked by individual Ashkenazic Jewish women by refraining from certain domestic chores. In the 1970s it was revived in a new form in North America as a time for Jewish women to gather and learn about the upcoming month—through story, song, prayer, art, dance, and text study. *Miriam's Cup* is a completely new ritual object with accompanying practices for the Sabbath, Passover, and menarche; it was created by a Boston Rosh Hodesh group in the context of one of their gatherings.[6]

In 1922 Judith Kaplan Eisenstein became a Bat Mitzvah at the insistence of her father, Mordecai Kaplan, founder of the Reconstructionist movement in Judaism. In her memoir, Eisenstein recalls how hard her father pushed for the Bat Mitzvah ritual. She felt that he seized her coming-of-age in order to "put into practice one of the basic tenets of his then unnamed philosophy of Reconstructionism, namely, the equality of women in all aspects of Jewish life."[7] The Bat Mitzvah ritual that Mordecai Kaplan enacted with his daughter was made to highlight not her adult femaleness but rather her adulthood. Only decades later, with the advent of secular and then Jewish feminism in the 1970s, was femaleness emphasized.

According to Riv-Ellen Prell, "Jewish feminists, over more than three decades, have *reenvisioned* Judaism, they have *redefined* Judaism, and they have *reframed* it."[8] In my recent observation of how the Bat Mitzvah ritual is being transformed by girls and women, I have witnessed all three of the above taking place. The result has been an expansion of the Bat Mitzvah into what is now being called by those participating in it a "process" rather than a mere event. With this change in the perception of Bat Mitzvah from a static, one-time occurrence to a flow of development in terms of physical as well as emotional, spiritual, and intellectual changes the girl undergoes, several new aspects of Bat Mitzvah are emerging. I would like to identify and characterize these.

Arnold Van Gennep has distinguished three phases of ritual. The first is the separation of the individual from his or her present peer group. The second phase is the transition from one state (childhood/boyhood/girlhood) to another (adulthood/manhood/womanhood). These two culminate in the final phase, called incorporation, during which the one who has been separated returns to the community, transformed forever.[9] However, in my observation of pre-Bat Mitzvah girls and their mothers since 2001, I have witnessed the emergence of a new phase in the coming-of-age process for Jewish girls, which I call the preparation phase. In addition, among the girls I observed, there was no separation phase; if anything, the first phase was the coalescing of the peer group. This change may be due to the fact that a new demographic has been identified by the marketplace and the media: 'tweens. These are girls age nine through twelve who strive to be adolescents even though many of them have not even reached puberty yet. They choose to wear clothes and makeup to emphasize their budding sexuality; they choose to listen and dance to popular music; they sometimes begin to test limits with their parents to see how far they can go in terms of staying out late or experimenting with alcohol and drugs.

Rabbi Sue Levi Elwell, who created programs for pre-Bat Mitzvah girls at Ma'yan, the Jewish Women's Project of the JCC of Manhattan, contends:

> The pre-bat mitzvah year is a perfect time to focus on girls' growing awareness of themselves, in relationship to their peers, their families, and the various communities of which they are a part. The preparation for the Bat Mitzvah itself can be seen in the larger context of preparing our daughters for lives of intentional choices, thoughtful commitments, and joyful service.[10]

Some parents, especially mothers of Jewish girls, are finding that the Bat Mitzvah ritual is an effective way to slow down the accelerated maturation process of their 'tween daughters driven by the media, music, clothing, and cosmetics industries. From 2004 to 2008, I helped create and lead four groups of pre-Bat Mitzvah girls and mothers. Two groups were sponsored by the Hadassah-Brandeis Institute (HBI) in Waltham, Massachusetts. Two groups took place at Mayyim Hayyim Community Education Center and Mikveh in Newton, Massachusetts, in a program called "Beneath the Surface."

In the groups from the HBI, girls and mothers met monthly for about ten months in two separate groups with two separate programs. The girls' program was based upon *The J-Girl's Guide: The Young Jewish Woman's Handbook for Coming of Age*[11] and led by a pair of college women. The mothers' program was led by me and was a combination of support group and text study.

Girls and mothers joined together in pairs for the last group meeting. During this session, the pairs had some private time during which they gave each other blessings. All in all, the girls were quite enthusiastic about their meetings with the two college women, comfortable with having their mothers in the same house but not in the same room. The mothers stated that they wished they had had more time with their daughters over the ten months during which the groups met. The separation seemed to be doubly difficult for them because they were, in fact, experiencing the loss of the "little girls" their daughters had been until quite recently both in their lives and in the context of the group.

The group sessions at Mayyim Hayyim were designed with significant time for mothers and daughters to be together as well as separate. Participants seemed to thrive on the different groups, one with their peers and one with their family member. The separate time was devoted to topics that participants could speak more freely about without a mother or daughter present. The topics covered were "Dealing with My Parents/Being the Parent of a Girl"; "What I wish my Bat Mitzvah to be/My Bat Mitzvah or non-Bat Mitzvah experience"; "What does it mean to be Jewish?"; and "The most important female figure in my life and why." During the last two sessions, mothers and daughters were to create a special short ritual that could be done using the water at the *mikveh* [ritual bath]. A description of one such ritual follows, created by a mother and her adopted daughter.

It was important for this mother and daughter to celebrate the girl's roots, physical and spiritual, because, in becoming a Bat Mitzvah, she reached into adulthood the way a tree reaches toward the sky. Therefore, this pair decided to buy a tree native to the land where the girl was born, water it with water from the *mikveh*, and then plant it in their backyard. They wrote a poem together for the occasion:

Prayer for
Tree Giving
Girl Growing

Seed. Soil. Water. Light.
Is what a tree needs for life.
God. Girl. Torah. Study.
Is what makes a Bat Mitzvah blossom.

Living. She. Beauty. Trunk.
This is my tree.
Living. She. Beauty. Soul.
This is me.

She is a tree of life to hold onto.[12]
Cherish them forever.

This ritual allowed the mother and daughter to reaffirm their relationship with each other in the context of a Jewish sacred space representing birth. The *mikveh* ritual is often compared to a rehearsal of birth in the warm waters from which the person emerges after total immersion. In the mother-daughter program, "Beneath the Surface," there was no total immersion because that experience was to be set aside for the time that the girl actually became a Bat Mitzvah. In this pre-Bat Mitzvah phase, the idea of birth was hinted at in the use of water to refresh the tree, the participation of mother and daughter together, and the notion of Bat Mitzvah representing the girl's "birth" into Jewish womanhood.

Two more pre-Bat Mitzvah rituals will further demonstrate the importance of this new preparation phase of the Jewish coming-of-age celebration. The first ritual was created by Andrea Cohen-Kiener for her daughter, Sarah, in the late 1990s in West Hartford, Connecticut. It took place in the kitchen of the synagogue where Sarah would become a Bat Mitzvah before the whole congregation of men and women the following week. The immediate goal was to bake *challot* [loaves of ritual Jewish bread] for lunch after the Bat Mitzvah. The ultimate goal was to welcome Sarah into the community of Jewish women.

Cohen-Kiener deliberately chose one of the traditional "women's" mitzvot—namely, challah baking—for this pre-Bat Mitzvah ritual.[13] Her aim was to go deeply into this mitzvah with Sarah and the other women who comprised this challah-baking community for the day. Therefore, as forty women and girls took turns forming the dough, letting it rise, punching it down, braiding it, and baking it, they also sang, shared wisdom about baking and cooking and other "women's" work, joked, and reminisced about their own Bat Mitzvah and coming-of-age experiences.

When asked about her goal in creating this ritual, Cohen-Kiener stated, "I have to do this in a way that feels open to women, women's knowledge, that feels like you're being initiated into the community of Jewish women."

She also said it was necessary to transform the challah baking from a mundane household task to a communal spiritual activity and celebration. She wanted to incorporate her oldest living relative's know-how and her grandmother's baking tips into the ritual as well. After forty women had baked fifty *challot*, imbuing the loaves with the earthy holiness she hoped would grow in her daughter, Cohen-Kiener observed privately, "*This* was the Bat Mitzvah, not the ceremony in the shul!"

The third pre-Bat Mitzvah ritual was one I created for my daughter, Laura, in 2001 in the living room of our home in Newton, Massachusetts. I called it "Make Your Own Midrash/Make Your Own Sundae."[14] With Laura's permission and help, we came up with a list of her closest female friends and their mothers, my closest friends, and some of her teachers. I sent out invitations, and with each one I included the name of a woman from the Hebrew Bible and some instructions. Each guest was to bring a blessing for

Laura in the form of poetry, art, music, story, dance, or any other medium they chose. However, this blessing was to be one that the particular biblical woman would give to Laura. The flesh-and-blood women and girls attending the ritual were embodying the biblical women, giving Laura gifts of ancient and contemporary wisdom. My goal for this ritual was to impart women's knowledge and experience to Laura, thereby affirming her uniqueness and empowering her to become an adult who would stand on the firm foundation of generations of Jewish women who preceded her and stood with her. In a remark paralleling what Cohen-Kiener had observed about the pre-Bat Mitzvah ritual for her daughter, one of Laura's teachers said, "This is the most beautiful Bat Mitzvah I've ever been to!"

What is common to these three preparation rituals is their location outside the synagogue proper. They took place in the synagogue kitchen, the *mikveh*, and the home. All of these are women's domains, places that, although not part of the public sphere of Jewish practice (mostly in synagogue or school), are part of the private, more historically typical women's sphere. The synagogue kitchen, *mikveh*, and the home even point to the three "women's" mitzvot: *challah, niddah,* and *hadlaqat nerot.*[15] However, these preparation rituals transform the mitzvot assigned to women into experiences meaningful to girls coming of age.

The *challah* ritual brings Sarah's and Andrea's particular community of women together to welcome Sarah as a new adult. The *mikveh* ritual of mother and daughter watering the tree symbolizes the unique mother-daughter bond that the two share as well as the path of Torah upon which the girl is embarking with her mother and with the entire community of Jewish women. The home-based ritual of women and girls creating midrash demonstrated the power of women's interpretations of the Hebrew Bible, which have historically remained undocumented until now. This ritual gave Laura the mandate from our community of women to interpret Torah for herself and, in so doing, to perpetuate her heritage of living the Torah.

These three rituals also share a sense of birth/rebirth. In each, the girl is being initiated by her mother and the community of women around her into the adult world of Jewish women. One could say that this is the girl's second birth; this time she is born into a women's community shared by her mother. She is also born into the adult Jewish world shared by men and women. Initiation in the women's world will give her the foundation she needs to thrive in the larger Jewish and secular worlds.

In conclusion, I would like to propose naming the pre-Bat Mitzvah phase of the Bat Mitzvah ritual "the *kavanah* phase." *Kavanah* comes from the Hebrew root meaning "to arrange, direct, be firm." A *kavanah* is an utterance before prayer, before blessing, before embarking on a transformative experience. Women and girls are making the process of becoming a Bat Mitzvah more meaningful by sanctifying space and time for "the *kavanah* phase" in this coming-of-age ritual.

## NOTES

[1] Ben Elijah al-Hakam, Joseph Hayyim, *Ben Ish Hai* (Baghdad: nineteenth century).

[2] Understand "daughters" to signify a girl in a close relationship with an older woman and not referring only to biological or adopted daughters.

[3] See Penina Adelman, *Miriam's Well: Rituals for Jewish Women Around the Year* (New York: Biblio Press, 1986, 1996). See also Penina Adelman, "A Drink from Miriam's Cup: Invention of Tradition among Jewish Women," in *Active Voices: Women in Jewish Culture* ed. Maurie Sacks; Chicago: University of Illinois Press, 1995).

[4] Chavva Weissler, "New Jewish Birth rituals for Baby Girls," unpublished paper delivered in an earlier version at the 1977 annual meeting of American Folklore Society.

[5] Adelman, *Miriam's Well*, 1996 edition, 1-2.

[6] See note 3.

[7] Judith Kaplan Eisenstein, "A Recollection of the First U.S. Bat Mitzvah," http://www.ritualwell.org.

[8] Riv-Ellen Prell, *Women Remaking Judaism* (Detroit: Wayne State University Press, 2007), 11.

[9] Arnold Van Gennep, *Rites of Passage* (London: Routledge, 1960).

[10] Rabbi Sue Levi Elwell, "Bat Mitzvah: Preparing Girls for Womanhood in a Changing Judaism," http://www.ritualwell.org.

[11] Penina Adelman, Ali Feldman, and Shulamit Reinharz, *The J-Girl's Guide: The Young Jewish Woman's Handbook for Coming of Age* (Woodstock: Jewish Lights Publishing, 2005).

[12] From the Torah Service liturgy, referring to the Torah as a "tree of life," Proverb 3:18.

[13] They are *challah, niddah* [observance of the laws of family purity including refraining from contact with one's husband during menstruation], and *hadlakat nerot* [lighting Sabbath candles].

[14] For a fuller description of this ritual, see Penina Adelman's introduction to *Praise Her Works: Conversations with Biblical Women* (Philadelphia: Jewish Publication Society, 2005). "Midrash-making" is a creative process the Jewish people have been engaged in since Sinai, a way of making meaning from the biblical text in each generation.

[15] See note 13.

# More Bar than Mitzvah: Anxieties over Bar Mitzvah Receptions in Postwar America

## Rachel Kranson

"The way things are going, the inauguration of the first Jewish president of the United States is going to be a let-down for the man," joked a member of Great Neck, New York's Temple Beth El in 1961. "The ceremony probably won't be able to stand comparison with his Bar Mitzvah."[1] This lighthearted jab at Bar Mitzvah parties represented just one example of a general current of anxiety surrounding the increased extravagance of Jewish life-cycle celebrations in the years after World War II. Throughout the postwar period, Jewish intellectuals, journalists, and especially clergy derided Bar Mitzvah receptions that, in the words of one Long Island rabbi, "stressed the 'bar' more than the 'mitzvah.'"[2]

These critics' concerns over opulent receptions intertwined with their worries over American Jews' increased affluence in the postwar years. They considered consumer patterns to be a reflection of morals and ethics, and they did not feel that showy life-cycle celebrations exhibited what they believed to be proper Jewish values, such as education, social justice, and solidarity with worldwide Jewry. Indeed, the same leaders who lambasted Jews for their extravagant life-cycle celebrations often applauded when Jews lavished their wealth on expensive trips to Israel, on religious books, on Jewish charities, or on their local synagogue's building fund. For these critics, extravagant receptions proved that the abundance of America, rather than enabling American Jews to perpetuate the best elements of Jewish culture, served rather to cheapen and degrade Jewish values and Jewish heritage. In the years after World War II, the Bar Mitzvah ritual served as a lightning rod for debates over the fate of Jewish life within an atmosphere of American affluence.

The Bar Mitzvah ritual was first formalized by Jews living in the German Empire in the sixteenth century. At age thirteen, boys were thought to have reached religious maturity. They marked their new position by publicly reading from the Torah or *Haftorah* [prophetic writings] for the first time and, beginning in the seventeenth century, delivering a speech that demonstrated their religious knowledge. As a Bar Mitzvah, or a "son of the commandment," the boys would then be responsible to perform the full array of religious rituals, which included wearing ritual garments such as *tefillin* [phylacteries] during times of prayer and joining a *minyan* [prayer quorum] three times a day.

The record of how this ritual spread into Eastern Europe and the Sephardic world remains unclear, but probably that expansion did not happen until the eighteenth and nineteenth centuries.[3]

By the time that Eastern European Jews began to migrate en mass to the United States at the turn of the twentieth century, the Bar Mitzvah had become a firmly established ritual. But whereas in Eastern Europe the immediate family might have embellished the Bar Mitzvah observance with a light repast, Jewish immigrants in America transformed the Bar Mitzvah party into a gala event. In the years before World War I, the families of American Bar Mitzvah boys would host luncheons for guests at their homes. By the 1920s, it became popular among those who could afford it to invite friends and family to Bar Mitzvah "affairs," complete with a banquet and orchestra, at catering halls and hotels.[4] For American Jews, a party following the service had become part and parcel of the Bar Mitzvah milestone.

The years after World War II drastically changed the economic profile of American Jews. Most had moved up from their working-class or modest middle-class backgrounds into a lifestyle of solid, middle-class affluence.[5] Along with this upward mobility came an increasing number of Jews eager to celebrate the Bar Mitzvah milestone with great fanfare. During the decades after World War II, observers reported Bar Mitzvah parties featuring six-course meals, sculptures of the Bar Mitzvah boy made of ice and chopped liver, baseball- and luau-themed decorations, dancing girls, comedians, and elaborate Torah-shaped cakes upon which relatives of the Bar Mitzvah solemnly lit candles.[6]

The growth of extravagant Bar Mitzvahs during the postwar era emerged as a prominent theme in the Jewish press during the decades after World War II. In the pages of *The Reconstructionist* in 1960, Stanley Meisler compared his own Bar Mitzvah reception, "a buffet dinner on a paper plate eaten at a small East Bronx apartment," to that of his younger brother's celebration, which featured showgirls, a comedian, and a sit-down dinner at a Broadway nightclub. And while Stanley's Bar Mitzvah gifts had amounted to a mere $125, the younger Meisler collected $1,200 in checks and savings bonds. The author attributed this celebratory escalation to the greater income enjoyed by his family's social circle in the fourteen years since he had celebrated his own Bar Mitzvah milestone, while his tongue-in-cheek language revealed his own ambivalence over the merits of this transformation.[7]

Wielding a lighthearted tone that did little to mask their serious concerns about the rising extravagance of the receptions, comic writers often found humor in the differences between pre- and postwar Bar Mitzvah celebrations. In the pages of his temple's literary magazine, an author writing under the name of A. Begelman poked fun at how an informal day of ritual celebrations had been transformed into a lavish, decorous affair:

> Time was when Bar Mitzvah was only a big day not THE big day. You learned to read [from the Torah], you went to shul [synagogue] on that big Shabbos [Sabbath], dovvened [prayed] well enough and watched your friends jump for the candy that your mother and her friends threw down from the women's section upstairs. Later there was a Kiddush [a light meal with sanctified wine], some schnapps [liquor], sponge cake, herring. Then you went home and the family and friends came in for a good, long party at which you saw what loot the company was good for – the fountain pen, of course, a tallis [prayer shawl] maybe from the frummer [more pious] wing of the family, and a dollar from this one and that one that mama quickly put aside for necessities; after all, who had money to throw away then?
>
> So times have changed. The religious part of the Bar Mitzvah hangs on—for sentimental reasons, at least. But nobody has a Bar Mitzvah at home unless he's an atheist, perhaps. You need a hall. People dress up. There are the before-meal drinks, cocktail knishes and caviar on crackers. There are 100 guests for a small affair.[8]

With his contrasting depictions of pre- and postwar Bar Mitzvah celebrations, this writer conveyed his impression of how drastically the ritual had been transformed in the interim. His somewhat nostalgic portrayal of the older Bar Mitzvah, laced with Yiddish words and religious symbols, recalled modest celebrations based largely at the synagogue and the boy's home. His description of the postwar Bar Mitzvah, which with the exception of the "cocktail knish" included little Jewish imagery, portrayed a formal event that lacked the warmth, charm, and Jewish flavor of the older celebration. Bar Mitzvah parties had gained in opulence but lost their authenticity.

In much stronger language, postwar rabbis soundly condemned Bar Mitzvah receptions. Debates over these parties loomed particularly large in the Reform movement, where the shapers of classical Reform had tried to eliminate the Bar Mitzvah ceremony altogether and replace it with the Confirmation observance. In the view of the nineteenth century leaders of Reform, Confirmation, a ritual that annually honored a cohort of teenagers who completed a course in religious education, improved upon Bar Mitzvah in a number of ways. First, the service honored the accomplishments of both boys and girls while the Bar Mitzvah celebrated only boys, and so Confirmation felt more in tune with the Reform movement's policy of equality between the sexes. Secondly, many Reform leaders felt that thirteen-year-old boys lacked the maturity to be initiated as full, adult participants in Jewish religious life and contended that Confirmation, which focused on older teenagers between the ages of fourteen and sixteen, more effectively served this purpose. Finally, the Bar Mitzvah celebrated a boy's facility with Hebrew language, and the shapers of Reform had de-emphasized the use of Hebrew for ritual purposes. The Confirmation ceremony, they believed, represented a more modern and appropriate approach to Judaism.[9]

By the postwar era, however, the Bar Mitzvah celebration had become common practice even among Reform Jews. According to a survey conducted by the movement's National Federation of Temple Brotherhoods, 92 percent of Reform temples celebrated Bar Mitzvah in 1953, while a poll taken in 1960 reported that 96.4 percent of Reform congregations commemorated the event. The Reform movement's adoption of the Bar Mitzvah ritual, instituted by the demands of the laity rather than by the recommendations of the clergy, caused consternation among many Reform rabbis. As the invention of a Bat Mitzvah ceremony for girls nullified complaints regarding the non-egalitarianism of the Bar Mitzvah ritual, and as the Reform movement began to incorporate more Hebrew language into its services, condemnation of lavish Bar Mitzvah receptions became a primary concern for those rabbis who opposed incorporating the ritual into Reform Jewish practice. One such rabbi, Joshua Trachtenberg of Teaneck, New Jersey's Temple Emeth, told *Time* magazine in 1959 that the superficiality of the Bar Mitzvah ritual typified the inherent dangers of the Reform movement's return to ritualism. He characterized Bar Mitzvah as an "empty ceremonial" followed by a reception that displayed "the conspicuous waste which is the hallmark of such celebrations."[10]

The preponderance of opulent receptions became an issue once again in the early 1960s as Reform clergy debated the growing popularity of Bat Mitzvah, a ceremony for girls that paralleled Bar Mitzvah. Many Reform rabbis urged their colleagues to include the Bat Mitzvah ritual on the grounds that anything else would be inconsistent with the Reform movement's stance on equality between the sexes. Other Reform rabbis felt, however, that the inclusion of Bat Mitzvah would only serve to multiply the "social evils" associated with the Bar Mitzvah ceremony. As Rabbi Harold Silver explained in 1962, "Just when the rabbis believe that they have stemmed the tide somewhat in our movement today regarding the toning down of these wild Bar Mitzvah celebrations, the grim spectre of having to wage religious battle all over again with parents and their *daughters* is just more than the average rabbinical heart can take."[11]

Though they had never promoted the practice of Confirmation as a replacement for Bar Mitzvah, rabbis of the Conservative and Orthodox movements joined their Reform colleagues in their frustration with lavish Bar

Mitzvah receptions.  In 1961, for instance, Conservative Rabbi Elias Charry derided the Bar Mitzvah gathering as "an elaborate and costly birthday party at which the chief celebrants are the adults and the poor Bar Mitzvah boy is the real victim."  Charry went so far as to suggest that his movement de-emphasize or even exchange Bar Mitzvah in favor of an initiation rite geared toward sixteen-year-olds.  That same year, Modern Orthodox Rabbi Leonard Gewirtz argued that American Jews had reduced Bar Mitzvah to "an occasion to show off their wealth, often with a general disregard for Jewish religious practice." Gewirtz believed, in spite of all evidence to the contrary, that opulent Bar Mitzvahs would inevitably lead to a decline in Orthodox observance.[12]

In rare cases, congregational leaders placed strict limits on Bar Mitzvah parties or banned the rite altogether.  The rules of the Hillcrest Jewish Center of Queens, a Conservative institution, stipulated that the public celebrations following a Bar or Bat Mitzvah had to be limited to the barest essentials.  And Congregation Solel, an experimental Reform synagogue on Chicago's North Shore, prohibited Bar Mitzvahs entirely.  "After a two year study of this popular ritual, we decided it did more harm than good to the child, the school, and the congregation," their rabbi explained.[13]

In this climate of unease over Bar Mitzvah parties, both the Conservative and Reform movements adopted standards for synagogue decorum that implored their members to tone down their receptions.  The Conservative movement's standards for synagogue practice, adopted by the biennial convention of the United Synagogue in 1955, gently, and somewhat vaguely, reminded constituents that the receptions following Bar Mitzvahs and weddings should be considered a *seudah shel mitzvah*, or a religiously commanded meal, and must therefore be in accord with the religious spirit surrounding the event.[14]  The Reform movement made a far stronger statement against Bar Mitzvah receptions in 1964, when the Central Conference of American Rabbis adopted a report that lambasted the "steady and alarming deterioration in the character of the Bar Mitzvah 'affair.'"  The report urged members of the Reform movement to exhibit simplicity and restraint in their Bar Mitzvah receptions, warning them that the "extravagant consumption, the conspicuous waste, and the crudity" of these parties "were rapidly becoming a public Jewish scandal." [15]

In characterizing the preponderance of lavish Bar Mitzvahs as a "public Jewish scandal," these rabbis revealed their concern that these receptions tarnished the reputation of Jews in American society.  And in fact, during the postwar years, the opulence of Bar Mitzvah parties emerged as a topic of general, sometimes contemptuous interest in the public discourse.

The national postwar press began to feature Bar Mitzvahs in 1952, when

*Life* published "*Life* Goes to a Bar Mitzvah," a feature article highlighting the reception of Carl Jay Bodek, the son of a wealthy Philadelphia contractor. The article dutifully mentioned Carl's recitation from the Torah but devoted its most detailed and ebullient coverage to the "lavish party" that followed the service. Underneath photographs of Carl cutting his Torah-topped Bar Mitzvah cake and dancing with his father and rabbi, the magazine gleefully reported that the party, which "was held in large tents erected on Bodek's seven-acre estate," employed the services of three orchestras and a string quartet, eighteen waiters, and four Pinkerton detectives to "guard the 310 guests' furs and jewels." *Life* also published a photograph of Carl surrounded by the presents he received, including "seven suitcases, four toilet sets, a set of gold clubs and a traditional present, a gold watch." That a popular magazine like *Life* would publish descriptions of a Bar Mitzvah reception that seemed extravagant even by postwar standards contributed to fears that these large parties could potentially contribute to antisemitic stereotypes of Jewish wealth, greed, and vulgarity.[16]

Herman Wouk's 1955 description of a Bar Mitzvah reception in his best-selling novel *Marjorie Morningstar* added to public interest in the celebration. Wouk detailed the elaborate catering flourishes at Marjorie's brother's Bar Mitzvah banquet, a party that included "the flower-decked ballroom, the spacious dance floor, the waiters in blue mess jackets, the murmuring orchestra behind potted palms, the fine linen and silver on the tables, [and] the camellias by each lady's plate." The climactic moment of the party occurred when the Bar Mitzvah boy entered the ballroom, accompanied by a flaming cauldron of brandy sauce that the headwaiter poured on top of each guest's grapefruit. Wouk enlisted one of his characters, department-store owner Mr. Goldstone, to mock the waste of money that this showiness represented. "Caterers, restaurants, great angle they got," said Mr. Goldstone. "Anything they can set fire to they charge ten times as much. Set fire to a twenty-cent flapjack, crepes suzette for two dollars. Maybe we could use it in our store, Mary. Sell a pair of flaming shoes, fifty dollars instead of five dollars."[17]

Assailed by critics who felt that Wouk's rendering of a Bar Mitzvah viciously ridiculed the habits of American Jewry, Wouk defended his description in *This is My God* (1959), a book that explained his own religious beliefs and practices:

> In my novel, *Marjorie Morningstar*, I did my best to portray a Bar-Mitzva with accuracy and with affection. I thought I succeeded pretty well, but for my pains I encountered the most bitter and violent objections from some fellow Jews. I had, they asserted, made a sacred occasion seem comical. . . . We Jews are a people of great natural gusto. In the

freedom of the United States, where for the first time in centuries we have known equality of opportunity, we have made of the Bar-Mitzva a blazing costly jubilee. I do not see anything wrong with that. The American coming-out party is not too different.[18]

The criticism Wouk received for his portrayal of an opulent Bar Mitzvah pointed to the great unease American Jews felt over the consumption and display associated with Bar Mitzvah parties. Though the postwar years saw a marked decrease in American antisemitism, many Jews continued to feel threatened by negative publicity. They could not, as did Wouk, view Bar Mitzvah as the benign, Jewish counterpart of the American coming-out party. To have such a showy Jewish celebration featured in a best-selling book widely read by non-Jewish Americans made many American Jews feel self-conscious and even angry with Wouk for exposing a contentious issue. To wit, upon reading that Wouk did not see any problem with American Bar Mitzvahs becoming a "blazing costly jubilee," Union of America Hebrew Congregation (UAHC) President Maurice N. Eisendrath acidly responded, "he wouldn't."[19]

Two years after the release of *Marjorie Morningstar*, Bar Mitzvahs entered the public arena once again during a 1957 New York State Supreme Court case. The case involved the parents of a twelve-year-old boy who sought to pay for their son's Bar Mitzvah reception with the $600 that he had been awarded in a personal-injury lawsuit. Since their son was a minor, the courts had the power to decide whether or not to release the child's funds for this purpose. Justice Hofstadter, who presided over the case, seized the opportunity to make a public statement on what he felt to be the abuses of Bar Mitzvah celebration. "The Bar Mitzvah ceremony is a solemnization of a boy's becoming a 'son of the commandment' and should encourage him in the path of righteousness. It was never intended to be a vehicle for mere entertainment and display. . . . It would be more fitting if the funds were utilized to initiate or continue his education in faith and morals," Hofstadter stated. Though the court finally allowed the parents to use $200 of their son's award to pay for the party, the ruling represented an unmistakable, public condemnation of lavish Bar Mitzvah celebrations. This court case, discussed in synagogue bulletins and studies of Jewish communal life during the late 1950s, contributed to the notion that Bar Mitzvah receptions had become a public disgrace.[20]

Fearing that the growth of Bar Mitzvahs might sully the reputation of American Jewry, rabbis used their pulpits to try to convince their congregants to reconsider their aesthetic choices. In 1950, Rabbi Roland Gittelson warned his congregants that Bar Mitzvah receptions that employed outlandish or off-color entertainment both demeaned the religious ritual and offered a negative impression of Judaism and Jewish life:

I have sat on occasion at Bar Mitzvah luncheons and dinners . . . where
the songs and jokes I heard made me blush.  And after 31 months in
the United States Marine Corps, I don't blush easily. . . .  I have listened
to lyrics and observed behavior which, believe me, would be far more
appropriate at the opening of a new burlesque house than to the most
important religious occasion in the first 13 years of a boy's life!  On
one occasion right here in this congregation when a Christian minister
who knew the family well was invited as a guest to the Bar Mitzvah
service and luncheon, I was so ashamed for him during the lunch that
with my food only half consumed I took him out for a walk to relieve
our common embarrassment.

In this sermon, Gittelson conjured up a scenario that may have struck a
chord with many postwar American Jews.  On the one hand, during the postwar
era, Jews enjoyed greater acceptance among their non-Jewish neighbors than
in the previous decades.  Many enjoyed cordial and friendly relationships
with their non-Jewish colleagues and neighbors, and they invited non-Jews to
their Bar Mitzvah receptions.  However, American Jews' sense of belonging
and approval still felt quite new and tenuous.  Gittelson acknowledged this
tension by reminding his congregants that the non-Jews at their parties would
be making judgments about Jews and Judaism based on their impressions of
Bar Mitzvah receptions.  He tried to convince his congregants that their Bar
Mitzvahs could alienate their non-Jewish friends and perhaps even endanger
their newfound acceptance in America.  He begged them, therefore, to hold a
"warm, gracious, appropriate, dignified, decent party . . . at which anyone you
know, Gentile or Jew, can drop in unannounced from beginning to end and
you can look him in the eye and say 'today is the happiest day of my life, my
boy read from the Torah today.'"[21]

Not only did rabbis express their disapproval over the content of Bar
Mitzvah parties, but they also suspected that American Jews valued the
receptions more than the religious aspects of the ritual.  As one rabbi wrote in
a 1956 article for *American Judaism*, "we offset the value of the Bar Mitzvah if
we forget that the social aspect is supposed to be a minor way of celebrating
its religious significance, not vice versa."[22]

The suspicion that the social aspects of Bar Mitzvah had eclipsed its
religious significance plagued not only religious leaders but also scholars such
as sociologist Will Herberg.  In his classic study *Protestant, Catholic, Jew* (1955),
Herberg argued that within the "triple melting pot" of American religious life,
Catholics, Protestants, and Jews were equally guilty of exploiting their faith to
advance their social needs rather than to worship God.  In the case of Jews, he
contended, Bar Mitzvah represented a prime example of a religious ritual that,
in its postwar, American incarnation, had come to serve an entirely secular

purpose. "Bar Mitzvah is usually nothing but a lavish and expensive party, with the religious aspect reduced to insignificance, if not altogether ignored," he wrote. As proof of this assertion, he cited the "typical Bar Mitzvah invitation" that announced the date and location of the reception, only to add "in tiny type in the corner: 'Religious Services at 10:30 a.m.'" For Herberg, this secularization of Jewish religious practice confirmed, for better or for worse, that Jews had become fully ensconced into American society.[23]

For critics of postwar Bar Mitzvah receptions, these parties had eclipsed the spiritual dimension of the service and distorted authentic religious practice. Rabbis grew irate, for instance, when rituals invented by bandleaders and caterers began to take on religious significance for the celebrants. Long Island's Rabbi Harold Saperstein expressed his astonishment when a congregant asked him for religious guidance in deciding which relatives should light the candles of the Bar Mitzvah cake. The rabbi complained, "She couldn't understand when I told her that lighting candles at a Bar Mitzvah reception was not part of any Jewish tradition but a gimmick introduced by caterers."[24] He found himself even more disturbed when he witnessed a ceremony in which a small girl carried a *tallis* [prayer shawl] into the banquet hall, which the parents then placed on the shoulders of the Bar Mitzvah boy. This ceremony, he felt, exploited Jewish symbols for the entertainment of the guests, "as though there had been no Bar Mitzvah [in the synagogue] and this [performance] made the experience holy."[25] As new rituals like the candle-lighting ceremony began to take on religious meaning for postwar American Jews, their rabbis feared that these recently invented rituals would detract from the older, rabbinically sanctioned Bar Mitzvah practices. Instead of accepting these new rituals as legitimate aspects of the Bar Mitzvah observance, many rabbis dismissed them as inauthentic, perhaps even dangerous, intrusions into the Bar Mitzvah ritual.

Though a scholar rather than a rabbi, Yeshiva University historian Abraham G. Duker argued forcefully that the Bar Mitzvah rituals invented by caterers had a deleterious impact on postwar Jewish life. "The trend in this area is towards increasing extravaganza, and as a by-product, also increasing costs," Duker wrote in 1950. He contended that these for-profit rituals had a "disastrous" effect on poorer Jews, who felt compelled to participate in them for social and religious reasons even when they could not afford to pay for them easily. For Duker, allowing profit-earning businesses to invent Jewish ritual made it difficult for working-class Jews to be involved in Jewish life.[26]

A telling letter printed in *American Judaism* seemed to echo Duker's concern that some American Jews, viewing the reception as an integral aspect of the Bar Mitzvah experience, felt compelled to pay for extravagances that they could not afford. Appearing among a series of comments debating the value of the Bar Mitzvah ritual, this letter, signed by one Mrs. R. Abrams, inquired, "In all the discussion about Bar Mitzvah, hasn't anyone something to say about the financial burden? We wanted a Bar Mitzvah for our son, but changed our mind because we couldn't afford it. Isn't the religious value of the ceremony offset when it becomes so difficult to pay for?" While many postwar synagogues did require a modest fee for Bar Mitzvah instruction, the costs surrounding the synagogual aspects of the ritual fell well within the budgets of most postwar American Jews. But for the many American Jews who lived in an increasingly affluent community, expensive receptions had become an integral aspect of the milestone. Mrs. Abrams and her family, unable to pay for the party, preferred to forgo the Bar Mitzvah altogether.[27]

Rather than expressing concern over the less-affluent Jews who could not afford to pay for elaborate Bar Mitzvah parties, however, most religious leaders focused their critiques on those newly affluent Jews who, they felt, were particularly susceptible to spending needless amounts of money on gaudy affairs. Rabbi Erwin L. Herman, director of regional activities for the UAHC, directed his vitriol towards Bar Mitzvah caterers, whom he accused of taking advantage of newly wealthy American Jews. He lambasted the caterer as "the shepherd who leads us with uncomplaining conformity down the road of social acceptance. We have been good sheep—and like good sheep, we have been clipped. Enough! It is time to state without equivocation that we have had it, and to admit that we have been had, in the process." Herman contended that American Jews, who had only recently come to enjoy the benefits of secure, professional incomes, felt particular pressure to prove their financial status through conspicuous display. In Herman's formulation, caterers exploitatively preyed upon American Jews' insecurity with their newfound wealth. He encouraged American Jews and their leaders to resist their offerings.[28]

As postwar Jews adjusted to their new economic status, their religious leaders enjoined them to use their money in a way they deemed consistent with Jewish ethics and values. These rabbis feared that Bar Mitzvah parties reflected social self-aggrandizing rather that what they considered to be more proper Jewish values, such as charity, education, or a commitment to the larger Jewish community. Chicago's Rabbi Ira Eisenstein, for instance, argued that the Bar Mitzvah party actually contradicted the ethical ideals that the synagogue hoped to transmit to its youth. "In school we try to inculcate the power to discriminate between what is important and what is trivial, between the good and the merely glittering," he wrote in his temple bulletin. "Then comes the Bar Mitzvah party which so often neutralizes all that the school has attempted to teach, and influences the child to believe that ostentation is better than modesty, and that money spent on elaborate entertainment is better than money spent on books or charity to the synagogue." For rabbis like Eisenstein, teaching American Jews how to properly use their wealth constituted an important part of their religious education.[29]

As religious leaders sought to educate their constituents about how to use their money appropriately, they assigned relative worth to various expenditures. Many deemed elaborate Bar Mitzvah parties to be a frivolous expense, preferring instead that Jews use their resources on what they felt were more worthy causes. Rabbi Roland Gittelson, for instance, suggested to his congregants that it would be more in keeping with Jewish values to forgo the large Bar Mitzvah reception and spend the money on a contribution to the synagogue. As he told his congregants during a 1950 sermon, "I can think of no better way to reinforce the real religious emphases of your son's Bar Mitzvah . . . than by taking the additional money you might have spent for a public spectacle and giving it in honor of the Bar Mitzvah to your Congregation's building fund."[30]

Similarly, Rabbi Edgar Siskin of Glencoe, Illinois, used the issue of Bar Mitzvah as a springboard upon which to discuss ethical economic values. In his Rosh Hashanah sermon in 1963, he implored parents of Bar Mitzvah–aged youth to resist their children's requests for opulent Bar Mitzvah receptions when so many worthy charities were in desperate need of funds. "Individual parents must have the gumption to stand up for decent moral values and tell their children, No!" he exclaimed. Instead, Siskin urged parents and their children to donate to humanitarian and religious causes such as peace and civil rights, aid to Israel and their local synagogue, and providing sustenance for the impoverished Jews of the Middle East and Eastern Europe.[31]

Increasingly during the postwar years, many American Jews did try to insert more meaning into their Bar Mitzvah celebrations by incorporating the State of Israel into the event. Some celebrants traveled to Israel in addition to, or in lieu of, a reception. Others joined the Jewish Agency's "National Bar Mitzvah Club," launched in 1962, which enlisted Bar and Bat Mitzvah youth into a three-year educational course before taking them on a study tour of Israel at the age of sixteen.[32]

The editors of *The Reconstructionist* applauded the trend of including Israel into the Bar Mitzvah rite. In 1963, they congratulated New York Senator Jacob Javits on taking his son to Israel on the occasion of his Bar Mitzvah, expressing their hope that this would become a model for other Bar Mitzvah celebrations. "Considering what some *bar mitzvah* parties cost these days, the trip would be a bargain," they gushed. "And consider the difference to the boy: instead of being exposed to the eating, drinking and dancing, which have nothing whatever to do with his entrance into the household of Israel, he would find himself upon the soil where the words he chants echoed millennia ago." In suggesting that Bar Mitzvah be celebrated with a trip to Israel rather than a party, the editors of *The Reconstructionist* joined the chorus of religious leaders who disparaged the content of Bar Mitzvah celebrations rather than the actual expense. After all, travel to the Middle East required a financial investment at least as large as the costs of a large party. For these leaders, it was not Jewish affluence itself but the ways that American Jews had chosen to use their newfound affluence that provoked anxiety. They hoped that Jews would choose to invest their wealth in causes that they judged worthy, such as the State of Israel, rather than in Bar Mitzvah receptions, which struck them as a frivolous waste.[33]

For the leaders of postwar Jewry, lavish Bar Mitzvah receptions emerged as a touchstone for far-reaching anxieties that extended well beyond the boundaries of synagogue catering halls. On the one hand, postwar rabbis feared that the extravagance of Jewish life-cycle celebrations would trigger anti-Jewish stereotypes of Jewish greed and vulgarity and compromise the acceptance that American Jews had just begun to enjoy in the United States. Secondly, they worried about cultural loss among American Jews. They believed that the practices of Bar Mitzvahs, many of which had been developed by catering halls, would eclipse what these leaders thought of as more-authentic Jewish practices. Finally, these critics expressed concern over the ethics of American Jews who spent vast sums of money on large and expensive parties when, at least in their opinion, their resources should have been put to better use.

Concerns about marginality, cultural loss, and the allocation of communal resources tortured the leadership of American Jewry in the decades after World War II. On the one hand, as American Jews, they were experiencing unprecedented, and very new, levels of affluence and acceptance. At the same time, they were keenly aware that many Jews around the world did not share their happy situation. They mourned the losses of the Holocaust, supported the struggle of survivors who were trying to rebuild their lives, and followed the plight of displaced Jews in the Middle East and around the world. Hovering uncomfortably between these two poles of triumph and unspeakable loss, American Jewish leaders felt an enormous sense of responsibility to provide cultural and financial leadership for the rest of the Jewish world. They worried when they saw American Jews behave in ways that could jeopardize their new feeling of security. They worried when they saw American Jews spend money on parties when their resources might be called upon at any moment to support victims of anti-Jewish violence or to ease a crisis in Israel. Any prevailing custom that struck them as inauthentic made them wonder whether American Jews were capable of sustaining Jewish culture in a post-Holocaust world.

Anxiety over the rapid accumulation of wealth experienced by many American Jews during the postwar years underlay the critique of Jewish Bar Mitzvahs. Many Jewish leaders saw these extravagant parties as proof positive that American Jews used their good fortune to degrade and cheapen Jewish life rather than to enhance its finest qualities. In their writings and sermons, they tried to teach American Jews how to use their resources differently. For these critics, the way American Jews celebrated life-cycle events connected directly to the viability of Jewish life in America and around the world.

## NOTES

[1] A. Begelman, "The Modern Bar Mitzvah," *Man about Town: The Literary Magazine of the Temple Beth El Men's Club* 11:3 (December 1961): 5.

[2] Papers of Rabbi Harold Saperstein, American Jewish Archives, ms. 718, box 6, folder 3, Kol Nidre Sermon, 1960.

[3] Ivan G. Marcus, *The Jewish Life Cycle: Rites of Passage from Biblical to Modern Times* (Seattle: University of Washington Press: 2004), 82-105.

[4] Jenna Weisman Joselit, *The Wonders of America: Reinventing Jewish Culture* (New York: Henry Holt, 1994), 90-94.

[5] A study among American college graduates in 1947, for instance, revealed that more Jews than non-Jews earned their living as professionals, proprietors, managers, and officials, though fewer of their parents had enjoyed these high-income occupations. This survey attested both to the rapid upward mobility of postwar American Jews as well as to their relative economic growth compared with Americans of other backgrounds. Cited in Nathan Glazer, "The American Jew and the Attainment of Middle-Class Rank: Some Trends and Explanations," in *The Jews: Social Patterns of an American Group* (ed. Marshall Sklare; Glencoe: The Free Press, 1958), 141.

[6] For instance, see Rabbi Erwin L. Herman's "Bar Mitzvah A La Carte," *American Judaism* 11:4 (Summer 1962): 4-5. The article describes a number of particularly fanciful Bar Mitzvah receptions that he attended, including a party with a three-ringed circus, complete with a live elephant, as well as a party in which the caterer released a slew of parakeets.

[7] Stanley Meisler, "Big Bar Mitzvah," *The Reconstructionist* 26:2 (4 March 1960): 21-24.

[8] A. Begelman, "The Modern Bar Mitzvah," *Man about Town: The Literary Magazine of the Temple Beth El Men's Club* 11:3 (December 1961): 5, 33.

[9] Roland B. Gittelson, "Bar Mitzvah in Reform Judaism," *American Judaism* 6:1 (September 1956): 14-16.

[10] "How Much Religious Education Do You Want for Your Children: Brotherhood Section," *American Judaism* 3:1 (September 1953): 23-24; Benjamin Efron and Alvan

D. Rubin, "The Reality of Bar Mitzvah," *CCAR Journal* 8:3:31 (October 1960): 31-33; "Rabbi's Report," *Time* (13 July 1959).

[11] Rabbi Harold Silver, "Today I am a Woman," *CCAR Journal* 9:4:36 (January 1962); for a history of how Bat Mitzvah developed in the United States, see Paula Hyman, "The Introduction of Bat Mitzvah in Conservative Judaism in Postwar America," *YIVO Annual* 19 (ed. Deborah Dash Moore; Evanston: Northwestern University Press and YIVO Institute for Jewish History, 1990), 133-46; and Regina Stein, "The Road to Bat Mitzvah in America," *Women and American Judaism* (eds. Pamela S. Nadell and Jonathan D. Sarna; Hanover: Brandeis University Press, 2001), 223-34.

[12] Elias Charry, "Ben Torah: Bar Mitzvah at Sixteen," *Conservative Judaism* 16:1 (Fall 1961): 52-55; Leonard B. Gewirtz, *The Authentic Jew and His Judaism* (New York: Bloch Publishing, 1961), 83. For a study of how Jewish Orthodoxy managed to thrive, rather than decline, in situations of postwar abundance, see Etan Diamond, *And I Will Dwell in their Midst: Orthodox Jews in Suburbia* (Chapel Hill: University of North Carolina Press, 2000).

[13] Morris Freedman, "New Jewish Community in Formation," *Commentary* 19:1 (January 1955): 37; Arnold Jacob Wolf, "Experimental Synagogue in Suburbia," *The Reconstructionist* 26:7 (13 May 1960): 16.

[14] "United Synagogue of America Standards for Synagogue Practice," printed in *Conservative Judaism* 10:4 (Summer 1956): 22-25.

[15] "Report of Committee on Guide for Synagogue Decorum," 75th Annual Convention of the Central Conference of American Rabbis (1964), *CCAR Yearbook* 74 (Philadelphia: Press of Maurice Jacobs, 1965), 60.

[16] "Life Goes to a Bar Mitzvah," *Life* (13 October 1952): 170-72.

[17] Herman Wouk, *Marjorie Morningstar* (Garden City: Doubleday, 1955); cited from later printing (New York: Signet, 1957) 93-95.

[18] Herman Wouk, *This is My God* (Garden City: Doubleday, 1959), 142-43.

[19] Maurice N. Eisendrath, "Paean of Praise, Wouk Style," *American Judaism* 9:3 (1960): 6.

[20] "Schindler v. Deeves," *New York Law Journal* (19 September 1957), quoted in "Bar Mitzvah and the Courts," *The Bulletin: Temple Beth El of Northern Westchester* 10:4 (December 1957-January 1958). Temple Beth El of Northern Westchester Collection, ms. 728, box 5, folder 1, American Jewish Archives; also cited in Albert I. Gordon, *Jews in Suburbia*, (Boston: Beacon, 1959), 205.

[21] Rabbi Roland Gittelson papers, ms. 704, box 35, folder 5, "Bar Mitzvah and Confirmation," sermon delivered on March 24, 1950, American Jewish Archives.

[22] Roland B. Gittelson, "Bar Mitzvah in Reform Judaism," *American Judaism* 6:1 (September 1956): 15.

[23] Will Herberg, *Protestant, Catholic, Jew* (Chicago: University of Chicago Press, 1983), 196, 208. On the growing secularization of American religions, see chapter 11, "Religion in America in the Perspective of Faith," 254-81.

[24] Papers of Harold Saperstein, ms. 718, "New Approaches to Judaism," sermon delivered on May 31, 1957, box 3, folder 1, American Jewish Archives; "What is Jewish Tradition?," sermon delivered on Sukkos 1963, box 3, folder 4, American Jewish Archives.

[25] Papers of Harold Saperstein, ms. 718, "The Need for Jewish Dignity," sermon delivered on January 4, 1963, box 3, folder 4, American Jewish Archives.

[26] Abraham G. Duker, "Emerging Culture Patterns in American Jewish Life," *The Publications of the American Jewish Historical Society* 39:4 (June 1950): 383.

[27] Mrs. R. Abrams, "High Cost of Bar Mitzvah," *American Judaism* 6:4 (April 1957): 7.

[28] Rabbi Erwin I. Herman, *American Judaism* 11:4 (Summer 1962): 4-5.

[29] Cited in Albert I. Gordon, *Jews in Suburbia* (Boston: Beacon, 1959), 205.

[30] Rabbi Roland Gittelson papers, ms. 704, box 5, folder 35, "Sermon: Bar Mitzvah for My Son?" delivered on March 24, 1950, American Jewish Archives.

[31] Papers of Rabbi Edgar Siskin, ms. 64, box 2 folder 4, "Fathers and Sons," Rosh Hashanah Sermon, delivered on September 19, 1963, American Jewish Archives.

[32] *The American Jewish Year Book* lists the National Bar Mitzvah Club in its 1964 directory as an organization that "seeks to enhance meaning of the Bar and Bat Mitzvah ceremonies; to further Jewish education; and to develop personal identification with Israel through a three year program which culminates in a summer study-tour of Israel." *American Jewish Year Book* 65 (1964): 372.

[33] "A Pattern for Jewish Boys Everywhere," *The Reconstructionist* 28:19 (25 January 1963): 4-5.

# Becoming Orthodox Women: Rites of Passage in the Orthodox Community

## Leslie Ginsparg Klein

In the 1975 yearbook of an Orthodox girls' high school, students included an illustration that outlined the life cycle of Orthodox Jewish girls. The drawing identified what these high school–aged girls viewed as the stages of their lives and their progress into adulthood. The two-page spread included images of birth, childhood, school days, graduation, marriage, motherhood, and old age. The girls' vision of their future lives can be traced to both the influences of their school and their experiences as students in a single-sex Orthodox high school.

This essay is part of a dissertation on Orthodox girls' education in the 1960s through 1980s. It focuses on Bais Yaakov high schools. Bais Yaakov, founded in Poland in 1917, was the first widespread school system for Orthodox girls, and it remains the dominant model of Orthodox girls' schools in America. Every major Orthodox community has at least one Bais Yaakov school. Bais Yaakov typically attracts the daughters of Yeshivish families, families whose brothers and fathers connected themselves to *yeshivot* [institutions of high Jewish learning for men] and their leaders, rather than Chasidic *rebbes* or Modern Orthodox pulpit rabbis. The most fundamental and defining difference between Yeshivish Orthodoxy and Modern Orthodoxy lies in the attitude toward secular American culture and knowledge, with the Yeshivish community being more restrictive and insular.

This essay discusses four schools located in New York. The first, Beth Jacob High School of America (BJHS), located in Brooklyn, was considered a particularly right-wing Yeshivish school.[1] The second school, Bais Yaakov Esther Schoenfeld (BYES), located on the Lower East Side of Manhattan, was a more moderate Bais Yaakov. The third school, Bais Yaakov Academy (BYA), also located in Brooklyn, started as a branch of BYES. BYA eventually grew larger and outlasted its mother institution. It shared BYES's reputation as a moderate Bais Yaakov. The fourth school, Yeshiva University's Girls' High School, was commonly known as Central. Central, which also had branches in Manhattan and Brooklyn, was a Modern Orthodox school and contrasts with the more fundamentalist Bais Yaakov schools.

When looking at schools and students, it is important to remember that prescriptive materials from schools are not necessarily descriptive of the actual behavior of students. School yearbooks and newspapers, whether quoting the Bible or the Beatles, reveal girls' attitudes toward the cultural ideals they encountered in school, the Jewish community, and the outside world. Together with the New York State Education Department archive, school archives, and oral histories, these sources present both student and school perspectives. They illuminate the rites of passage schools presented; how students related to the messages the schools presented; and the alternative culture, with its own rites of passage, that girls' created, with school influence, for themselves.

Traditional Judaism, as alluded to in the Bible and clearly expressed in the Talmud and rabbinic writings, held essentialist views on men and women. Men and women had clear, defined, and different roles that suited what Judaism considered their different emotional make-ups. The woman's primary role in Judaism is centered in the home. Biblical and rabbinic sources referred to her as the *akeret HaBayit*,[2] understood as the foundation of the home, a role that included maintaining the physical and spiritual aspects of the home. Traditional Judaism imbued the work of housekeeping, cooking, and child-rearing with a higher, holier purpose,[3] and it expected women to set the religious tone in the home and raise children with good Jewish values.

Traditional Judaism also stressed the role of women as enablers. The Talmud in Tractate *Berachot* 17A asked how women accrued merit in this world. The assumption behind the question is that men received merit through fulfilling the command to study the Torah. But women, because they needed to devote themselves to family and home responsibilities, had no obligation to study. The Talmud answered that women accrued merit through their husbands and children, by enabling their husbands and children (though ostensibly it referred only to sons) to learn Torah. The ideal form of life in nineteenth and twentieth century Europe, which became even more popular in postwar America, had men studying Torah full time in a Kollel, a study program for married men, while their wives shouldered the primary responsibility as the breadwinners of the family.[4]

In twentieth century Orthodox society, these views manifested themselves in the strict separate spheres of men and women. The private sphere, the home, belonged to women. The public sphere, which included all public expressions of religious worship in the synagogue, belonged to men. Jewish law, as defined by Orthodoxy, allowed only men to be counted among the ten required for a *minyan*, the religious quorum required for public prayer services. Women also remained ineligible to lead services, serve as a *chazzan* [cantor], and participate in the reading of the Torah. Men served in all the leadership roles associated with the synagogue and organized Jewish life.

For boys and men, Orthodox culture had a very obvious rite of passage, the Bar Mitzvah. Celebrated at age thirteen, the Bar Mitzvah inducted a boy into adulthood and into synagogue life, where he could now count toward a *minyan* along with other adult men and be called up to the Torah. While other Jewish denominations instituted a Bat Mitzvah, with girls reading from the Torah, Orthodoxy continued to believe that the practice of women leading prayer services transgressed Jewish law.[5]

As traditional Orthodoxy maintained strictly separate spheres for men and women, this major rite of passage could only apply to men. For women, whose role in Judaism centered on the home, their only rite of passage would be marriage. With marriage, a woman entered adulthood. She took on her new role as keeper of the Jewish home and future mother to Jewish children. She took on new legal obligations, such as lighting Sabbath candles and keeping the laws of family purity. For much of Jewish history, even up until the early twentieth century, marriage commonly took place around the same age as the Bar Mitzvah.

In the twentieth century, with the common age of marriage rising and the promulgation of compulsory school laws, Orthodox girls spent the years preceding marriageable age in high schools. Accordingly, the leaders of Orthodox girls' schools directed and prepared girls for marriage and for that rite of passage into their definition of Jewish womanhood. School leaders espoused the message that this role had immense value and responsibility and strongly encouraged girls toward this life choice.

In 1966, Rabbi Uri Shraga Hellman, one of the principals of BJHS, began his letter to students by quoting the Tractate *Berachot* passage. Printed in the yearbook, the letter went on to describe the purpose of a Jewish girl's life and the purpose of a Bais Yaakov education as intellectually internalizing the value that learning Torah is of paramount importance in Judaism. Hellman instructed students to put that value into action by sending their children and husbands to learn. In an allusion to a famous Talmudic story, he quipped, "This is all the Torah of Bais Yaakov on one foot, and the rest is commentary." If one had to sum up the entire purpose and ideology of Bais Yaakov in one sentence, what the school viewed as most important, it would consist of telling students to get married and encourage your husband to learn Torah. This is how Hellman explained to students the purpose of their education, not something academic or intellectual in nature or even directly related to their own development. Hellman ended his letter by telling students that while schools customarily give diplomas upon graduation from school, the students will get their true diploma only when they fulfill the words of this Talmud passage.[6]

In the 1967 yearbook, Rebbetzin Vichna Kaplan, the head of BJHS, discussed what the ideal Bais Yaakov graduate would be like. Kaplan defined her as someone who chooses to marry a man learning Torah full time in Kollel because, "I hope that in the years that you spent in Bais Yaakov, you learned the *hashkafa* [religious outlook] that a woman can receive her share in Torah only through encouraging and strengthening her husband toward learning, and by guiding her children in the ways of torah." A student's marriage, not anything related to her academic development, determined a graduate's measure of success.[7]

The message of becoming wives and mothers appeared in BYA as well. In a letter to one of the first graduating classes in 1968, BYA principal Rabbi Ephraim Oratz charged students with the responsibility of forging the image that would forever form the seal of BYA. But what Oratz hoped to be the image of a graduate of his school centered on becoming a wife and mother, not on any academic or professional goal.[8] Playing on the name Bais Yaakov, he wrote, "Are you, Bat Yaakov [daughter of Jacob], prepared to assume your beautiful and lofty role in life and to establish your own Bais Yaakov, your home, which is not merely the glitter of furnishings, but the sanctuary that is illuminated with G-dly splendor."[9]

Schools measured the success of students by their adherence to traditional values. For these school leaders, Bais Yaakov high school served as a prelude to and preparation for marriage. Accordingly, they tried to ensure that students continued on to this rite of passage into Jewish womanhood.

In the 1979 BJHS yearbook, a single teacher, herself an alumna, wrote a poem comparing the experience of graduating with the ultimately more important and more meaningful experience of getting married:

> The beautiful gold ring you wear and promise never to remove will give way to another ring—shinier and brighter—that you will never take off. That blue gown you marched in with such pride will be replaced by another gown that you will also march in with pride. And that piece of paper with the pink ribbon tied around it that was presented to you and which you cherish so is only the forbearer of another piece of paper that will also be presented to you but which you will cherish more.[10]

The teacher trumpeted the importance of the wedding ring, gown, and *ketubah* [Jewish marriage contract] over the class ring, graduation gown, and diploma. The school did not present graduating as a rite of passage; rather, it placed paramount importance on marriage. It encouraged students to keep marriage as their ultimate, defining goal.

Even at Modern Orthodox Central, which strongly encouraged students to continue on to college and pursue their education, school leaders emphasized the importance of marriage. In 1966, a member of Central's administration instructed students that they had two purposes in life. The first was to learn in order to keep the commandments. The second was to prepare themselves to be future mothers in Israel. The male administrator stated that he hoped Central's education had provided them with a Jewish education and prepared them to be "true mothers in Israel."[11]

While right-wing and moderate Bais Yaakov schools differed in their approaches regarding secular education and school rules, both models of Bais Yaakov schools equally encouraged students toward marriage. Even Modern Orthodox Central, which sharply contrasted with Bais Yaakov schools in its advocacy for secular higher learning and more lax rules, likewise encouraged students toward marriage. Within the Orthodox community, marriage was such an essential part of the structure of society and fundamental rite of passage for girls entering womanhood that schools from across the spectrum equally pushed marriage as an essential life choice.

Students wrote about their roles and futures as well. From their writings and from interviews, it seemed that they internalized the values their schools presented. Student writings displayed an enthusiastic embrace of traditional domesticity. A student essay in the 1964 BJHS yearbook showed students' acceptance of their role as Jewish mothers in accordance with how it was defined by the school: "Who is responsible for educating the next generation? Who is responsible for the future of *am yisroel* [nation of Israel]? . . . This high task was given into the hands of the Jewish mother. . . . she should feel the holy obligation."[12]

In 1965, Central students rejected external messages they heard about pursuing careers and reaffirmed the message their teachers and administrators advanced:

> How many times, in years gone by, have we been lulled to sleep by stirring orations beginning: "The Youth of today are the leaders of tomorrow"? Now, for a senior, these rather trite words take on an ominous meaning. "'Me?'—you say, cringing slightly—'the leader of tomorrow?' I just want to get married and raise a family." Think for a moment, dear senior. Even if you do not become a doctor, lawyer, nurse, psychologist, or artist, you will still have a very important task to fulfill. In raising a family, you will be instilling into your children the values that will remain with them for the rest of their lives. Even if you are not a leader of THIS generation, you will be a molder of the leaders of the NEXT generation. So, senior, whatever you become, don't take your tasks lightly, for YOU are . . . Tomorrow.[13]

This sentiment did not change over time. Decades later, in the 1982 BJHS yearbook, the members of the senior class reaffirmed their commitment to their role as Jewish women: "This yearbook symbolized our graduation and our crossing over from being the next generation to creating it. And so, we dedicate ourselves to being future mothers of Israel."[14]

While Bais Yaakov schools pushed their students into the private sphere, with marriage as their only potential rite of passage, Bais Yaakov also provided students with the means to generate their own rites of passage. Whereas in centuries past girls went straight from the private sphere of their parents' home to their married home, in the twentieth century girls left their homes and went to school. As students in Bais Yaakov schools, girls found themselves inhabiting a public sphere similar to that of their brothers in yeshiva.

For example, at Bais Yaakov, students also had the opportunity, to a small extent, to replicate male prayer services. Every morning, girls prayed together as a group, with one student serving as the *chazzanit* [literally, a female cantor] and leading the prayers. In the activities pages of the BYA yearbook, a picture of the "Chazaniyos" appeared alongside other club pictures, which displayed members of the school band, newspaper staff, honor society, and student council. Within the total female environment of Bais Yaakov schools, girls ran all aspects of communal life. Girls served as class presidents, headed religious education and community service committees, and occupied various other leadership roles not available to women in the Yeshivish Orthodox community.[15]

With schools creating their own religious society and small public sphere, schools gave students plenty of alternative rites of passage. Students turned school rituals, color wars, theatrical productions, and school ceremonies into rites of passage. Students in both schools devoted pages to that year's color war. Student writing indicates that they became very involved in each year's color war and that winning was a momentous occasion. Additionally, schools put on a musical production each year. Yearbooks contained pages covering the production as well. Being the chair of one of the many committees involved in putting on the production earned a student a place and a picture in the yearbook.

Even those rituals designed to lead to homemaking, such as learning how to make a chicken Kosher during senior year, became schoolhouse rites of passage. Students wrote about that class session as one of the defining events of being a senior.[16]

Additionally, while faculty might not have considered graduation as a rite of passage, students certainly did. In the page of images representing the life cycle, students attributed importance to school days and graduation, which would have been approaching as the students drew this picture. Students viewed school life and graduation, both phenomena new to Orthodox Jewish life in the twentieth century, as important steps on the road to adulthood. Interestingly, students did not include college or career, two stages of life Bais Yaakov school leaders discouraged, in their life cycle.

While at first glance Orthodox girls' schools seemed to have been restricting girls' rites of passage narrowly to marriage and adopting the role of wife and mother, at the same time the schools served to create a new stage of life and a whole other set of rites of passage, generated by girls themselves, for becoming Bais Yaakov graduates and twentieth century Orthodox women.

## NOTES

[1] Beth Jacob is the anglicized version of the term Bais Yaakov.

[2] The source of the term is Psalms 113:9. There are countless sources on women in home and family. See, for example, Mishna Yuma 1:1, Tractate Ketuboth, Tractate Sanhedrin 110a, Commentaries on Proverbs 14:1.

[3] Hasia Diner and Beryl Benderly, *Her Works Praise Her* (New York: Basic Books, 2002), xvi.

[4] Tractate Berachot 17a.

[5] See, for example, Moshe Meiselman, *Jewish Woman in Jewish Law* (New York: Ktav and Yeshiva University Press, 1978).

[6] *M'gama*, Beth Jacob High School of America yearbook (1966), 15.

[7] *M'gama* (1967), 8-9.

[8] *Hamaayan*, Bais Yaakov Academy yearbook (1968), 5.

[9] *Hamaayan* (1968), 5.

[10] *M'gama* (1973), n.p.

[11] *Elchanet*, Yeshiva University High School for Girls of Manhattan yearbook (1966), n.p. See also *Elchanet* (1967), n.p.

[12] *M'gama* (1964), n.p. My translation from the Hebrew.

[13] *Elchanet*, Yeshiva University High School for Girls of Brooklyn yearbook (1965), n.p.

[14] *M'gama* (1982), n.p. My translation from the Hebrew.

[15] See, for example, *Hamaayan* (1972-1978), n.p.; and *Hamaayan* (1983), n.p.

[16] See, for example, *Elchanet* (1970), n.p.; *Elchanet* (1963), 56; and *Beth Jacob Teachers Seminary and High School Alumnae Bulletin*, June 1979, 2, Beth Jacob Teachers Seminary of America Archive.

# Talking about the Jewish Wedding Ritual: Issues of Gender, Power, and Social Control

## Irit Koren

## INTRODUCTION

This essay focuses on the ways in which a small yet growing number of Modern Orthodox women in Israel endeavored to challenge, resist, or adapt the Orthodox wedding ritual and, in so doing, transform it so that it would serve as an expression of their own identity, values, and ideals.[1] The Jewish women I have interviewed identified themselves as both Orthodox, or at least committed to Orthodox *halakhah* [Jewish law], and as feminists, or at least as being conscious of feminist principles.[2] Some of these women found themselves confronted with a tension between these two aspects of their identities, as the values embraced by feminism and Orthodoxy are often at odds.

Orthodoxy, generally speaking, implies an obligation to traditional halakhic practice as developed by the Talmudic rabbis and their followers. Given that these rabbis believed their halakhic system was based upon divine oral law passed from generation to generation alongside the divinely revealed Torah, or written law, Orthodoxy promotes its own authenticity by viewing individuals as bound to submit to divine authority and, therefore, rabbinic law.[3] Thus, Orthodox ideology perceives *halakhah* as "transhistorical," lifting its believers beyond everyday life, and as "ahistorical," meaning it does not pertain to history and therefore resides beyond a specific time and space. Feminist theory, on the other hand, challenges the notion of a nonrelative truth, "implied by the bedrock status accorded to an exclusively male tradition of rabbinic interpretation."[4] The Orthodox view internalizes a gender hierarchy, seeing women as subordinate, a view that is "linked to the fact that men have greater obligations in the study of Torah and in performance of *mitzvoth* [religious commandments]."[5] In contrast, feminism de-emphasizes gender differences, attributing them to social constructions rather than viewing them as divine, objective, and fixed.[6] Therefore, "feminism can be seen as undermining the deepest foundations upon which rabbinic Judaism—as an authoritarian system—depends for its survival."[7]

The Orthodox movement has, therefore, regarded feminism with suspicion, perceiving its endeavor for equality as foreign to Jewish thought and, thus, as something to be rejected. Moreover, it seems that this "rejection has become a key precept of Modern Orthodoxy's sense of self."[8]

Orthodox feminism evolved as an answer to this tension, beginning in the United States in the 1980s and spreading to Israel soon afterward. In some ways it struck a deeper root in Israel because Israeli women, as native speakers of Hebrew, had more access to sacred texts.[9]

As demonstrated in the interviews, these feminist women who have chosen to remain in the Orthodox fold describe their religious identities and their feminist identities as equally integral to their personal identities. They do, however, differ in their characterization of the relationship between their two identities. Some feel marked tension, whereas others found these two outlooks more easily compatible and even mutually enriching. Regardless of the degree to which they felt tension, all of the women in my study devote conscious thought and effort toward accommodating their Orthodoxy with their feminism. Therefore, they are necessarily committed to reengaging and challenging their tradition rather than rejecting it as a whole.

I investigated the process by which these women attempt this accommodation in a specific context: the wedding ritual. As I explain later, this ritual is a point of contention for many feminist women. Using the wedding ritual as a case study enabled me to demonstrate how women negotiate between the boundaries of *halakhah* and the maintenance of feminist values in relation to themselves and vis-à-vis their society. In order to further understand the women's social context, I also interviewed some of their relatives (the mothers, fathers, and husbands) and some of the rabbis who performed the weddings. I collected the data for this study through in-depth narrative interviews.

The women I studied comprise a fairly homogeneous group.[10] All were in their midtwenties to midthirties at the start of their marriage. For women in the Orthodox society, this age is significant. Women are expected to wed at the beginning of their twenties, preferably soon after they finish their army service or *sherut leumi* [special civil service for religious women]. All these women lived in Jerusalem while single, specifically in the neighborhoods of Rehavia, Katamon, and Baka.[11] All of these women's marriages took place within the past decade and all of them are well educated.[12] As the women expressed in their interviews, the years they lived as single women in these specific neighborhoods had an impact on their identity and religious perspective. Living in this specific context enabled them to be exposed, through synagogues, friends, political movements, and so on, to feminist ideas and acts that they had not encountered beforehand. Therefore, they had had some years to grapple and redefine their religious outlook and identity prior to their marriages.

Since these women identified themselves in their interviews as religious, they felt constrained (to varying degrees) to abide by Jewish law[13] and, thus, they evinced a desire to have an Orthodox wedding. They did not feel that they could take the path of some non-Orthodox women who opt for civil secular ceremonies that are not acknowledged by the Orthodox Rabbinate, the only body authorized to perform Jewish marriages in Israel. Thus all marriage ceremonies in Israel must confirm to Orthodox *halakhah*.

The Jewish wedding ritual is a significant cultural icon. The performance of the wedding ritual by its participants is a "mode of communication, framed in a special way and put on display for an audience."[14] Thus, it promotes and reflects the community's ideals, boundaries, and values. This function of the ritual explains why many Orthodox leaders and rabbis are hostile and unsympathetic toward any attempts made by women to challenge and change any aspects of their wedding ritual. It seems that "Even the slightest symbolic change in ritual creates a dissonance with primeval memories, associations, and traditional patterns of worship that have nurtured the spiritual self-image of Jewish women for centuries."[15]

These defined, rigid boundaries and a social setting that is suspicious of changes combine to make these women's attempts at transformation of the wedding ritual much more difficult than for those who do not see themselves as bound to Orthodox *halakhah*. The latter group, in contrast, is able to freely choose the elements they like and "trot out and juggle around"[16] other elements that seem archaic and irrelevant to their lives. For these people, "designing the ceremony seems no different than designing the reception."[17]

## THE ACT OF *KIDDUSHIN* AND GENDER POWER RELATIONS

The transformative aims of the women's discourses and the discourses of those in their social environment can be understood only in the context of the traditional wedding ritual as it is performed in Israel (and throughout the Orthodox Jewish world) today.[18]

The typical Orthodox ritual comprises a series of steps. Although the blessings and structure of the wedding are uniform in any Orthodox community, there are a variety of customs that change from community to community. The ritual I am describing henceforth is typical of the Modern Orthodox Ashkenazi [European Jewish] community in Israel,[19] and it differs in a few aspects from the typical wedding of the Modern Orthodox community in the United States.[20]

First, before the wedding ceremony itself, the groom signs the *ketubah*, a contract delineating his financial and sexual obligations toward his wife. Then he is led, with loud singing and dancing, to his bride, who is awaiting him in her "queen"-like chair. Upon reaching her, he covers her face with a veil. He turns and walks to the *huppah* [marriage canopy], still accompanied by the wedding guests, and awaits the bride there. The bride, similarly, proceeds to the *huppah* accompanied by more guests. Once again, this escort is done with loud singing and dancing. In most cases the guests will remain standing throughout the *huppah*. This is different than the Jewish American wedding, in which a formal procession takes place with the guests sitting quietly, viewing the entrance of each participant.

Upon reaching the *huppah*, the bride circles the groom seven times accompanied by her mother and mother-in-law to be. She then stands besides her groom, and they both face the crowd. The rabbi stands near the couple, facing the guests as well. This staging is also unlike the typical Jewish American wedding, in which the couple stands with their backs to the crowd, while the rabbi faces them and the guests.

These dissimilarities in performance and staging represent the different values of the communities in Israel and in the United States. These values relate to the degree of formality that the congregation attributes to the wedding ritual, the focus of attention of the community (e.g., the rabbi or the couple), and the influence that cultural surroundings have on the community. For example, the formal procession in the Jewish American wedding reflects a procession "which is part of every Jewish and Christian wedding in the United States" and has no halakhic significance.[21]

Only now does the formal two-part ritual begin. The first part is the *kiddushin* [acquisition] ceremony, in which, following recitation of the betrothal blessing and the blessing over wine, the man fulfills the active role of betrothing the woman by addressing to her the Hebrew words *harei at mekudeshet li* [you are hereby consecrated unto me] while giving her a ring. After this, the *ketubah* is read aloud, separating the two parts of the ritual. Now the second part, the *nisu'in* [marriage], begins, and the *sheva berakhot*, the traditional seven wedding blessings, are read by a man or several men. At the end of the ritual the groom shatters a glass by stamping on it. Finally the bride and groom walk together to a private room and stay there for a short while until they come out and join the rest of the crowd.

The *kiddushin* act is based on the ruling of the Mishnah.[22] The Mishnah states: "A woman is acquired [in marriage] in three ways and acquires her freedom in two. She is acquired by money, by deed, or by intercourse . . . and she acquires her freedom by *get* [divorce bill given to her by her husband] or by her husband's death" (Mishnah, Tractate *Kiddushin*, 1:1). The ritual just described includes all three modes of acquisition. The ring given to the bride symbolizes her acquisition by money, the *ketubah* symbolizes her acquisition by deed, and standing under the *huppah* and the couple's entrance into a private room after the *huppah* symbolize her acquisition by intercourse. Many rabbis and religious leaders have argued that the acquisition established through this act does not mean ownership of the man over his wife. Rabbi Maurice Lamm, a prominent contemporary Orthodox rabbi, echoes this argument. He claims that the *kiddushin* act is not an act of acquisition but rather implies exclusivity: "When a man 'takes' a wife, he chooses one woman and, with her consent, makes her his life-long partner. She has no other husband."[23] What is markedly absent, however, from this analysis is that the bride does not perform a mutual act of *kiddushin*. It is exactly this point that has produced numerous feminist critiques leveled against the traditional wedding ritual, specifically targeting the *kiddushin* as an act of acquisition and, therefore, of oppression.[24]

The Jewish legal scholar Judith Wegner points out that the framers of the Mishnah view marriage first and foremost as the transfer of ownership of a woman's sexuality from her father to her husband.[25] Wegner continues and states that in the mishnaic catalogue of various types of chattel and the legal procedures for acquiring them, wives head the list. Wegner suggests that the Mishnah's framers listed the different types of property along with the wife to indicate both a formal and a substantive analogy between the acquisition of the woman's sexuality and the acquisition of chattel. Thus, the traditional text's view of the woman's sexuality (but not necessarily of the woman herself) as chattel is further expressed in the unilateral nature of the espousal ceremony, whereby the man recites a formula to the woman, who does not make any verbal reply. Even if she were to speak, her words would have no effect, since she is not legally capable of acquiring her groom's sexuality in the way that he is capable of acquiring hers. In other words, it is specifically forbidden by *halakhah* for the woman to "acquire" her husband in a mutual act of acquisition.[26] Moreover, some rabbis rule that not only do her words lack the power to acquire the husband, but they also cancel the man's act of acquisition and, therefore, she must be silent in response to this ritual act.

There are some harsh implications to this legal arrangement—the transformation of the woman's sexuality to a possession of her husband's—especially since it is still valid in the rabbinical courts in Israel as well as in the rest of the Orthodox Jewish world. Most significantly, a Jewish woman wed by the laws of the Torah can be divorced only by her husband's act of giving her a traditional *get* [bill of divorce]. Should her husband stubbornly refuse or otherwise be unable to release her in this way, she will remain a *mesurevet get* or an *agunah*, unable to remarry.[27] In this matter, Jewish law discriminates openly and explicitly between men and women.[28] A *mesurevet get* or *agunah* who chooses to live with another man pays a heavy price. Her children by that man are considered *mamzerim* [bastards], and under religious law neither they nor their offspring are allowed to marry Jews. Because all marriages between Jews in Israel are governed by Orthodox religious law, such children and their descendants are unable to marry in the State of Israel. In contrast, a married man can have children by another woman without legal sanction.[29]

The inequitableness of the wedding ritual is not just pronounced in its legal structure. Performatively speaking, throughout the whole ritual, the bride is symbolically invisible both in her physical appearance—her face being covered most of the ceremony with a veil (while her husband is standing beside her uncovered)—and vocally—her voice is not heard at any point during the ritual. These components mark the "Jewishness" of this ritual in regard to gender relations. They reflect the rabbis' "point of view of the man in relation to the woman whom he is 'marrying' while she is 'being married.' Similarly, in the subsequent act of giving the ring and reciting . . . the man is the initiator of the marriage link."[30] This socially constructs the male as the publicly visible, active subject and the female as the "invisible," passive object.

This article focuses on the discourse of the brides and those in their surrounding social environment about their wedding ritual and, specifically, about the act of *kiddushin*.

## THE COMPETING DISCOURSES

The term "discourse" is used to explain a variety of practices (e.g., conversation, performative acts, art, media, literature) that produce a social reality and understanding of any given social phenomenon. The verbal expression of my interviewees about their weddings, therefore, reflects the ways they understand, interpret, and express themselves in relation to this ritual. Thus, in this article I have limited the term "discourse" to spoken language alone. This perception of discourse follows Teun van Dijk's definition, which reads, "The emphasis on the interactional and practical nature of discourse is naturally associated with a focus on language use as *spoken* interaction."[31]

The discourse analysis I have undertaken below can be viewed as an ethnography of speaking, as "It studies the speech acts, events, and situations—everyday and informal as well as formal and RITUAL—that constitute the social, cultural and especially verbal life of particular societies."[32] In this sense, discourse can be "considered the focus of the language-culture-society-individual relationship, the place in which culture is conceived and transmitted, created, and re-created."[33] In other words, it "is constitutive in both conventional and creative ways: it contributes to reproducing society (social identities, social relationships, systems of knowledge and beliefs) as it is, yet also contributes to transforming society."[34] Therefore, understanding language is important because it creates social meaning and is fundamental to the construction of the social essence.[35]

In this article I wish to show how spoken language has the power to maintain the continuity of tradition, on the one hand, and to transform tradition, on the other hand. I include a summary of the discourses of the different groups, yet I have stressed the discourse of the brides and the rabbis because I see them as the most influential in this context.

## THE BRIDE'S DISCOURSE

When the interviewed brides were asked about their understanding of the wedding ritual and, specifically, about the act of *kiddushin*, they invoked the religious language of Jewish *halakhah* [religious law] and text, thus expressing and reflecting on their religious knowledge. In her interview, Shira, for example, a lawyer in her professional life, opposed the religious act of *kiddushin*, yet she expressed this resistance by using language that refers to her knowledge of religious law and text:

> The rituals assume that from the moment that the man gives the ring to the woman and says to her whatever he says to her, then what he really does by this act is he stakes an exclusive claim on her sexuality. Now this whole concept is not acceptable. It is a feeling that if he betrays me so it is bad! But if I betray him it is horrible! This concept is amazing. In all the matters that relate to my sexuality I am consecrated to one man, but he, on the other hand, can fool around and even if he is a pimp, they [the religious court] don't obligate him to give a *get*.

Shira clearly communicated her own interpretive understanding of the legal meaning of the *kiddushin* act. Although she did not cite Talmud or Mishnah, it is clear that her understanding stems from knowledge of Jewish legal texts—a knowledge that is continually conveyed throughout her interview. Her profession as a lawyer has also informed her discourse, as she continuously referred to civil legal terms in addition to Jewish ones. Other brides also made the connection between the act of *kiddushin* and the acquisition of a woman's sexuality, couching it in religious halakhic and textual terms. For example, Miri, who studies Torah in the *beit midrash* [religious house of study] at Hebrew University, asked: "What does the *kiddushin* mean? From a halakhic point of view it is an act of acquisition." Shelomit, a Talmudic scholar and teacher, stated: "I couldn't ignore the rule of the Mishnah, which states that the 'woman is acquired in three ways.'" By using the discourse of religious knowledge, these brides entered into a realm that, until recently, belonged only to men.

Some of the brides went beyond merely using the halakhic language and reappropriated it for their own uses. For example, Rivki demonstrated a nonliteral understanding: "It was clear to me that halakhically the *kiddushin* are not an actual acquisition and it is only symbolic." Like Shira, Anat also used specific terms related to religious laws but gave them her own nuance:

> The whole meaning of the ritual wasn't easy for me. That is, the fact that he consecrates me. So I gave my own interpretation. *Kiddushin* [to consecrate] means also to single someone out [*leyached*]. That means that he singles me out from the rest of the women in the world and I also single him out from the rest of the men in the world. But at the same time it was clear to me that although I single him out, I still am not consecrating him to me.

Some of the brides, throughout their interviews, expressed their initial belief that the use of this knowledge would put them on equal footing with the rabbis. That is to say, they thought they would be perceived as partners in the halakhic discussion about the boundaries of the wedding ritual, yet this was not the case. Their different stories demonstrated that, for some of the rabbis, the brides' ability to justify changes based on religious knowledge did not make a difference. These women, knowledgeable or not, were not viewed as equal partners in discussions on halakhic matters, precisely because of their gender. Thus, instead of focusing on their actual legal argument, the focus often shifted to their motivation for changing the ritual. This attitude toward women's knowledge and their desire to change tradition is not only in regard to the wedding ritual. Rather, this stance toward women's attempts to increase their participation in any ritual or "roles in public life have been overall adamantly resisted. . . . It is neither women's knowledge that is questioned nor the halakhic validity of what they propose. Rather, it is their motivation—that is, their *use* of knowledge—that is scrutinized, suspected, and impugned."[36]

## THE FAMILY

Overall, the grooms expressed indifference to and little concern for the wedding ritual and, specifically, for the act of *kiddushin*. Although they articulated their excitement regarding the beginning of a new life together, they did not focus on the wedding or on the ritual itself.

Some spouses articulated their increasing awareness of the problematic elements that the ritual entails only after their wives raised the issues with them. Even those who came to this conversation with more knowledge and consciousness about the issues emphasized the gap between their feelings toward the ritual compared to the feelings of their future wives.

The grooms supplied few explanations to account for their stance and, specifically, their indifference or low interest in the wedding ritual and the *kiddushin* act. For example, one expressed that as a man the feminist issues engendered by *kiddushin* did not concern him as much; another groom emphasized his equal and mutual relationship with his spouse, which innately contradicts the idea of acquisition. Another expressed confidence that in a case of a divorce, he would never use his advantage as a man within the religious system.

Although the language these grooms invoked was of total or partial indifference toward the wedding ritual, they did not generate an insensitive discourse. Rather, they expressed empathy to the distress their spouses felt because of the wedding ritual. They tried, in the name of their love and duality, to reach some compromises that would soothe their spouses' anxiety and soften the patriarchal elements of the ritual.

The mothers who were interviewed for this research generated a complex discourse. This discourse reflected, on the one hand, their partial identification with their daughter's unhappiness with certain aspects of the wedding ritual, and, on the other hand, their identification with Jewish tradition. Compared to their daughters, these mothers pronounced a more conservative approach regarding tradition and ritual. In this regard, they viewed themselves as the guardians of the tradition—those who need to place borders around the tradition to protect Judaism from radical or even moderate changes.

Part of the mothers' discourse described how they first learned about feminism from their daughters and how, as a result, they began to identify and feel empathetic to the difficulties their daughters found with the tradition and, particularly, the wedding ritual. The mothers' language revealed a perception of themselves as integrally connected to their daughters, and thus they experienced things as a continuation of their daughters' experiences.

Although the mothers identified this connection to their daughters, they also emphasized the gap that exists between their viewpoints and those of their daughters. While they admitted that some changes in the wedding ritual are necessary, they also stressed that these changes need to be done gradually and with rabbinic approval.

Overall, the mothers expressed the need for continuity and the importance of the community. Stressing gradual change through an ongoing relationship with the establishment, these mothers feared radical changes, which they saw as leading to a break from the community and to a distortion of the familiar face of tradition. It seems like the mothers viewed themselves as socialization agents and, thus, as the guardians of the tradition, including the wedding ritual. By supporting the wedding ritual as it is celebrated today, they were able to retroactively confirm the choices they made about their own wedding ritual and to communicate the idea that they and their daughters are part of a chain. Moreover, this emphasis on the chain of tradition influenced the tone of their discourse as well. While the daughters' discourse was populated with religious terms that expressed their knowledge, the mothers used the language of emotions to describe their relation to the tradition. It seems like the emotional attachment that these mothers felt toward the tradition was one of the causes of their unwillingness to fully support the changes that their daughters envisioned.

Regarding the question of changing the wedding ritual and, specifically, the act of *kiddushin*, the fathers, much like the grooms, were indifferent to this act and to the wedding ritual in general. Instead, they emphasized the importance of the relationship of the couple. Yet, there is a distinction between their discourses and that of the grooms. The difference relates to the fact that the fathers' discourse focuses on three main social and institutional structures: the maintenance of the legal and/or social and/or religious systems. Avi and Shmuel accordingly demonstrate this position:

> I would say to my daughter do what ever you want to do in another place, but [here] do a ritual that would be accepted. That you will be married according to what is accepted through the rabbinate institution in Israel. . . . I am not saying that I wouldn't want to change what is accepted in Israel, but first of all one needs to do what is acceptable, so no one will question if the marriage is according to the halakhic law and the Israeli law. . . . There is the ritual, there is the legal issue, and there is the relationship between the husband and the wife and that's what is important, OK. And I think that the relationship between the husband and the wife is not affected by the fact that the ritual is not mutual.

> From a pragmatic point of view I would not suggest to any one of my daughters to get married in a Conservative wedding because, unfortunately, it is not acceptable by the rabbinate in Israel . . . there is no civil marriage in Israel and Jewish religious marriage is defined as only Orthodox, and I am not in favor that my daughters will fight for principles. There is no use for it. . . . Let's assume they would solve the legal problem regarding the Conservative wedding, so I would have no problem that they would be married that way, or even in a Reform wedding, but not in the Israel of today, or [at least] not with my friends.

Each of the fathers stressed his motivation to keep the ritual, more or less, as it is, but their motivation was based on different considerations. Both Avi and Shmuel highlighted the importance of performing the ritual according to the laws of Israel. Shmuel's position is especially interesting. Although he is principally in favor of separating religion and state, he emphasizes that until this happens his daughters should remain in the traditional structure for political reasons. He accentuated the social implications in addition to the legal structure. He relates what he said to his daughters: "Why don't you do your wars on other people? Instead you embarrass the parents who put all the money for the wedding and invite all the friends, and at the end all the [feminist] principles blow everything up."

It is worth noting that in the statements, and throughout their entire interviews, Avi and Shmuel, as well as the other fathers, frequently used some form of the word "acceptable," indicating their internalized concern for established institutions. To sum up, the fathers spoke about the importance of maintaining the different structures from a practical and utilitarian point of view.

## THE RABBIS' DISCOURSE

It is possible to divide the rabbis' discourse into two parts. One part concentrates on the language of religious law and terms, similar to the discourse of the brides. Another part of their discourse, which was much more significant in terms of its length, was their use of mythical and transcendental language to talk about the wedding ritual. Rabbi Zvi displayed such language:

> I see a lot of wisdom in the fact that a man marries a woman. I see something mythical about it. . . . I still think that a certain definition of masculinity is that the man can marry [*lase'et*] a woman, meaning in the simplest way that he can carry her [*nosee*], and I think a woman wishes to be carried [*nise'et*]. I think that there is something beautiful in the image of Boaz and Ruth;[37] in these mythical biblical images: that a man goes to a well and can pick up the stones [when he meets his beloved].[38] Yes, all these mythical pictures are powerful pictures in my mind. They are stronger than the postmodernist language, which we live by: that besides some physical differences everything is completely equal.

After describing his ideas about gender relations through the play on the Hebrew word *lase'et*, which means both to marry and to carry, Rabbi Zvi continued to delineate how this mythical idea is embodied in the act of *kiddushin*:

> From this concept [the mythical view of male and female] I think comes the idea of *kiddushim*, of this ability to carry. And you wrap this

idea in the language of *kiddushin*, when in the ancient Jewish language, *kiddushin* were done through acquisition. The acquisition is not the center. The acquisition is the objectification through which this whole idea [of manhood and femininity] came into the world.

Rabbi Zvi recognized the element of acquisition, the essence of the *kiddushin*, yet he wished to interpret it in a different way. In an effort to use language to construct reality, he viewed the *kiddushin* as embodying a deep, universal, romantic, and mythological truth that relates to the basic relationship that is created between a man and a woman—the man who carries and the woman who wishes to be carried. It is precisely this notion that is reflected in the fact that only the man can consecrate [*lekadesh*] the woman, while the woman can only be consecrated. Zvi therefore transformed the meaning of the *kiddushin* act from one that has legal and halakhic meanings and consequences to one that expresses a romantic and mythical relationship. Ironically, his discourse, which seeks to negate postmodern language, is a modern and Western discourse. It is a language that emphasizes romantic love, which is in itself a modern concept associated with marital relationships.

The other rabbis also used terms that were beyond the halakhic meaning of the *kiddushin* act. For example, Rabbi Shlomo compared the bride to the Shekinah through the use of metaphorical language,[39] thereby replacing the physical dimension of the bride with metaphysical and spiritual dimensions. The other rabbis I interviewed expressed a similar perspective that the act of *kiddushin* reflects the true reality of gender relations as it ought to be in this world. It is a dynamic of carrying versus being carried, activeness versus passiveness, and centrality versus marginality. Yet the relationship between the couple stems not from the man's public activeness but precisely from the centrality of the woman, from her sexual strength, from her silence, and from the fact that the wedding ritual is nonreciprocal. Therefore, the act of *kiddushin* is tied not only to a cosmological truth but also to a deep psychological and sociological need.

The rabbis' discourse also reveals a delineation of the halakhic boundaries of the wedding ritual and, therefore, also expresses what can be changed. The rabbis clarified why they drew the limits where they did, citing their emotional connection to the tradition, the halakhic limitations, the social pressure they are under, and the strict rules of the Rabbinate that they must follow.

To conclude, the rabbis' discourse is uniquely marked by their use of metaphorical language. Although this language originates in their authority, they are also aware of restrictions to this power based on social, political, halakhic, and emotional considerations.

# SOCIAL LOCATION AND HIERARCHICAL AXES

It is my contention that there is a direct correlation between the social location of each group and their discourse as described above. As a result of my work on this issue, I have identified three hierarchical axes that are instrumental in establishing the social location of each of the five interviewed groups in this context. These axes are (1) gender, (2) religious knowledge, and (3) authority.[40] These axes were not chosen randomly; rather, they represent two significant cultural concepts: power and control; that is to say, they are based on who has more power and control throughout the negotiations regarding the ritual. These concepts are embodied in each of the hierarchal axes and enabled me to determine if the interviewed group is dominant or subordinate on each axis.

## THE GENDER AXIS

In Judaism, men are considered more powerful than women and, thus, have more control over them.[41] As I have demonstrated above, this is also the case in the wedding ritual, in which men are perceived as more powerful than women in terms of their status. Therefore, from the outset gender plays an important role in establishing power and control within the marital relationship. Thus, men are dominant on the axis of gender in the religious context.

## THE KNOWLEDGE AXIS

The Jewish world has always perceived the study and the acquiring of religious knowledge as one of its highest and worthiest goals. In spite of this ideal, there have always been marginal groups who could not participate in such an endeavor due to social status or lack of means. As a result of their subordinate social status, women constitute one of these groups. The widespread assumption was that women would naturally misunderstand religious texts or would use their knowledge in the wrong way. Therefore, women were not encouraged and were even forbidden from studying Jewish texts and, as a result, largely remained ignorant in many halakhic matters.[42] Tamar El-Or sums up the phenomenon of religious literacy in the Jewish religious society and claims that "religious-halachic knowledge forms the primary power centre in the organization of the daily life of religious Jewish individuals and communities. It is the material from which the imperative conceptual, moral, political, and ideological fabric is woven. This knowledge lies in the hands of 'knowing' me."[43]

In the ultra-Orthodox and even in the modern religious society, men are still considered to be more knowledgeable and, therefore, to be more powerful than women. Since they are the "knowing ones," they have the tools to interpret and to develop religious laws and, thus, they have more control than women in the religious system.

## THE AUTHORITY AXIS

It is possible to divide the concept of authority into two categories: (1) the authority within the family—that of parents over their children; and (2) the authority within society—that of the rabbis and, specifically, the rabbinic institution that governs all the members who participate in the ritual. Within the family, the parents are perceived as more authoritative than their children for obvious reasons. The brides and the grooms described in their interviews their need to negotiate with their parents about the changes they wished to make to their ritual. Many times the negotiation concluded with the children relinquishing their desires to appease the demands of their parents. The brides and grooms explained their submission to their parents' desires by saying that they wished to respect their parents, to avoid conflict, and to maintain the relationship. This dynamic testifies to the fact that the parents were more powerful and had more control over their children than vice versa.

Viewing the concept of authority from a broader social perspective, the rabbis and, moreover, the Rabbinate are perceived as more authoritative than the rest of the participants in the wedding ritual, since they are the ones who dictate the borders of the traditional wedding. However, this authority is not without its own hierarchy. On the one hand, the interviewed rabbis referred to their limited ability to change certain aspects of the wedding ritual, since they were worried that the Rabbinate might take away their authority to perform marriages in the State of Israel. On the other hand, it was individual rabbis who forbade the brides' and grooms' requested changes, as the brides and grooms have described in their interviews. Since the wedding ritual is acknowledged in Israel only by the Rabbinate and since ultimately the rabbis have to be willing to perform the ceremony, the brides and grooms were forced to accept the rabbis' decisions (unless, of course, they choose to marry outside of Israel or in a ritual that the state does not acknowledge). The rabbis, therefore, acted as delegates of the Rabbinate. Therefore, in this context, the rabbis are more powerful and have more control than the rest of the interviewed groups, but the Israeli rabbinic institute has the ultimate power and control.

## BETWEEN DISCOURSE, SOCIAL LOCATION, AND POWER

The mapping of each group onto each one of these hierarchical axes can explain the unique discourse that stemmed from each group.

The brides were subordinate on the gender and authority axes but dominant on the knowledge axis. The brides in this study were unique in their ability to attain religious knowledge. These brides are part of the literary revolution taking place in the modern religious society, which has been described by Tamar El-Or.[44]

The brides' knowledge, in turn, enabled them to access the religious law and, therefore, question the ideas, notions, motives, and limits of these laws. This eventually encouraged them to enter negotiations with their groom, parents, and rabbis regarding their wedding ritual. The brides felt not only that they owned the religious knowledge (at least to some extent) but also that they could use this knowledge as a source of empowerment to try to make changes. However, this ability was limited when they met the others who were involved in these negotiations, especially in their encounters with the rabbis, who acted as mediators between the brides, *halakhah*, and the larger Rabbinate.

The locations of the brides on the three hierarchical axes can explain why their discourse emphasized law and religious language. This is a discourse that strengthens their dominant position and, therefore, empowers them. This knowledge enabled them to first interpret the different ritual acts, then negotiate for their desired changes, and finally act, to some extent, to effect change, ultimately reclaiming and reconstructing their wedding ritual.[45]

The grooms were dominant on the axes of religious knowledge and gender and subordinate on the axis of authority. Their dominance on the axis of religious knowledge results not only from being men in the Jewish religious system but also from their education in *yeshivot* [religious schools that specialize in the study of Jewish text].

One could expect that since the grooms are dominant on the knowledge axis they would produce a similar discourse to that of the brides, using the language of knowledge in Jewish text and law. Although some of them did refer to the Jewish law, it was not the main concern of their conversations. This can be explained by the fact that, for these men, being dominant on the knowledge axis is taken for granted. Being born into this privilege, they have no need to use their knowledge in order to feel more empowered.

Rather, the discourse of the grooms can be characterized by the separation between the halakhic realm and the personal realm. They mostly demonstrated indifference toward or lack of consciousness about the wedding ritual and the act of *kiddushin*. This discourse can be explained by the grooms' dominance on the axis of gender. Their ability to be indifferent toward the act of *kiddushin*, with its legal implications, can be best understood by the fact that they do not feel threatened by this act. In case of divorce, they are situated on better legal grounds than their spouses. Therefore, they can afford to separate the *halakhah* construct—a hierarchical ritual—from their feelings toward their marriage and their future wives. Hence, their discourse stresses the personal realm. They invoke the language of love, romance, and their shared life together as more significant to them than the wedding ritual and the wedding day.

The mothers were dominant on the authority axis as parents, yet they were subordinate on the gender and religious knowledge axes. Their dominance on the authority axis explains why their discourse concentrated on the need to maintain the traditional borders of the wedding ritual and, in general, maintain the Jewish tradition. This discourse emphasizes the way these mothers perceived themselves as socialization agents responsible for maintaining cultural and religious order within the family. The mothers most likely viewed themselves as guardians of Jewish life because they had internalized a long-existing social message that has perpetuated this perception. The historian Paula Hyman describes the origins of this message: "When life in the modern Western world led most assimilating Jewish men to abandon traditional Jewish culture and limit their religious expression to periodic appearances at synagogue and the performance of some communal service, their wives absorbed the dominant societal expectations of women as the guardian of religion."[46]

This process accounts for the mothers' domination in the realm of their home, where they have become the guardians and the agents of Jewish tradition. In relation to the men and even to their daughters, the mothers were subordinate on the religious knowledge axis. They did not engage in extensive study of Jewish text. The subordination on this axis can explain the lack of language involving Jewish text and law and the proliferation of emotional language involving Jewish tradition.

Finally, the mothers' subordination on the axis of gender can also explain their identification with and empathy for, at least to some degree, the aspirations and the frustrations of their daughters in reference to the religious system.

The fathers are dominant in all three axes: gender, religious knowledge, and authority. Their dominance on the gender axis explains their general lack of empathy for and identification with their daughters' desires to change the wedding ritual. Moreover, this location can also explain their indifference to the wedding ritual or, at least, their choice to downplay the meaning of acquisition embodied in the act of *kiddushin*. Instead, like the grooms, they emphasized the importance of couplehood and maintaining a loving relationship.

The fathers and grooms were also similar regarding the lack of references to law and text in their language. Like the grooms, their status as knowledgeable is a given in their social system.

Despite their similarities with the grooms, the fathers also shared a dominant position on the authority axis with the mothers. However, their dominance on this axis has an additional dimension that is absent from the mothers' authority. The fathers' authority not only is maintained within the small family unit but also exists in the larger context of their society. The power they have as men results from the religious authority that both society and religious law bestow upon them. Therefore, their identification with the different institutional systems (e.g., social, religious, political) is stronger than that of the mothers and, hence, is articulated in their discourse. Therefore, the fathers' discourse emphasized the importance of remaining within the different institutional frameworks and the need for social and legal approval of the wedding ritual. In other words, their discourse preserves their status in the religious and social system.

The rabbis are dominant on all three axes, and as a result they produced a mythical and metahalakhic discourse. Although the rabbis seem to be located on the three hierarchical axes at positions similar to the fathers, their actual status is higher on the authority axis because their authority to make religious decisions is absolute, as I have explained above.

Since the rabbis' discourse derives from their absolute dominance on the authority axis (compared to the other participants), it is not accidental that their discourse is ideologically based. Many times ideology is produced by the social elite precisely in order to justify and maintain the social order without using physical force. Moreover, it is also not surprising to discover that gender ideology—an ideology of "difference that elaborates and legitimates the attribution of a range of traits, roles, and statuses to men *or* women"[47]—is intertwined with the discourse about the wedding ritual. In this context ideology is a powerful tool used to convince the unconvinced about the importance of maintaining the religious Jewish ritual.

In the specific case of Jewish marriages, rabbinic ideology finds its expression in a mythical discourse. This mythical discourse perpetuates an ideology centered on gender power and relations, giving credence to broader considerations than the halakhic construction of the wedding ritual. Using a transcendental-spiritual-mythical language to discuss wedding rituals stabilizes and reinforces the power of the religious authority and maintains the status quo of gender roles. The rabbis' discourse distinguishes clearly between men and women and constructs gender roles not as culturally derived but as natural. Although part of this discourse makes women the center of the ritual, it does not really subvert the established gender roles and power. Rather, it strengthens them because the final result is the justification and maintenance of the *kiddushin* as a nonreciprocal act with all its legal implications. This perception leaves almost no room for fluidity and mobility in gender roles. Thus, the power of the rabbis' discourse strengthens social stereotypes regarding masculinity and femininity and presents them as an inherent truth. The usage of mythical images and transcendental language (e.g., Jacob and Rachel, Ruth and Boaz, the Shechina) makes the narratives of the rabbis more significant because "Myth deals with imagery, that is, with symbolic language, and it is grounded in the existential archetypes of the narrating society."[48] When the couple speaks with their rabbi and hears this language, it evinces many layers of meaning for them. It touches a deep core regarding nationality, history, and belief, reminding them of the connection between the present and the past. Hence, it has a significant influence.

The mythical and transcendental language used by the rabbis is not unique to them. Susan Sered states that many cultures use "biological and transcendental language in order to construct two essential different genders: male and female. Thus the 'natural' and the 'supernatural' language serve 'as powerful tools for idealizing and enforcing difference and hierarchy.'"[49]

In talking about the ways the *kiddushin* reflects an ultimate truth about the psychological needs and essence of male and female, the rabbis create two different types of beings—the man who needs to be the carrier and, hence, the one who consecrates, and the woman who needs to be carried and, hence, to be consecrated. These explanations illuminate why the rabbis so naturally shifted from the halakhic language to the mythical and transcendental language (i.e., referring to the bride as Shekhina).

The ideology that the rabbis so naturally create becomes an interpretive tool for them, which, ironically, strives to diminish the hierarchical and oppressive elements in the wedding ritual and, thus, ease the distress of the brides about these elements. Their language then tries to reconcile between the halakhic stance and the modern feminist stance. However, there is a need to acknowledge the power of the rabbis' discourse, which has the ability to maintain the social order and the masculine power perpetuated by the act of *kiddushin*. By ascribing to this ritual act a cosmic truth, they legitimize and sanctify it. Hence, they leave almost no room for criticizing and changing the legal construction of the wedding.

## CONCLUSION

The different discourses convey the tension that exists between the participants' subordination to the authorities and their search for autonomy and self-expression.   In the course of this article, I demonstrated that the different groups of interviewees are situated differently on three hierarchical axes and, therefore, the discourses they produced are also positioned differently within the social pyramid.  As Rosalind Coward and John Ellis argue, understanding language as a symbolic system, one cannot comprehend the revolutionary potential individual subjects have despite their location in the social construct.[50] Coward and Ellis argue that discourse has the power to make social change, even if this change might be minor because they are limited by other social forces.  The power of the brides' discourse lies in its criticism of the powers of the *halakhah*, the religious institution, and society to determine the wedding ritual.  It has the power to create a refreshing and new way of thinking about the traditional Jewish wedding.  Moreover, their discourse demythologized the act of the *kiddushin* and, consequently, the hegemonic ideology.  In this sense, the brides' discourse can be defined as feminist discourse, which, similarly to gender or feminist performance, can be seen as "imbricated in identity politics."[51]  It allows women to "rewrite themselves and the cultural texts that have defined them."[52]

More than just the power to reinterpret the different ritual acts, this discourse motivated the brides (with their grooms) to create some significant changes, specifically visual changes, within the wedding ritual.  However, the brides' discourse did not have the strength to create fundamental changes in the construction of the *kiddushin* act and, therefore, could not change significantly the legal status of women and the imbalance of power that results from the construction of this act.

The rabbis' discourse and its tendency to mythologize the *kiddushin*, on the other hand, had the power to actually shape the limits and boundaries of the wedding ritual.  As the rabbis employ their own unique discourse, their identification of *kiddushin* as an act of acquisition no longer reflects only the demands of *halakhah* but rather creates a gender ideology.  In other words, the rabbis were able "to constitute the given by stating it, to create appearances and belief, to confirm or transform the vision of the world and thereby action in the world, and therefore the world itself."[53]

Since the rabbis' discourse receives its legitimacy from different institutions (religious, social, political) and from the people themselves, its power to "constitute the given" is more effective than the other discourses, which do not enjoy this legitimacy.  In this sense, "the power of the elite . . . is a dominant force."[54]  At times, this discourse even silences other discourses and any of their efforts to resist and to change the social order.  In this way, one ideological discourse becomes sacred while the other discourses become marginal.

The brides (along with their husbands) who wished to create change in the religious system found themselves in an ironic situation. The women who chose to press for change while recognizing limits were, consciously or not, contributing to the perception of this monopoly of halakhic power, and, in turn, the rabbis' power.

Just as Bar-Itzhak demonstrates how the stories that mythologize and demythologize the society of the kibbutz reflect the tension between preservation and contemporary complexities in that society, the same occurs in the case of the wedding ritual. The existence of two linguistic movements, mythologization—expressed by the rabbis' discourse—and demythologization—expressed by the brides' discourse—reflects a social tension. On the one hand lies the desire to defend and maintain the tradition, with its ancient roots as it is; on the other hand exists the desire to display the tradition, with all its imperfections and complexities.

As for the discourses of the grooms, mothers, and fathers, they have the ability to either support or divert the power of the brides' discourse. If these groups choose to offer support, the brides have more leverage to stretch the boundaries of the wedding ritual. Brides who had the support of those around them were able to create more significant changes than the brides who had no social support for their wishes. That is, these discourses can create an additional pressure on the rabbis and the Rabbinate.

This article has revealed that women are not simply passive objects within given patriarchal constructs. Rather, they can choose to be active subjects who work within those same constructs in order to activate change by creating an alternative discourse followed by action (which I did not discuss in this article).[55] The brides in my research, being dominant on the axis of religious knowledge, demonstrated their ability to be social and cultural agents of change. The article, therefore, highlights the specific resource of religious knowledge that can act as a significant tool to create a unique and powerful discourse. Discourse is the first critical step necessary for women to initiate change in a religious system; it is the articulation of the problematic elements in a system and the protest against these elements that must take place before actual change can occur. Thus, the power of discourse is not an abstract power but rather has concrete influence on reality.

Finally, I wish to refer to the words of the anthropologist Clifford Geertz, who wrote, "seeing heaven in a grain of sand is not a trick only poets can accomplish." In this article, I intended to follow the Geertzian course of seeking out in these grains of sand the heaven of a much broader phenomenon. Although I focus here on one religious ritual, I believe that these women's discourse represents a larger phenomenon. These women illustrated the struggle faced by citizens of a modern, increasingly transnational world to remain at home with their religious traditions and to reconcile their modern identities with premodern ritual practice.  Thus, while this article compares different discourses regarding the wedding ritual, it is more broadly about the ways men and especially women deal with the tension between tradition and modernity.

## NOTES

[1] A different version of this article will be published in *Revisioning Ritual: Jewish Traditions in Transition* (The Jewish Cultural Studies Series; ed. Simon J. Bronner; Oxford: Littman Library of Jewish Civilization, forthcoming, 2011).

[2] The fear of being identified as feminist and, thus, the hesitancy to define oneself as feminist has been discussed elsewhere.  For example, see Harriet Lerner Goldhor, *The Dance of Anger: A Woman's Guide to Changing the Patterns of Intimate Relationships* (New York: Harper Paperbacks, 1985).

[3] Yehuda Mirsky, "Modernizing Orthodoxies: The Case of Feminism," in *Lihiyot Ishah Yehudiyah* [To Be a Jewish Woman] (Kolech Proceedings vol. 4; ed. Tova Cohen; Jerusalem: Kolech–Relgious Women's Forum, 2007, in Hebrew), 40-41.

[4] Tamar Ross, *Expanding the Palace of Torah: Orthodoxy and Feminism* (Waltham: Brandeis University Press, 2004), 24.

[5] Ibid., 16.

[6] Christel J. Manning, *God Gave Us the Right: Conservative Catholic, Evangelical Protestant, and Orthodox Jewish Women Grapple with Feminism* (Piscataway: Rutgers University Press, 1999), 6.

[7] Ross, *Expanding the Palace of Torah*, 24.

[8] To learn more about the development of Modern Orthodoxy as it has stemmed from Orthodoxy, see Mirsky, "Modernizing Orthodoxies"; to learn more about the tension between Orthodoxy and modern women, see Manning, *God Gave Us the Right*; Lynn Davidman and Shelly Tenenbaum, eds., *Feminist Perspectives on Jewish Studies* (New Haven: Yale University Press, 1994).

[9] Mirsky, "Modernizing Orthodoxies," 45.

[10] I was looking for women who defined themselves as religious and feminist and for whom the wedding ritual was a point of contention.  These women had similar characteristics, and thus the group came out as a fairly homogenous group.

[11] These neighborhoods are the venue of several liberal Jewish study centers and of various types of social, religious, and spiritual activities.  Their populations include a sufficient concentration of immigrants from English-speaking countries.

[12] Most of these women had a graduate degree and some had a PhD degree or were in the process of getting one.  In addition, most of them spent a significant amount of time, after high school, going to women's *yeshivot* [house of religious studies], where they learned materials that men learn in their *yeshivot*, such as Talmud.  This fact is significant since different research projects demonstrate how women's education has an impact on the personal processes they go through and on their identities.

[13] In this article, *halakhah* refers to Jewish law as interpreted by Orthodox rabbis, which is the *halakhah* that the women I studied had to challenge in order to formulate the type of wedding rituals they desired. Accordingly, all the rabbis I interviewed were Orthodox.

[14] Richard Bauman, "Performance," in *Folklore, Cultural Performances, and Popular Entertainments: A Communications-Centered Handbook* (ed. Richard Bauman; New York: Oxford University Press, 1992), 41.

[15] Ross, *Expanding the Palace of Torah*, xiv.

[16] Vanessa Ochs, *Inventing Jewish Ritual* (Philadelphia: Jewish Publication Society, 2005), 217.

[17] Ibid.

[18] To learn more about the problems that the wedding ritual comprises and about the actual changes these women made to their wedding ritual, thus transforming and renewing the typical traditional wedding, see Irit Koren, "The Bride's Voice: Religious Women Challenge the Wedding Ritual," *Nashim* 10 (2005): 29-52.

[19] I have chosen to focus on the Ashkenazi ritual because most of the brides I interviewed were Ashkenazi and were wed according to Ashkenazi customs.

[20] To learn more about American Orthodox wedding customs, see Rela Geffen, *Celebration & Renewal: Rites of Passage in Judaism* (Philadelphia: Jewish Publication Society, 1993); and Ochs, *Inventing Jewish Ritual*.

[21] Daniel H. Gordis, "Marriage: Judaism's 'Other' Covenantal Relationship," in *Celebration & Renewal: Rites of Passage in Judaism* (ed. Rela Geffen; Philadelphia: Jewish Publication Society, 1993), 108.

[22] The Mishnah is considered to be the first written recording of the oral laws, which, according to tradition, were given to the Jewish people on Mount Sinai.

[23] Maurice Lamm, *The Jewish Way in Love and Marriage* (San Francisco: Jonathan David, 1980), 151.

[24] Susan Aranoff, "Two Views of Marriage—Two Views of Women: Reconsidering *Tav Lemetav Tan Du Milemetav Armelu*," *Nashim* 3 (2000): 199—227; and Susan Okin, "Marriage, Divorce, and the Politics of Family Life," in *Marriage, Liberty and Equality: Shall the Three Walk Together?* (ed. Tova Cohen; Ramat Gan, 2000, in Hebrew), 7-26.

[25] There is a certain age at which the woman does not need her father's consent, but even then, through this act she transfers her sexual rights to her husband's ownership. In the wedding ritual this transformation is not expressed in any performative way.

[26] Judith Wegner, *Chattel or Person? The Status of Women in the Mishnah* (New York: Oxford University Press, 1988), 66-72.

[27] An *agunah* is a woman whose husband has disappeared or is otherwise unable to give his wife a *get* [bill of divorce]. A *mesurevet get* is a woman whose husband abuses the power given to him by *halakhah* and refuses to grant her a *get*. For more information on *agunot* and *mesuravot get*, see http://www.agunot.org.

[28] During the tenth and eleventh centuries, Rabbi Tam (Gersom ben Yehudah) issued a ruling in Ashkenaz Europe. According to this rule, when a man initiates the divorce, the woman needs to agree to accept his *get*. This rule was supposed to balance the power relations between men and women in cases of divorce. Nevertheless, the gap between men and women in this context is still significant, since in case of her refusal

he can get permission to divorce her as long as he gets 100 rabbis to agree. Moreover, the implications for their children from another spouse, while they are still married, are different, as I have explained above.

[29] Orit Kamir, *Feminism, Rights, and Law* (Tel Aviv: Broadcast University, 2002, in Hebrew), 142-46.

[30] Harvey Goldberg, *Jewish Passages: Cycles of Jewish Life* (Berkeley: University of California Press, 2003), 121.

[31] Teun A. Van Dijk, "Discourse as Interaction in Society," in *Discourse as Social Interaction: Discourse Studies: A Multidisciplinary Introduction* (vol. 2; ed. Teun A. Van Dijk; London: Sage Publications, 1997), 4.

[32] Joel Sherzer, "Ethnography of Speaking," in *Folklore, Cultural Performances, and Popular Entertainments: A Communications-Centered Handbook* (ed. Richard Bauman; New York: Oxford University Press), 79.

[33] Ibid.

[34] Norman Fairclough, *Discourse and Social Change* (Cambridge: Cambridge University Press, 1992), 65.

[35] Bauman, "Performance," 43.

[36] Tova Hartman, *Feminism Encounters Traditional Judaism* (Waltham: Brandeis University Press, 2007), 18.

[37] Boaz and Ruth are biblical characters from the Scroll of Ruth.

[38] This is a reference to the story of Jacob, who is able to remove a heavy stone from a well by himself when he sees Rachel, his future wife, for the first time (Gen 29:10).

[39] The Shekinah is held by many to represent the feminine attributes of the presence of God (*shekhinah* is a feminine word in Hebrew), based especially on readings of the Talmud and later on the mythical philosophy in Judaism called Kabbalah.

[40] Susan Sered, Romi Kaplan, and Samuel Cooper compare different groups' discourses in the context of different social hierarchical axes and in the context of different religious ritual. It is interesting to compare their findings with my findings. See Susan S. Sered, Romi Kaplan, and Samuel Cooper, "Talking about Miqveh Parties or Discourses of Gender, Hierarchy and Social Control," in *Women and Water: Menstruation in Jewish Life and Law* (ed. Rahell Wasserfall; Hanover: Brandeis University Press, 1999), 139-65.

[41] See, for example, Rachel Biale, *Women and Jewish Law* (New York: Schocken, 1984).

[42] Amos Funkenstein and Adin Steinsaltz, eds., *The Sociology of Ignorance* (Tel Aviv: Misrad Habitachon, 1988, in Hebrew), 75-76.

[43] Tamar El-Or, *Next Year I Will Know More: Literacy and Identity among Young Orthodox Women in Israel* (trans. Haim Watzman; Detroit: Wayne State University Press, 2002), 29-30.

[44] Ibid.

[45] To see more about the changes they did accomplish, see Koren, "The Bride's Voice."

[46] Paula E. Hyman, *Gender and Assimilation in Modern Jewish History: The Roles and Representation of Women* (Seattle: University of Washington Press, 1995), 25-26.

[47] Susan S. Sered, "Religiously Doing Gender: The Good Woman and the Bad Woman in Israeli Ritual Discourse," *Method & Theory in the Study of Religion* 13:2 (2001): 154.

[48] Haya Bar-Itzhak, *Israeli Folk Narratives: Settlement, Immigration, Ethnicity* (Detroit: Wayne State University Press), 34.

[49] Sered, "Religiously Doing Gender."

[50] Rosalind Coward and John Ellis, *Language and Materialism: Developments in Semiology and the Theory of the Subject* (London: Routledge and Kegan Paul, 1977).

[51] Deborah A. Kapchan, "Performance," in *Eight Words for the Study of Expressive Culture* (ed. Burt Feintuch; Champaign: University of Illinois Press, 2003), 135

[52] Ibid.

53 Pierre Bourdieu, "Symbolic Power," in *Issues in the Sociology of Education* (ed. Denis Gleeson; trans. Colin Wringe; Nafferton: Driffield, 1977), 117.

[54] Bar-Itzhak, *Israeli Folk Narratives*, 48.

[55] For discussion of changes made through action, see Koren, "The Bride's Voice."

# The Making of a Rabbi: *Semichah* Ordination from Moses to Grosses

## Jonathan Gross

Many times in Jewish history the Torah was almost lost from our people. Only because of the heroic actions of great men and women was the Torah able to be passed down throughout the generations despite oppression and persecution. One such hero was Rabbi Yehudah Ben Baba. The story of his heroism is related in *Messechet Avodah Zarah* 8b. During the Hadrianic persecutions in 135 CE, the Roman government issued a decree that made rabbinic ordination a capital crime. The law stated not only that the granter and the recipient of ordination would be sentenced to death but also that the town in which the ordination was performed would be destroyed and the area upon which the town stood would be laid to waste. In defiance of the decree, Rabbi Yehudah Ben Baba ordained five of his students who would go on to be the leaders of the next generation. So as not to bring guilt upon a particular town, the location of the ordination was between two cities and wedged between two mountains that could not be laid to waste.

Upon seeing that they were detected by the authorities, the rabbi said to his students, "Flee, my children!" But they said to him, "O Rabbi, what about you?" "I," he replied, "will lie still before them as a stone that cannot be turned." While his students fled through the passage formed at the base of the two mountains, Rabbi Yehudah Ben Baba held off the Romans. The Gemara [part of the Talmud] relates that the Romans could not move him until they drove 300 iron spears through his body and made his corpse like a sieve.

Rabbinic ordination—*semichah* in Hebrew—is thankfully not always as dramatic and heroic as the story of Rabbi Yehudah Ben Baba, but in many ways it is a rite of passage for a student of Torah, albeit not in the same literal sense it was for Rabbi Yehudah Ben Baba and his students.

*Semichah* literally means "leaning." When Moshe [Moses] appointed Yehoshua [Joshua] as his successor, he did so by laying his hands on or leaning on Yehoshua, symbolically transferring a portion of the divine spirit. This event began a long chain of ordination that lasted over a thousand years. The *semichah* of the Talmudic period, like that of Rabbi Yehudah Ben Baba, meant that the student was being ordained by someone who could trace his own ordination back to Moshe himself. Although Yehudah Ben Baba was able to keep *semichah* alive in his day, the chain was tragically broken by the fourth century CE because of persecution.[1]

Throughout the ages there have been a number of attempts to re-institute *semichah* and begin a new authoritative chain. These attempts were based on the ruling of Maimonides found in his laws of *Sanhedrin* 4:11: "It appears to me that if all of the sages of the land of Israel were to agree to appoint judges and give them *semichah* then they would have [genuine] *semichah*. They would have the authority to rule in cases of fines as well as the authority to grant *semichah* to others."

The most famous of all historic attempts to re-institute the chain of *semichah* was in the fifteenth century, when Jacob Berab of Sefad convened a rabbinic summit to grant *semichah* to four outstanding scholars, among them Rabbi Yosef Caro, the author of the *Shulchan Aruch*. This and other such attempts were always contested by opposing rabbinic authorities and were subsequently never accepted by the Jewish masses. In a sense, this fate was predicted in the same passage in the works of Maimonides: "If [there is a possibility to restore *semichah*] then why did rabbis [such as Rabbi Yehudah Ben Baba] take such pains to maintain *semichah*? Because Israel is scattered and it would be impossible for all to agree. If there was always one who had *semichah* from the chain of Moshe then there is no need for consensus." With the establishment of the modern State of Israel in 1948, there was another failed attempt to restore *semichah*. The latest attempt is the Sanhedrin initiative started with the *semichah* of Rabbi Yitzchak Halberstam in 2004.[2] Today, countless institutions offer rabbinic ordination referred to as *semichah*, but to my knowledge there is no institution that actually claims to be connected by direct lineage to the *semichah* of Moshe.

I received my *semichah* from Yeshiva University's Rabbi Isaac Elchanan Theological Seminary (RIETS). To earn *semichah* from RIETS, a candidate must complete four years of intensive study, sit for regular written and oral examinations on areas of Jewish codes and laws, take a number of courses in practical rabbinic skills such as counseling and speech, and fulfill an internship requirement in one of a number of rabbinic fields. There is no annual graduation; rather, every four years there is a public ceremony called the *chag HaSemichah* that celebrates all those who completed their requirements over the last four years. Although my *semichah* does not have a direct lineage to the *semichah* of Moshe, in many ways it is similar. The *chag HaSemichah* ceremony is less a graduation for an academic degree and more a religious celebration and a rite of passage.

## ADMISSIONS

Admission to RIETS is unique in that a person is admitted based not on his knowledge alone—stellar moral character and religious observance are prerequisites for admittance into the study hall. In *Messechet Brachot* the Gemara relates that, under the administration of Rabban Gamliel, no student was allowed into *Beit Midrash* [study house] if his "inside was not like his outside"—that is, if his personal character did not meet the high ethical standards that were expected of a student of the Torah. There was actually a guard at the door, and those who did not meet the standard were barred from entering. When Rabbi Elazar Ben Azaria replaced Rabban Gamliel as the *Nasi* [leader], his first official action was to remove the guard and allow anyone access to the yeshiva. In that tradition, the Yeshiva University *Beit Midrash* is open to all who want to study Torah. On any given day the *Beit Midrash* has visitors not enrolled in the Yeshiva who come to study and learn. The open-door policy does not apply for those who want to receive *semichah*. Those who receive *semichah* will eventually leave the walls of the *Beit Midrash* and become leaders in the Jewish community. Thus, the yeshiva feels a responsibility to hold the students to a high moral standard no less than its responsibility to hold the students to a high academic standard. A graduate of questionable moral scruples not only damages the reputation of RIETS and its thousands of graduates, but he also damages the entire Jewish community by lowering the esteem of all Torah scholars. Even worse, as an unqualified rabbi, he can potentially lead an entire community astray.

At RIETS there is no guard at the door, but character references from rabbis and teachers are part of the admissions process. In addition to written and oral entrance exams, the dean of the yeshiva meets personally with every applicant before they are accepted. Over the four-year program every student is expected to choose at least one of the forty rabbis as his personal mentor. In addition to the regular subject material, rabbis regularly lecture on textual passages that address character development and self-improvement. The rabbi-student relationship extends beyond the walls of the *Beit Midrash*. It is normal for a student to spend a Shabbat at the home of his rabbi, to join his rabbi for a Passover Seder or other holiday meals, and to have his rabbi officiate at a marriage or *bris* [circumcision]. The rabbi observes the student's personal development over his years at yeshiva and will confidently endorse the student's candidacy for *semichah*. The *chag HaSemichah* is more than just the conferment of a diploma; it is a personal achievement for both the rabbi and student.

## TORAH STUDY

*Semichah* does not require a student only to demonstrate his mastery of information for an exam. One who has *semichah* is expected to embody the Jewish value of Torah study for its own sake. The Hebrew term for Torah scholar is *Talmid Chacham. Chacham* means wise. *Talmid* means student. The implication is that one who seeks wisdom from the Torah knows that he is always a student and always has more to learn.

The *semichah* curriculum involves a finite section of Jewish law from *Yoreh Deah*, a section of the *Shulchan Aruch*, but the expected curriculum of a *Talmid Chachahm* is infinite. The yeshiva student's day begins early with morning *minyan*. After a short breakfast the student meets his study partner [*hevruta*] in the *Beit Midrash* for his morning study session. This session that goes until noon is preparation for the main lecture in Talmud, *shiur*. The students are expected to prepare on their own all the relevant sources and commentaries that will apply to the passage being taught at the *shiur*. Before *shiur* the students break for lunch. The *shiur* is an advanced lecture in Talmud that lasts anywhere from an hour to two hours. After *shiur* the students pray *minchah*, the afternoon service, and then they have their afternoon study session, when they study the assigned passages of Jewish law that are requirements for *semichah*. The main text is the *Shulchan Aruch*, but the students are also expected to have learned the Talmudic and post-Talmudic sources upon which the rulings of the *Shulchan Aruch* are based as well as commentaries on the *Shulchan Aruch* and contemporary authoritative responses to practical cases.

After the afternoon study session, the students break for dinner, after which the students reconvene for the evening study session, which runs until 10:00 pm. While the morning and afternoon sessions are spent studying texts in depth and not covering a great deal of ground, most students use the evening session to study other texts at a faster pace with less depth. The day ends with the *Ma'ariv* [evening] service.

The yeshiva is a culture that values learning. The most valuable commodity is time, and students are constantly trying to find more time into which they can fit more learning. There are exams in yeshiva, but grade point average is not the motivation for the passion, excitement, and love for the Torah that is felt in the *Beit Midrash*. Just as food nourishes the body, the Torah is nourishment for the soul. The students' desire to learn Torah is motivated by their desire to draw close to their creator through understanding His divine word.

Just as a wedding marks the end of a courtship for a couple but the beginning of a lifelong commitment, the *chag haSemichah* marks the end of the student's formal training but the beginning of a lifelong passionate relationship between the student and the Torah.

## TRADITION

Although I do not have *semichah* that traces its way back to Moshe, on my mother's side of the family I am from a very long line of rabbis and Torah scholars. My mother's father, Rabbi Yosef Maza, was a rabbi for fifty years in a large *shul* [synagogue] in South River, New Jersey. Growing up, I always admired my grandfather, but it was only when I started studying in yeshiva that I was truly able to connect with him on a deep level. The texts that I was learning in yeshiva were the exact same texts that my grandfather had studied as a yeshiva student.

My grandfather's commitment to Torah never ceased, and even in illness and old age he continued to spend hours every day immersed in Torah study. It was my grandfather who encouraged me to become a rabbi. While he was still the rabbi in South River, my grandfather discovered a Jewish community in the nearby city of Manalapan, New Jersey, which had no synagogue. With his own savings he purchased a small house and had it converted into a synagogue. He also purchased an apartment for himself and my grandmother in a nearby retirement community. His love of Torah and the Jewish people would not allow him to stop being a rabbi, but he also knew that it would eventually be time for him to step aside and allow the community of South River to hire a new, younger rabbi. The *shul* he established in Manalapan would allow him to continue to teach Torah and serve the Jewish people in retirement.

God had other plans. When I was in college, my grandfather was diagnosed with Parkinson's disease. The disease severely affected his mobility, and he could not walk to synagogue on Shabbat without help. My mother sent me every Shabbat to assist my grandfather so that he could continue to serve the people. For four years I spent almost every Shabbat with my grandfather in Manalapan. Those were among the best Shabbats of my life. On Friday evening, when my grandfather and I returned from *shul*, my grandmother would have Shabbat dinner waiting for us. After dinner we would sing Shabbat songs that my grandfather remembered from when he was in yeshiva, and then we would learn Torah together late into the night. We completed an entire tractate of Talmud together, a project that took us almost three years to complete.

As my grandfather's health deteriorated, I began to take on more and more responsibilities at the synagogue. I would lead services, give the sermon, and even officiate at Bar Mitzvahs, weddings, and funerals. At that point the rabbinate seemed like the most obvious and natural career path for me. My grandfather did not live to see my *chag haSemichah*, but before he died he had the pleasure of knowing that one of his grandchildren would continue in his footsteps and serve the Jewish people as a rabbi and teacher of Torah.

The Torah that I learned with my grandfather stays with me to this very day, and I hope that one day I will have the privilege of learning the same pages of the Talmud with my own children and sharing the insights that I learned from their great-grandfather, whom they will know only through the Torah that he left behind. Receiving *semichah* was my rite of passage that connects me to the past. I hope that as a rabbi and teacher of Torah to the Jewish people I will fulfill my primary role of facilitating my congregation's connection to the past and the future through the study of the Torah.

## NOTES

[1] Jewish Encyclopedia: *Semikhah*. JE sites other sources that *semichah* may have lasted until as late as the twelfth century.

[2] Information on the project can be found at the Sanhedrin Web site: http://www.thesanhedrin.org.

# Perspectives on Evaluating New Jewish Rituals

## Vanessa L. Ochs

In my research on emerging Jewish rituals and their adaptation in America, I have observed that when people initially encounter a new ritual practice, after the first shock of novelty has passed, they typically ask three questions: Is it authentic? Is it permissible, either according to *halakhah* [Jewish law] or according to the standards or customs of my rabbi, community, or family? And finally, the question that is especially unanswerable: Will it endure?

I should say that that shock of novelty hits some more strongly than others. Speaking from personal experience, I admit that when I witness a new Jewish ritual, when I am without my ethnographer's hat to wear or hide behind and I am there just as myself, I do not inquire immediately about authenticity, permissibility, and endurance. The first question I ask, particularly when caught unaware, is usually "Where is the door?" If I am told to stand in a circle and hold hands, or take a partner, or close my eyes, I disappear. When it comes to new ritual practices, many share my gut reactions of fear, disgust, anger, and suspicion. If this offers any consolation, these responses are not so different from the initial reactions people had to medical practices, such as organ transplants or fertility treatment using new technologies, when they emerged on the horizon as possibilities. First there was horror, followed by some interest once the new methods have been proven, and then full embrace, if the technologies, shown to be effective and lifesaving, become commonplace.

People react strongly and then inquire cautiously because the rituals that already work for them, the ones that feel "right" or "natural," matter so much. They are enactments that hold them together and express and affirm sacred (or holy, or powerful) commitments. People hesitate to alter old rituals that are just a little creaky, out of date, or even altogether dissonant, fearing (imagining a cosmic balancing scale, perhaps) that adding a new one might jeopardize the integrity or sturdiness of the familiar and precious rituals. While people may, in theory, be proud of Judaism's radical guise, its capacity to imagine a world more perfect than the one we inhabit, they tend, in practice, to be fiercely protective of Jewish rituals as a conservative force, preserving memory, transmitting identity and values, and specifying acts of piety, sensitivity, and obedience—whether or not they themselves ever practice them. To maintain a protective stance in the face of a tradition that feels vulnerable despite its venerability, to remain a responsible (even if disengaged) guardian, it seems logical to set up a gate-keeping mechanism that preserves the borders between what should and should not be added or changed.

While I, like many, do eventually come round after the passage of time, given my own proclivities, had I been a rabbi in the Middle Ages, I might have joined my colleagues who tried to suppress, say, the popular folk practice of breaking a glass at a wedding—thought, by Jews and non-Jews alike, to ward off evil spirits and to be too reminiscent of the popular practices of the host culture in which Jewish were living. I might have opposed the Bar Mitzvah ritual and wedding *chuppah* [canopy] because I could glean their origins in church practice. Would I have been readily persuaded to accept casting sins into the water, *taschlich*, which many rabbis initially opposed because it risked introducing levity and frivolity into an otherwise theologically heavy day? Perhaps, but only because I could not refuse such a fine excuse to take some fresh air. In modern times, I would surely empathize with those rabbis who panicked when machine-made, square matzos were first introduced and sold in—heaven forefend—boxes, and who proclaimed that these were a "dangerous instrument of modernity leading inevitably to assimilation and apostasy, and would uproot the Torah."[1] Mostly, though, I would miss the old, round matzos. Passover without them would not be Passover, and my heart would break. I overstate my point here, but it is clear where I am going: some people are especially slow to come around.

In retrospect, those turnarounds seem rapid. We experience a new ritual, we decide that we hate it or never will get used to it, or it offends all that we hold to be holy and genuinely Jewish, however we define that. And then, all of a sudden we cannot imagine our lives without it; a Seder table without Miriam's cup feels as incomplete as a Seder table without Elijah's cup (yes, his cup was once new too and seems to have been introduced because it settled certain arguments about having a fifth cup at the Passover Seder).

The very concept of a new ritual can appear paradoxical. Rituals are supposed to be so old that their origins are obscure. We are not supposed to wonder what to do or what it means or worry about how long it will last. We are just supposed to know, but not just as a cognitive memory. Ritual is a cultural muscle memory that is supposed to well up, touching some primordial core. Rituals should not feel tentative or made up—they are supposed to feel natural, timeless, graceful, inevitable, venerable, full of power and resonance; they should be self-evidently worth preserving. We do not want religious rituals rote and meaningless, but we do want them rote and comforting. Otherwise, how can a new ritual hold us together; how can it have cosmic significance if we are practicing it with self-consciousness? Or, as a nonpracticing secular

Jewish colleague tells me, if he is going to go to a Jewish ritual, such as a wedding, a Passover Seder, or a *bris*, it better be done the right way. And what is the right way, I asked? With only the slight twinkle of self-consciousness visible in his eyes, he said, "How it was done in the fifties, in Long Island," done the way it feels graceful and natural to him. I do understand where he is coming from, almost literally, having been a Long Island baby boomer myself, although I cannot say I share my colleague's fondness for the suburban Judaism that the countercultural peers of my generation collectively rebelled against and replaced, over time, with practices that were less formal, less hierarchical, and more insistently spiritual in style. Not that I liked these new practices initially, but I got used to them and embraced many.

Acknowledging how averse I am to ritual innovation when it is not an object of study as well as the sluggish pace of my adjustment, I can better understand those who so resisted the new Jewish women's rituals when they emerged in the seventies. In vehement prose, Rabbi Meiselman, an Orthodox rabbi, called the practices futile and meaningless, claiming that celebrating the birth of a daughter "completely mocks the entire structure of Judaism." For this Orthodox rabbi, a "ridiculous ceremony" such as this celebration "destroys the meaning" of the male rituals and "is not necessary to make women feel significant." He dubbed women's ritual creativity "spiritual autoeroticism." Their dancing with Torah scrolls on Simchat Torah was but "a sexual provocation that distracts male worshippers from their concentration." And as for those who wish to wear a *tallit* [prayer shawl], it is a "tool for an ego trip or for the advancement of a . . . political movement."[2] As most are aware, all these dreaded and despicable practices Meiselman feared and saw perniciously bubbling up through liberal branches of Judaism have entered mainstream modern Orthodoxy. Those young enough may assume that such practices have gone on among the Orthodox for generations and that they are, in fact, "natural." Such rituals have found their way into some ultra-Orthodox and Chasidic communities: there are baby-naming ceremonies for girls, ceremonies for three-year-old girls to receive and light their first Sabbath candles, and Bat Mitzvah.

All Jewish rituals were once new. But it helps to forget that, and there are traditional strategies for doing so. In their imaginative writings, our sages and ancestors had their reasons for claiming that Eve went to the *mikvah* [ritual bath], Abraham prayed wearing *tefillin* [pylacteries], and Sarah lit Sabbath candles in her tent. This is midrash, magical and imaginative thinking. One does not have to be a sage to know that nowhere in the Torah does God command Moses to tell the children of Israel to cover their heads with yarmulkes and the women to wear wigs. Nowhere are there Sabbath angels who make house calls after synagogue service—there is no synagogue, and biblical weeks ended happily without *havdalah* [ceremony to conclude the Sabbath]. Nowhere is there a commandment to have separate dishes for milk and meat—Sarah, our Sabbath candle lighter, prepared a lovely meat and dairy dish for Abraham's visitors that would promptly render a modern kosher kitchen *traife* [unkosher].

I want to begin by comparing the questions laypeople ask to a different set of questions: those that I as an ethnographer of contemporary Jewish life ask about the very same practices. As will be readily evident, the ethnographic questions are not asked to protect Judaism as a fragile entity. Rather, they are concerned with documenting and investigating Jewish religious creativity, however it is given shape in particular eras and locales. Research questions are no doubt shaped by a scholarly conviction that when religious practices change, religions still endure; more precisely, if practice could not change, the continued survival of any religious system, over time, would be threatened.

What then, goes on in the field? I will begin by approaching a new ritual first from a scenographic perspective, carefully noting what actions I see, what objects are introduced, and what script (or text, or program) is being provided and comparing these observations to any already-existing forms. How does it rehearse major Jewish themes of the past in new or altered forms? How does the ritual, in its language and actions, build upon, subvert, or reject Jewish rituals of the past? I will examine how it complies with a range of halakhic interpretations as well as contemporary ethical expectations, such as feminism. I will note who seems to be in charge, who is allocated more or less agency, and who has been designated as a main actor and who comes as a witness. I pay attention to the mood that is being created through manipulations of place, smell, light, music, dance, and food.

I notice how deftly or clumsily the new ritual is being introduced and carried out, and I notice how participants react through their comments and body language: are they anxious or comfortable, engaged or bored, reluctant or eager, resistant or accepting? I try to account for such reactions beyond personal proclivities. I gauge, in terms of audience, if the ritual appeals to those already committed or reaches out to those on the fringes, creating new points of entry. When possible, I ask the creators to narrate their stories of the ritual's genesis, including all the process and deliberation along the way, and afterward, I ask leaders and participants of differing levels of enthusiasm, Jewish engagement, and erudition to reflect upon their experience and evaluate it.

Outside any particular site-specific enactment of a new ritual, I read or listen to different people telling their own true, complex, and usually contradictory stories about how the ritual first came into being, from the genesis of an idea, through experimentation in early forms, to more stable iterations. How, for instance, were the early *Rosh Hodesh* [New Month] groups born? How did the orange get onto the Seder plate, and how does the story most frequently told deviate from the one the founders claim as authoritative? From a spiritual perspective, and this would be through discussion and direct observation, I try to note how a presence of God is referenced and made available to participants in this new practice, and how that presence is differently interpreted as the ritual occurs in a variety of settings, in different denominations and communities, over time.

When a new object is involved, such as Miriam's cup, Miriam's tambourine, or a Holocaust Torah, I consider how it corresponds to the existing inherited inventory of Jewish ritual objects, just as I would compare a liturgical innovation to established conventions. How does it reframe Jewish memory or reinterpret sacred Jewish narratives? How does it make the new ritual repeatable and transmittable from one generation to another? Does it intentionally disguise the radical nature of a new ritual within an innocuous, mundane, and traditional-seeming vessel? How democratic is it: is it simple to make or acquire, or is it complicated, requiring special skills and access to knowledge or money? Is it intended as a sacred object in and of itself or as an object that is facilitated for sacred experience?

Over time, I observe the ritual, live, photographed, or filmed as it keeps getting performed, and I note the variations as it is disseminated. I try to discover the multiple forces—say, in our age, the democratization of Judaism or feminist Judaism—that have led Jews to simultaneously originate similar new rituals that over time coalesce so thoroughly that they appear with instructions in rabbinic manuals. How are people beginning to write about the new ritual, in memoirs, in the Jewish (and sometimes secular) press, and in rabbinic deliberations? Along this vein, I study papers given on new ritual at academic conferences by scholars (who may also happen to be themselves generators or proponents of new ritual), noticing how their presentations describe and analyze the new rituals but also can reify them, particularly when the scholars have been actively engaged in creating, performing, and introducing them.

If my research questions can plausibly be answered as I go about chronicling the birth, transformation, and acceptance or rejection of new Jewish ritual, why are the questions laypeople ask about authenticity, permissibility, and endurance so much more difficult?

As for authenticity, I would like to suggest that any new Jewish ritual cultivates its authenticity only over time, through repeated, loving practice, through its capacity to hold multiple variations, resonance, and meanings.

In religion, authenticity, as I have been claiming for a long time, is a feeling about legitimacy and divine sanction, a cultural feeling and not a fact that gets substantiated with evidence (although it is commonplace for religious groups or movements to employ the term "authenticity" to support claims that their interpretation of text or tradition is the one that is most true and legitimate). Lapsed time changes the valence of a ritual that initially does not inspire a feeling of authenticity, giving it weight and steadfastness that clothes and supports it. With time, rituals become plausible, real, and ordinary. With time, too, comes the forgetfulness that facilitates cultural change and acceptance.[3]

As for permissibility, nearly every new Jewish ritual practice can feel transgressive, forbidden by God (who shows dismay by "causing lightning to strike"), by some authority (a rabbi or often one's Hebrew school principal), or by its inconsistency with local or familial practice [*minhag*]. For my mother, born in 1932 to a traditional Jewish family, nearly all the new practices she has encountered in her lifetime have initially felt transgressive. That extensive list includes synagogue prayers recited in English; Bat Mitzvah; *Rosh Hodesh* groups; baby-naming ceremonies for daughters; women counting in a *minyan*; women being called to have *aliyot* [opportunities to "go up" to read the Torah]; women wearing *kippot* [head coverings], *tallit*, and *tefillin*; and women serving as rabbis and cantors. It also includes saying the names of the matriarchs in the *Amidah* [major prayer, recited in standing position] and, at the Passover Seder, including Miriam's cup and a pillow for her (and not just my father) to lean on. My mother did not need an authority to tell her that such acts were forbidden; she knew it to be the case, and had she inquired and received permission, I believe she would have overlooked it. With different passages of time, with the growth of familiarity and the formation of new habits, all of these practices now seem permissible to my mother.

I think this reflects an awareness that while it may seem that a ritual's permissibility is decided by authorities, it is in fact ultimately decided upon by the folk—again, in their own time, which can be speedy or slow. Rabbis know this. In the Talmud, when the rabbis were contemplating ritual behaviors of which they were unsure, they gave each other this advice: *Puk hazei mai amma davar* [Look around, and see what people are actually doing].[4] Then legislate it. For example, when married women wanted to wear wigs to cover their heads as a sign of modesty, rabbis of the late nineteenth century were against it, preferring the more modest hat, kerchief, or shawl. But the wig-wearing women (especially as more could afford wigs) prevailed. Now, wearing wigs is the sign of the highest modesty and piety in certain communities, and it would be rabbis who would be the first to say the practice is *de rigueur*. Another example: rabbis did not initially appreciate, as I said, *tashlich*. But people did;

I suppose they liked it a lot. Now, when we open up a high holiday *machzor* [prayer book], the sages tell us exactly how to observe *tashlich*, when to observe it, and what they want it to mean. We can almost forget that it was not their idea in the first place. We can also imagine that Abraham and Sarah and little Isaac all went out to do *tashlich*, until we recall they did not yet have Rosh Hashanah.

And now endurance: it is almost curious that we move quickly ahead to ask about a ritual's longevity when we first encounter it. Can we realistically ask why some new rituals stick and others do not? There is no way to have anticipated that *etrogim* [citrons] would be shipped special delivery around the world each year for Sukkot. Who would have supposed that turning the *afikoman* [hidden piece of matzah] into a game of hide-and-go-seek at the end of a Seder would still be around or, for that matter, Hillel's bitter herb and Passover sandwich, to which so many add, as a condiment, haroset? In fact, it is only in hindsight that one could have predicted that lighting a Chanukah menorah would attract American Jews after it had nearly fallen away.

It is not possible to predict endurance; demanding proof of it, long before the fact, is yet another indication of the hurdles that protectors of Jewish tradition feel obligated to erect. That said, and I conclude here by offering observations that should reflect the concerns of both laypeople and scholars, I do think it is possible to evaluate new rituals, with an interest in refining them and enhancing the possibility that they might be around after the first, second, and even third appearances. Even if a new practice meets any or all of these criteria, we cannot know if it will endure, but we can assume that it just might.

Thus, these are some of the hallmarks that characterize the stronger new rituals, and I conclude with this checklist:

1. Does it make overt links to major Jewish themes, using familiar Jewish ritual objects, and creating links to Jewish times and values? Does it allow people to remember, mark time, synchronize their psyches with natural cycles—in a word, does it feel continuous with the Jewish past and still rooted in the present?

2. Does it use Hebrew and make scriptural reference in ways that feel familiar and artful?

3. Does it establish new communities and sustain existing ones? Does it create opportunities for bonding across lines that might otherwise be divisive: for instance, age, economic class, marital status, sexual orientation, and denominational and ideological identification? Does it strive to be inclusive, so that even those without Judaic knowledge will feel comfortable and

included? Does it allow for improvisation, personalization, and spontaneity? Is it user-friendly and self-explanatory?

4. On the level of meaning making, does it help to give sense and order to life? Does it carry people through painful changes and crises in life that might otherwise be unendurable? Does it articulate joy or grief?

5. Does it mark life events that have gone unmarked by a formal Jewish response? (Examples would include the onset of menstruation, pregnancy, giving birth, menopause, miscarriage, infertility, hysterectomy, healing after rape and abuse, and completing a course of cancer treatments.)

6. Does it confirm and evoke a capacious definition of the divine presence in the world? Does it offer realistic steps toward living one's life according to ever-higher moral standards?

The short-term endurance of potent new rituals, ones that already seem to be catching on, is often dependent upon people who put energy and intelligence into incubating them further, strengthening them, and broadening their access. New rituals need community ritual organizers, so to speak, to plead for their cause. They need to persuade first-time participants in the new ritual that shocking innovations ought to become tomorrow's hallowed traditions.

Which new rituals stick? Perhaps the ones people care most about, and the ones that are nurtured.

## NOTES

[1] Jonathan D. Sarna, "How Matzah Became Square," sixth annual lecture of the Victor J. Selmanowitz Chair of Jewish History, Touro College, New York, 2005.
[2] Moshe Meiselman, *Jewish Women in Jewish Law* (New York: Ktav, 1978), 60ff, 146, 154.
[3] I have explored this topic and many of the others addressed here more extensively in my book, *Inventing Jewish Ritual* (Philadelphia: Jewish Publication Society, 2007).
[4] Babylonian Talmud *Brakhot* 45a, *Eruvin* 14b.

# Memory, Questions, and Definitions:
# Images of Old and New Rites of Passage

## Ori Z. Soltes

### ONE: DEFINITION AND IDENTITY WITHIN ART
### AND JEWISH ART

Jewish identity is rife with questions regarding definition. What is "Jewish"? Is it an identity tag that refers to religion, to nationality, to ethnicity, to historical association, to affiliation with a particular body of customs and traditions, or to a combination of features that might fall under the rubric "civilization," as Mordecai M. Kaplan first argued seventy-five years ago?[1] Applied to art, that issue is multipliable in different directions. One might ask whether in using the phrase "Jewish art" one is referring to the identity of the artist (and then by what criteria is he or she judged to be Jewish—birth, conversion, conviction?) or to the nature of the art, in which case one asks whether it is Jewish by subject, symbol, style, content, or intent.

One might turn the definitional question in a completely different direction, which carries beyond the matter of Jewishness. One might ask how art—or perhaps "fine art" would be a more appropriate turn of phrase—is distinguished from craft. In the medieval period one could hardly distinguish the one from the other—the same anonymity usually appertained to sculptors and mural or panel painters as to tapestry weavers and furniture makers—and the closest identifiable category to what we might in our own time call "architects" were chief masons—but the extent to which they who supervised the construction of the cathedrals of the Romanesque and Gothic periods may be said to have designed them is more often than not almost impossible to determine.

Names emerge during the Renaissance, and with them a sense of definitional and categorical distinction that separated architecture, sculpture, and painting of various sorts (on walls, wooden panels, and eventually canvas) from gold- or silver-smithing or cabinetry-making and other crafts[2]—but many of the more important artists were first trained in their masters' workshops in a range of craft-skills. Such training was as endemic to the creation of their major works as preliminary sketches and drawings were.

One of the issues that emerged for visual art as it approached the last third of the nineteenth century was a sense that both hierarchy among the arts and division between fine arts and crafts arts offer false categories. The

Arts and Crafts Movement in England and its siblings across Europe, from *Liberta* in Sicily and *Modernismo* in Spain to *Art Nouveau* in France and Belgium and *Jugendstil* in Austria, all sought, in a fundamental way, to eradicate the line between "art" and "craft"—a chair or even an ashtray could be as invested with aesthetic significance as a painting or a statue.

One of the places where this sensibility was echoed outside of Europe was in Jerusalem, where the Bezalel Academy of Art that opened under the leadership of Boris Schatz in 1906 pursued a similar ideology of blurring, if not eliminating altogether, the line between "fine arts" and "craft arts." Bezalel's goal was, moreover, to create work that could be called "Jewish art"—Jewish national art—at a time when the very definition of "Jewish" was first acquiring a national parameter in active political and cultural senses.

Certainly, if Schatz failed—because of the definitional problem pertaining to both "Jewish" and "art" but especially to "Jewish"—on the other hand, he nevertheless offered the first steps in shaping what would eventually become Israeli art.[3] He also helped to further push open a door that had been slowly opening for at least a generation before him, regarding the consummate object matter of "craft" in a Jewish mode: Judaica. For centuries, guild restrictions and inhibitions had prevented Jews from becoming craftsmen and artisans of their own Jewish ceremonial objects.

Judaica had perforce been created throughout Christendom by non-Jewish artisans, who typically followed Western—essentially Christian—canons of style and symbol. So the definition of centuries of Judaica as "Jewish" would have to pertain to the Jewish ceremonial purpose it served rather than to the identity of the artist or the style, subject, or symbols of and on the object. But the eventual aftermath of Emancipation had been to open up new possibilities for Jews in a range of professions, including those that included work in metals in both secular and sacred contexts. And Schatz's Bezalel Academy took that idea and ran with it, seeking to turn out scores of competent Jewish producers not only of ashtrays and statues but also of Torah pointers and *hanukkiyot* [Chanukah menorahs].[4]

Jewish ritual objects fall into two general categories. There are those artifacts that pertain to the cycle of the year and its diverse celebrations and commemorations—from the candelabra, *kiddush* cups, and spice boxes of the weekly Shabbat and *Havdalah* [ceremony at the conclusion of Shabbat] celebrations to the often elaborate multileveled plates that occupy the center of the Passover Seder table. On the other hand are those objects that pertain to life-cycle events, from circumcision to Bar/Bat Mitzvah to wedding celebration to funerary and *yahrtzeit* [anniversary of a loved one's death] commemoration. One may view both these two categories and the ceremonial objects that pertain to them as also marking a series of interweaves between the individual and the community, on the one hand, and between memory and focus on the past and thought directed toward the future, on the other hand.

The range and nuanced aspects of both kinds of celebration and commemoration have expanded in the past several generations. Female baby-naming and male circumcision ceremonies have emerged, just as a broader spectrum of Jews has embraced Bat Mitzvah together with Bar Mitzvah; but weddings have become more evenly focused on both bride and groom for growing numbers of Jews. And on the other hand, new holidays, from Israeli Independence Day to Holocaust Memorial Day, have found their way onto the calendar. The array of Jewish artists eager to address aspects of Jewish being has exponentially expanded in the past generation. New ritual objects—such as the Miriam's Goblet that now adorns the Seder table in many Jewish homes—have joined the array of newly designed but familiar ceremonial objects.

The world of visual imagery and its concomitants that reflect the matter of definition and of both memory and hope—that partake of both celebration and commiseration—have been nothing short of explosive in engaging Jewish being in the world. Part of this ever-expanding world of visual imagery follows directly from the ideology of which Bezalel was part a century ago: it blurs or altogether eliminates the line between craft and art by producing sculptures that may double as ritual objects and ritual objects that stand on an equal footing with painting and sculpture as fine arts.

*      *      *      *      *

As Jewish artists emerged in the last century—and with exponentially increasing vigor in the past few generations—an obvious question that many of them asked is "how exactly do I and my work fit into Western art, when for the past sixteen centuries or so, Western art has essentially been Christian art?" Among the most stunning of responses to that question are those that apprehend the triptych form (which for Christian art symbolized the triune God embraced by Christianity) but radically adapt it. For example, Barnett Newman's 1950 *The Name II* is an all-white painting marked only by two thin gold vertical lines that turn the canvas into a conceptual triptych, thus re-articulating the subject matter of traditional Christian triptychs with a Jewish sensibility [fig. 1]. Instead of a figurative Christ—on the Cross, flanked by the two thieves; or on the Virgin Mother's lap, flanked by saints—the artist offers blank space. As Judaism embraces an invisible God, and as traditional Jews refer even to God's ineffable Name only by circumlocution—as *HaShem:*

Fig 1: Barnett Newman, "The Name II." 1950.
Magna and oil on canvas.

"The Name"—except when praying, the God of no-thing-ness, whose Name may not even be spoken outside prayer, has been "portrayed" by the absolute absence of color. But white also chemically encompasses the totality of color—so the invisible God contains all things within it.[5]

  Nearly two generations later, in the 1990s, Susan Schwalb created an entire series of paintings on wood panels—actual hinged triptychs that can hang on a wall or rest on a surface. Called *The Creation Series*, these works add to Newman's response two new elements. First, while retaining the abstract sensibility of his work, she adds color—browns, blues, as well as gold leaf, silverpoint, and copperpoint [fig. 2]. Nor is this arbitrary, for Schwalb was inspired by the opening series of illuminations—the cycle of creation, presented in an abstract, utterly nonfigurative style—found in the *Sarajevo Haggadah*, the fourteenth century manuscript with arguably the most

Fig 2: Susan Schwalb, "Beginnings." 1988. Silver point,
acrylic, gold leaf on wood. From the *Creation Series*.

renowned illuminations and illustrations in the medieval Jewish tradition. So,
part of her response to the question of fitting in as a Jewish artist is to impose
an abstract style, based on a specific medieval Jewish visual work, onto the
triptych form.

The second element that carries beyond Newman's formulation—and
like his, is in part conveyed by the titles of individual works within the series—
is that Schwalb introduces specific geometric and other elements that connote
femaleness. Most obvious among these is the downward-pointing triangle that
has been associated in art with the female pubis since the Neolithic period; and
the swirling, undulating lines of silverpoint encased in circles that suggest the
waters of the womb. Thus her *Creation Series* is not only about God's creation
of the universe but also about venerating female fertility and creativity in the
child-bearing, facilitating-the-survival-through-continuity-of-the-species sense
and redirecting that fecundity toward the creation of visual art.

Thus, Schwalb's engagement is relevant to this discussion on two fronts.
On the one hand, the instances when women artists have been acknowledged
before the twentieth century—or even been permitted to become artists when
their inclinations and talents pointed in that direction—have been relatively few

and far between. So reconnecting female creativity to the realm of visual art is taking on a subject that transcends national, ethnic, or religious categories, just as the matter of defining "art" versus "craft" does. On the other hand, the specifically "Jewish" aspect of Schwalb's symbolic and stylistic sources evokes the question that Jewish women might well ask—and that a growing array of contemporary Jewish female (and occasional male) artists have asked: to wit, "how do I, as a woman, fit in to Judaism, which in its traditional form excludes me from any number of key individual and communal roles, such as reading publicly from the Torah or reciting the *Kaddish* [the mourner's prayer] for my deceased father?"

## TWO: ART AND ARTIFACT ADDRESS THE BEGINNING OF THE LIFE CYCLE

This array of issues and questions, pertaining to definition and identity, to past memory and future hope, reflected in a range of different modes of what might be perceived as "Jewish art," is generally addressed and richly expressed in contemporary works that pertain to rites of passage. Thus the 2008 acrylic and mixed-media work by Washington, DC, artist Marilyn Banner, called *Prayer* offers a broad spiritual subject that encompasses both individual and communal aspects of celebration, commemoration, and simple communion within the human-divine relationship [fig. 3]. Into the acrylic paint she has embedded not only bits of chiffon, lace, and even some wallpaper but also two photographic transfers. One, in the lower right-hand side of the image, depicts her parents—perhaps even before they were married—and across from them, to the lower left, is an image of herself as perhaps an eighteen-month-old toddler.[6]

Add to these the childlike rendering of ghost-figures, flowers, and seven hearts—seven, the number of completeness within the Jewish tradition (among others) going back to antiquity—and the domination of the work by spring-like colors—sky blue, grass green, and flower violet—and what do we see in this fecund work? A religious concept become secularly spiritual; prayer as love and love as prayer—birth and rebirth, which are the most basic needs addressed by religion from its beginnings and expressed in visual art that has served religion from its beginnings.

Art and, within art, ceremonial objects pertain to prayer in pertaining to the human need to address divinity so that we survive—so that what has created us and what we therefore believe can destroy us blesses us and does not curse us. And the most fundamental aspect of survival and blessing is expressed, in nature, by spring and its color-laden explosions and in ourselves

Fig 3: Marilyn Banner, "Prayer." 2008.
Acrylic and mixed media on wood.

by the creation, through love, of the children who carry us from past to future.

Santa Monica-based artist Ruth Snyder also addresses a broad ceremonial and celebrational concept by means of a modernist mode, in her 1998 mixed-media collage *Life Cycle* [fig. 4].[7] A white, gender-ambiguous, but somehow female-seeming (at least to my eye) figure stands purposefully within a sea of abstract patterns. These are torn (literally) from diverse flotsam and jetsam—found objects and materials—that include tiny Chinese scroll writing and the odd letter (W) and numbers (1, 2, 4, 8). It is as if the penchant for text so emphatically ascribed to Jews has been turned inside out and upside down: the words are unintelligible to the uninitiated—but in Chinese, not Hebrew—and

Fig 4: Ruth Snyder, "Life Cycle #II." 1998.
Mixed media, collage.

the isolated letter and numbers add to the playful ambiguity of the entire
composition. Does the "W" stand for "woman" within the life cycle—near
to the "8," which is, after all the number referring to the day after birth when
a Jewish boy is circumcised, but which in the last generation has come to mark
ceremonies welcoming Jewish girls into the community as well?

But what of the other floating numbers? Does "1" symbolize God?
Does "2" stand for the parallel—male and female—aspects of the life cycle?
(There is a bare-breasted female figure discreetly posed in a grisaille image

hovering above the number "2.") What of the number "4" that surges along the upper right of the image, near the white figure and almost across from the "1"? Could it refer both to the Tetragrammaton—the ineffable four-lettered name of God—and to the four-directioned world contrived by God with all of its ambiguities? Ambiguity defines the Jewish life cycle in its traditional articulation—particularly from a female perspective—at every step: birth, circumcision, Bar Mitzvah, wedding (divorce), and funerary rituals all seem to have their exclusionary properties where women are concerned.[8]

There is no such gender ambiguity in New York-based Jenny Tango's 1995 mixed-media work, *Finally, a Son!* On the contrary [fig. 5]. Tango plays overtly on the very birth-time ambiguity that is a part of what flows somewhat covertly beneath the surface of Snyder's work. Tango has extracted her "characters" directly out of the world of Sholom Aleichem's *shtetl*—the "traditional" Jewish Old World as romanticized by so many American Jews and echoed as far as Broadway's *Fiddler on the Roof*. More specifically, this work is part of a series that focuses on the women of Chelm.[9] But she has leaped between the nineteenth and twentieth centuries, interwoven the question

Fig 5: Jenny Tango, "Finally, a Son!" 1992.
Mixed media on paper. From *Woman of Chelm* series.

of conversion out of Judaism and the long history of Jewish-Christian relations (culminating, almost offhandedly, with the Holocaust),[10] played on the imperfection of the perfect number "seven" when one of the (absolutely identically faced) daughters converts to Catholicism, and when in any case, the seven are merely daughters: only the birth of the single son will bring perfect satisfaction to parents previously limited by a slew of female progeny.

The son's birth affects a rebirth of parental joy (and even at that, it is the mother who is ecstatic, while the father is nowhere to be seen—is he in the synagogue, the study house, drinking with his friends, busy handing out cigars?) after the "death" of the undutiful daughter who married out of the tradition. If life-cycle events are among the most obvious events in every culture (including Jewish culture) that help define where individuals fit into the world, then Tango's piece is part of a growing legion of works that ask who fits in where by way of reference to this most fundamental, incipient, of life-cycle moments.

At first glance, Leslie Starobin's 1996 *Jewish Daughter* appears to approach the same territory from the opposite angle [fig. 6]. After all, we are confronted with a stylized blonde daughter and therefore—in what by the early twenty-first century refers to an era that seems as distant as that of the *shtetl*—a Barbie-doll beautiful daughter. But the plot quickly thickens. A single Hebrew word tattoos the image across her upper-right thigh—within touching distance of her crotch—*tzenuah* [modest (female)].[11] Her lower legs are less legibly marked with part of a long quotation in English—certainly from a street sign in one of the ultra-Orthodox neighborhoods in Jerusalem: "Jewish Daughter, dress modestly! We do not tolerate people passing through our street immodestly dressed!"

We can piece together the entirety of the warning/announcement because parts of it are repeated vertically across her upper left torso and head and on several other parts of the image—most obviously between the figure of the Jewish daughter (and now we know where the title of the painting comes from) and a tree with beautiful, bright-red fruit among its branches, and a serpent slithering up its trunk. We look back at the daughter and see that the same bright-red fruit is held in her hands and that her body is covered with leaves, protecting it from our peering eyes. Everything falls into place: this Jewish daughter is a direct descendant of Eve, construed by all three patriarchal Abrahamic traditions as a temptress.

Eve (who is nobody's daughter, except God's) is the archetype; every Jewish daughter, in general and in walking through "our streets" wherever they are, "immodestly dressed" in whatever fashion we (whoever we are) regard as "immodest," carries with her, from past to future, the burden of the crime that got humanity thrown out of the Garden of Perfection. While the Jewish tradition does not view that act as an original sin so fundamental that all humans are automatically born into it—and so egregious that only an extraordinary act of divine self-sacrifice can overcome it, as Christianity teaches—the sense that the first life-cycle moment for females, birth, is marked by the inherent danger of becoming an ongoing accessory to the fundamental crime is richly reflected in the framing of the words that overrun Starobin's image. But her clever Jewish daughter will prevail: like a figure by Modigliani,[12] she has one eye blue and one black—one looking outward and the other inward, where her communion with God need not depend on patriarchal parameters.

This initial series of images pertains to art forms—paintings, albeit with nontraditional mixed-media additives—not traditionally associated with rites of passage, for which traditional expectation would look toward various "craft" arts. But in New Yorker Tobi Kahn's 1986-1987 *NATYH, Baby-Naming Chairs* we encounter a reversal of this principle [fig. 7]. Aside from the fact that the chairs were made not to welcome sons but to welcome daughters

Fig 6: Leslie Starobin. "Jewish Daughter." 1996.
Acrylic and ink on paper.

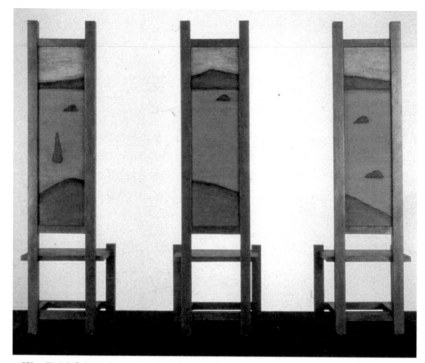

Fig 7: Tobi Kahn, "NATYH, Baby-Naming Chairs." 1986-1987.
Acrylic on canvas and wood.

into the Community of Israel[13]—so that Kahn, a modern Orthodox, male artist, sees his art as an instrument to balance the traditionally imbalanced male-female life-cycle equation at its first stage—he has deliberately blurred the line between "craft" and "art." These are indeed elegant high-backed chairs, constructed in a rigorous rectilinear Arts and Crafts style. Not only are they a far cry from the small Elijah's chairs of the medieval and postmedieval tradition (used for male circumcision ceremonies) in their scale, but, more to the point, their backs are enhanced by exquisite semiabstract landscapes.

These are precisely the sort of landscapes that one sees in Kahn's paintings, stretches of sea, shore and sky, rocks emerging from the waters, evoking peaceful, meditative times and places. There is more. Both in his paintings and here in these chairs, the artist uniquely mixes and thickens his pigments with plaster dust and slowly layers the image onto its backing, building it up in order to create textured, sculptural surfaces. Conversely, his sculptures are painted with this same plaster-and-pigment combination— which means that he constantly blurs the lines between painting and sculpture as well as between ritual objects and "fine art."

We can see this in reverse by referring, for example, to three 1985 works from his *Shrine Series*. Neither *ECCU* nor *BRUN* nor *EYKHAL* is a shrine of any definite sort [fig. 8]. They all somehow evoke a sense of shrineness, but they are all actually abstract sculptures, explorations of form, and also, as it turns out, color. Each has an arbitrary, contrived name—just as the group of baby-name chairs do—that reinforces the obligation placed by the artist onto the viewer's shoulders: to approach these works without name-based or medium-based preconception. So his media mix and meet at several verbal and visual points.

Where newborns are concerned, verbal and visual play are utilized by Israeli-born, New York-based Rachel Giladi, with regard not to the entrance of baby girls into the world but to babies of whichever gender for whom misfortune selected unmarried parents. Such babies, in the Hebrew language of the Jewish tradition, are called *mamzer* [a bastard][14]—and there is an entire Talmudic discussion of what constitutes a *mamzer*, the centerpiece of which is the limitations imposed on someone so labeled with regard to his (or her) ceremonial and other rights and obligations as a member of the Jewish community.

*Mamzer* is the name of Giladi's found-object work [fig. 9]. The artist has taken a plastic baby doll and mounted it on the wall with a piece of paper wrapped around its wrist. Instead of the baby's name or that of his mother or his birth weight or any other information that might ordinarily be contained on that paper bracelet, she has inscribed the word "*mamzer*." This photo-realist toy, hanging there with its arms a bit up and out—can one avoid thinking of criminals hanging or even of the Christ who is central

Fig 8: Tobi Kahn "ECCU," "BRUN" and "EYKHAL."
Acrylic on wood and bronze. 1985. From the *Shrine Series*.

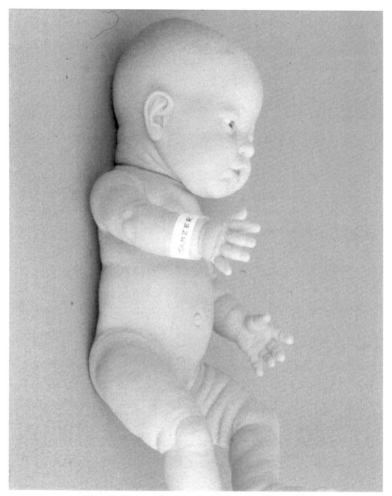

Fig 9: Rachel Giladi, "*Mamzer.*" 1995.
Plastic doll, paper and ink.

to the Christian tradition?—represents a baby with all of its plumpness and folds of soft skin. And are not all babies innocent and pure in the Jewish (as opposed to the Christian, original sin) tradition? So how can a *mamzer* be a semi-disenfranchised-from-the-community *mamzer*? What crime has she or he committed to justify that status?

The linguistics of the situation make it even more complicated, since not only can anyone be casually insulted by being called a *mamzer* just as anyone might be called a "bastard" in English, without literal reference to his parentage. But in one of those reversals of which language is fond,[15] the term can also apply to someone who seems to have inordinate success or good luck. Such a reversal, in the case of this term and Giladi's innocent hanging on the wall, underscores the idea that however we humans choose to structure our social hierarchies and however we decide to classify each other may have little to do with how God looks upon us and favors or disfavors us.

God is the prescriber of all proper behavior, and every tradition wants its children to absorb the guidelines for proper behavior from babyhood. In every tradition there are overlaps between individual and communal roles and responsibilities and between life-cycle and festival-cycle events. If in some traditional Jewish communities a Jewish boy receives his first haircut in a formal ceremony at age two, all Jewish boys become Bar Mitzvah at age thirteen—when he will first read from the Torah publicly, before the congregation—then at what age should a Jewish child begin to participate in Jewish festivals? The answer—at least in Santa Fe artist Ted Egri's circa-1985 *Succoth* [fig. 10]—is that it is never too early to begin the process of participation.

Fig 10: Ted Egri, "Succoth." Ca 1985.
Cast bronze.

Egri's cast-bronze high-relief sculpture presents a babe in its mother's arms reaching for a bunch of grapes hanging from the open-air roof of the *sukkah*—the structure[16] that, in its temporary and fragile construction, recalls the temporary booths in which the Israelites dwelled as they wandered for forty years through the wilderness, so that the old generation, born in slavery, could be succeeded by a new generation born in freedom. The fruits and vegetables with which the *sukkah* is traditionally decorated represent the richness of the fall harvest, the fecundity of nature, and the graciousness of God's blessings and generosity.

So this festival and this work are both about the cycle of life that interweaves the human microcosmic and natural macrocosmic realms. Egri's simplified sculpture is about the intertwining of the individual shifting into the community (in his or her babyhood) and the communal celebration (Sukkot) that marks both natural and historical cycles of continuity and memory. Moreover, the artist double puns with regard to art history—and thus addresses the abiding Jewish question of where his art fits into that history. For on the one hand we recognize the echo of endless representations of the Virgin Mary and Christ child—in many of which, the babe in arms, reaching for grapes, is symbolically reaching for his future martyrdom, since grapes and their wine are a symbol of blood and therefore, in the context of Christian art, of sacrifice.

But that association predates Christianity. Dionysius is the god of wine in the pagan Greek tradition—whose father is divine (none other than Zeus, king of the Olympian gods) and whose mother is human—who dies and is reborn. His constituents are promised rebirth after death. To assure this, they participate in the ceremony of symbolically consuming the god—in the form, earlier, of bull's blood and flesh and, later, of wine and bread—which ceremony will evolve, in Christianity, as eucharistic communion. A renowned mid-fourth century BCE sculpture by Praxiteles shows the infant Dionysius in the arms of the god Hermes, reaching for grapes. So on the other hand, Egri plays on this image, as well—except that, like the figures themselves, the grapes have been transformed: in his work they represent earthbound, not sacrificial, postmortem, joy. For in the Jewish tradition, wine commemorates the blood offerings in the Temple, connotes hope for a messianic-era restoration, and punctuates both life-cycle and festival-cycle celebrations with joy.

## THREE: RITES OF PASSAGE BETWEEN LIFE AND FESTIVAL CYCLE

The ultimate Jewish festival that embeds past into present—most emphatically through myriad gastronomic symbols—and ties the individual to the community is Passover. The act of turning the meal table into a symbolic altar—a space of sacred celebration, endemic to Judaism (we enter and exit every meal with formal blessings that connect us to God)—is expanded at the Passover meal, every detail of which is organized according to a prescribed order. And so the meal is called a Seder, meaning "order." The extended service that precedes the act of eating is an extended narrative of the Israelite experience in and coming out of Egypt, punctuated by focus on symbolic foods. Stated otherwise, the Seder liturgy is an extended answer to a series of stylized formal questions posed at the outset by the youngest child at the table capable of asking them. Thus, for whoever that youngest child is, the Seder at which he or she asks the four questions constitutes a rite of passage into a raucous communal experience.

Moreover, any number of details are designed to accentuate the role and participation of children—from the colorfully illustrated *Haggadah* [the liturgical "book of telling"][17] that offers one of the important art historical exceptions to the more frequent tendency not to disfigure God's words and words directed to God with human imagery, to the long tradition of hiding part of the central matzah and not concluding the Seder until the children have found it. Santa Fe artist J. Barry Zeiger's 1999 installation, *Seder Table*, turns the Passover table into a historical narrative by means of a range of found objects, disfigurations, and reconfigurations [fig. 11]. Lights festoon the table. These may be seen as symbols of the divine presence—there are four of them, connoting both the four directions of earthbound reality and the four letters of the ineffable Name of God, and in the context of the Passover Seder, the four questions, the four sons, the four goblets of wine, and other Passover echoes of the importance of that number within the Jewish tradition. Moreover, the kindling of lights at the outset of every Jewish Sabbath and festival recalls the beginning of the divine process of creation—of shaping an order [*seder*] to the universe, when "God said: 'let there be light!' and there was light."

But the table is otherwise laid with a range of objects, most obviously, beautiful blue and white crockery—most of it broken. We recognize the diasporic complications of breakage and scattering that have defined much of the history of the Jewish successors to the Israelites. And rather than passage from bondage to freedom, those successors have been pushed from one locale to another and have endured one destructive effort after another from many of their neighbors. Zeiger has, in fact, split his Seder table down the middle, but bursting up through that destructive seam is a series of birch trees: the ever-regenerating Jewish people rises from whatever ashes to which history has consigned it.

Fig 11: Jay Barry Zeiger, "Seder Table." 1997-2001.
Mixed media found objects installation.

Of course, the trees are shorn of every hint of leaf or fruit—but beyond their upper reaches the eye is drawn to large fluttering swaths of blue cloth—the color of the stripes and Star of David in the Israeli flag. Above the windows from which the cloth extends blunted Stars of David (made from tennis racquet presses) are centered by glowing lights. These last components form a compendium not only of hope but also of already-achieved fact: the rebirth of an independent Jewish state in the same space to which the wandering Israelites eventually made their way—in the aftermath of the most destructive moment in Jewish history.

Zeiger's entire installation is an exploration of the layered paradoxes of destruction and regeneration, death and rebirth, mourning and joy that define the Jewish condition. At the same time, his table that is no table but a work of art—his work of art that is no work of art in traditional painting-and-sculpting terms but in terms of the aesthetics of reshaping flotsam and jetsam into a work that makes the viewer think, hard—partakes of a reality endemic to both art history and Jewish history: a reality fraught with a dynamic tension between conserving the familiar and reforming the familiar into something new. This is a work of memory, questions, and definitions that views all of Jewish history as an ongoing rite of passage.

Passover is the seminal statement of that ongoing experience, and as a celebration it has continued to evolve from the limited shape prescribed in the Torah to the growing specifics added in the late Second Temple and rabbinic periods to those additions that we recognize as part of the medieval period to recent innovations.[18] One of the more important recent innovations, exploding in the 1990s, was the addition of a second goblet—an oblique balance for the Cup of Elijah—on the Seder table. Miriam's Goblet is filled with water, rather than the wine that fills the Cup of Elijah, for it recalls the important role of Moses' sister in providing water for the Israelites in the wilderness—the rabbinic tradition asserts that God provided her with a miraculous well that accompanied the Israelites through the wilderness but disappeared when Miriam died.[19]

The goblet symbolizes not only Miriam's rarely mentioned role (in the traditional Passover narrative) but also, by extension, all of the unmentioned women in the narrative and women as a whole in their essential role in birth and creativity—the very theme that centralizes the Passover story, from the birth of Moses (and it was Miriam, we recall, who watched over the basket that held him as it lay in the water in the rushes until the Pharaoh's daughter came along) to the birth of the Israelites as a covenantal people. Linda Gissen's 1997 *Miriam's Dance* is one among many such cups that now grace Seder tables. Her work both alludes to Miriam—most specifically in the painted figures dancing along the goblet walls, recalling Miriam's role in leading the Israelites in a song of thanksgiving and praise of God after their successful transit of the watery Sea of Reeds—and also hovers on that familiar border between useful object and work of art. For her painted glass goblet is "held" in the outstretched hands of a gold-painted sculpted bronze Giacometti-esque figure that could be Miriam herself [fig. 12]. In this case, we have, as it were, a double portrait

Fig 12: Linda Gissen, "Miriam's Dance."
1997. Acrylic on glass and gold
leaf on bronze.

of the heroine, as presenter of the goblet body and as leader of the dancers depicted along the goblet sides.

Nor is it the case that only women artists have added Miriam's cup to the Seder table—with its emphasis on the rite of passage of the People Israel through the Sea of Reeds and through the wilderness to Sinai and beyond Sinai toward the Promised Land—and the prayer that accompanies it[20] to complete contemporary Jewish participation in that rite of passage. Among male artists, Tobi Kahn, not surprisingly, includes this cup in the array of ceremonial objects that he created in his 1998 work, *RKADH, Miriam's Cup* [fig. 13]. Once again we cannot miss the blurred line between ritual object and

Fig 13: Tobi Kahn, "RKADH, Miriam's
Cup." 1998. Acrylic on bronze.

sculpture, as the stem of his cup assumes the copper-colored, sculpted form
of a female figure, standing on a gold-colored base, from whose upraised hand
a gold-colored goblet rises.

Passover as the consummate expression of the interweave between
individual and communal rites of passage, and between past and present and
present and future (we end the Seder with the messianic recitation "next year
in Jerusalem!"), has inspired an extraordinary range of kinds of art. Certainly
none is more compelling than the series of fourteen enormous semiabstract
acrylic-on-aluminum sculptures (and hundreds of drawings), focusing on the
Exodus, created by Connecticut-based artist George Wardlaw in the 1980s and
1990s; the series was inspired by the Passover narrative—in particular the ten
plagues. One of these, *Exodus II: Warning Signs*, is an 88" high, 106" wide, and

24" deep piece that suggests a cross between a black pyramid mounted on a massive platform and a stylized representation of the mountain ascended by Moses to receive the Torah [fig. 14]. The platform is made up of five layers, the number of books of the Torah, which is the foundation and platform for all of Jewish thought and history.

Wardlaw's work thus connects the experience of the Israelites as oppressed builders of Egyptian monuments and the moment of their painful reconfiguration at the foot of Sinai (painful because of Moses' extended forty-day sojourn on top of the mountain and the fear of abandonment that led to their construction of the golden calf). Its warning is reflected in the hundreds of subtly painted locust images swarming over its surface—alluding to one of the plagues that beset the Egyptians—and is directed to the Israelites and their descendants as well, who might too easily lose their faith or abandon the word and will of God.

This sculpture also recalls the synthesis of the ethnicity of Moses—the Israelite raised in the ultimate Egyptian household—and the spirituality of

Fig 14: George Wardlaw, "Exodus II: Warning Signs." Ca 1988.
Acrylic on aluminum. From *Exodus* series.

Jethro, his father-in-law, who joined the covenantal community when he heard about "all the goodness that God had done to Israel" (Exod 18:1-12). Such an ethnic-spiritual perspective also reflects a particular, personal rite of passage for the artist. Raised as a Baptist in a small southern town he was eventually inspired, in part by contact with the Judaism of Jack Tworkow, one of Wardlaw's key mentors when he was a young art student in New York City, to convert to Judaism years ago. We are reminded, then, not only of the blurred definitional line between artwork and ritual object but of the ambiguities ever-present in how we decide to label either of them as "Jewish" art or object, specifically with regard to the identity of the artist.

The passage from the Sea of Reeds to the other side of Sinai was as dangerous as the transit through the sea itself. The time until the arrival at the foot of the mountain is understood to have been seven weeks. That period is commemorated on the Jewish calendar by counting the time from the second day of Passover until the arrival at the day before the festival of Shavuot (which means "weeks"). In the era of the Temple, the period was marked[21] by the bringing of a daily dry-measure offering [*omer*] of barley flour to the Temple. In the modern era, *omer* counters, as they are known, have occasionally marked the passage of those weeks. Perhaps—who knows?—this visual custom was inspired by Christian counters of the days leading up to Christmas. Or was it the other way around?[22]

In any case, in the past generation, not only has the creation of *omer* counters become increasingly common, shaping them as interesting works of sculpture has yielded increasing diversity of *omer*-counter types. Among these is a harmonious 1996 work by Nashville artist Arnold Schwarzbart—not called "*omer* counter" but given a name, *The Time 'Till Sinai*, thus underscoring its identity as a work of art even if it is a ceremonial object that serves a specific ceremonial purpose [fig. 15]. Schwarzbart's work offers seven rows of triangular pyramid-shaped enamel on copper flaps that can be slid along dowels (a kind of Sinai abacus), the ends of which are embedded in the beautifully fired clay frame. Behind these, implanted within that frame, are forty-nine square lozenges of gold leaf, imprinted with Hebrew letters used as symbols for the numbers being counted down.

The Jewish calendar is rife with the importance of numbers and counting with precision. The most distinctively "Jewish" commandment among the ten[23] offered at Sinai pertains to the keeping of the seventh day of every week as a day of rest—it is what (explicitly in the reading of Exodus 20:8) links our behavior directly to God's since God rested [the Hebrew verb is *shavvat*] on the seventh day after completing the creation of the physical universe. Every

Fig 15: Arnold Schwarzbart, "The Time 'Til Sinai." 1997.
Clay, gold leaf, enamel on copper.[24]

Sabbath begins precisely at sundown, and every traditional Jew wants to mark that moment of passage from the weekdays into that pre-paradise time-space with absolute precision. The Sabbath candles, lit exactly at that moment of transition from one conceptual reality to another, recall the divine act of initiating the ordering process of the universe that culminated with the divine rest that we emulate every week by celebrating the Sabbath.[24]

  The odd, yet not so strange, thing is that the one time when the Jewish tradition becomes calendrically imprecise—even though it articulates itself in a precise manner—is at the end of the Sabbath. The ceremony of *Havdalah* that marks the transition back to the work week[25] does not take place at sundown, but rather—as if to prolong the pleasure of the Sabbath to the last possible moment—only when three stars have appeared in the sky. The thing is that one can fairly easily discern the moment when the first star appears,[26] and perhaps even the second, but by the time three are visible, many more than three are discernible. So the notion of waiting for that moment is a recipe for a delightful vagueness. The point is to make sure that, if one errs, that error extends the Sabbath beyond its theoretical endpoint, rather than abbreviating it.

As new visual directions have marked not only Torah-mandated annual festivals but also weekly Torah and post-Torah-mandated celebrations, the last generation has seen an explosion in the production of Sabbath- and *Havdalah*-related objects that operate on the line between "craft" and "art." So, for instance, Jennifer Karotkin's 1995 *Havdalah Set* places a trio of delicately sculpted objects, made of sterling silver, pearl, and fourteen-karat gold on a steel and silver plate that could just as easily be read as a platform for three small abstract sculptures [fig. 16]. How many of these would the uninitiated recognize as ritual objects? Certainly the tallest piece would be recognized as a wine goblet. Perhaps the medium-height "figure," tilting in to the others, might be identified as a holder for the *Havdalah* candle, with its sharp culminating spit intended to hold the candle in place.

But the most distinctive artifact in the arsenal of *Havdalah* celebration, the *hadas liv'samim*—the spice box, in which sweet-smelling herbs and seeds are placed as a symbol of the sweetness of the Sabbath and which is passed from person to person in the reluctant farewell to the Day of Rest—is its own oyster-like entity, without precedent in the traditional vocabulary of *Havdalah* spice boxes. Karotkin has allowed stylized vines to wrap their way up the stems

Fig 16: Jennifer Karotkin. "Havdalah Set." 1995.
Sterling, steel, pearl, 14k gold.

of the cup and the candleholder, and a gold leaf flutters from the candleholder spit—thus underscoring the nature of the Sabbath as a moment of Garden of Paradise calm within the turbulent week and between Eden and the messianic era, for which these objects are the instrumentation of farewell.

The light that is such a constant across the spectrum of Jewish celebration takes a particular place at the center of the ceremonial stage with Hanukkah. On the one hand, Hanukkah [the word means "dedication"] marks the defeat of the Seleucids by the Maccabee-led Judaeans and the cleansing and rededication of the Temple in Jerusalem in 165 BCE. On the other hand, the account of those events is found outside the Hebrew Bible—the first two books of Maccabees are read as canon by Orthodox and Catholic Christians, but neither by Protestants nor by Jews—and thus the holiday itself is a decidedly minor one throughout most of Jewish history. Nonetheless, for various reasons beyond this discussion, the holiday has grown, particularly in the modern era, in popularity (mostly, no doubt, related to the perceived need for a balance to Christmas in the annual cycle of the sun, at least in the past century or two).

In any case, the *hanukkiyah* [Chanukah menorah] has long been an object of visual passion—whether in all those times and places when non-Jews were necessarily its makers, or (the more so) in the last century when Jews have been freer to direct themselves to the production of Judaica. In some traditional circles, the tree-style *hanukkiyah*—with nine "branches" (one for each of the eight nights of the festival and a ninth with which to kindle all the others) rising from a "trunk"—is considered unkosher because its form "competes" with the tree form of the seven-branched Temple menorah. Since the advent of Reform Judaism in early nineteenth century Germany, that inhibition has diminished, and in the last generation, as in other areas that we have observed, the line between *hanukkiyah* as ritual object and as work of art is often stunningly blurred.

We are by now familiar with the underlying aesthetic principle of Tobi Kahn's mid-1990s *QUYA, Hanukkah Lamp*: a sculpture—on three legs, rather than one—inundated with plaster-suffused pigment [fig. 17]. The golden candleholders rise like the central buds from a series of petals opening up—not in response to the light of the sun but in order to present the candles that will offer light in the long dark night of December. Cynthia Schlemlein's 1997 sterling silver work is called *Zoe: Hanukkah Lamp*—so that, like Kahn, she has "named" her creation ("*zoe*" means "life" in Greek, so we might understand this work as an address of the concept of life as it relates to light and heat in the wintertime as much as to the stunning survival of the Jewish people symbolized by the Hanukkah story), thereby translating it away from the

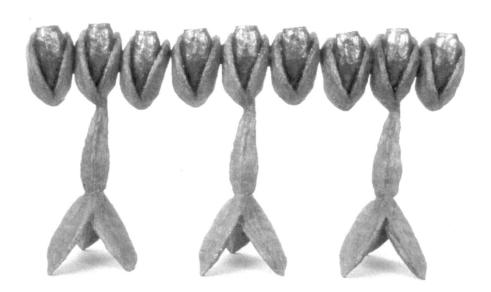

Fig 17: Tobi Kahn, "QUYA, Hanukkah Lamp." 1996. Acrylic on bronze.

normative ground of unnamed ceremonial objects. And, in fact, her work is far from "normative." Two vertically soaring and beautifully rendered wing forms hold up the delicate bowl around the periphery of which the candle flames burn [fig. 18].

The most enduring traditional rabbinical prescription for *hanukkiyot* is that the eight candles signifying the eight days of the festival be absolutely level, and in transgressing the line between ritual object and objet d'art Schlemlein has chosen—as many artists have in the past few decades—to ignore that prescription. Cleveland artist Bea Mitchell crosses that line even more radically in her 1994 bronze sculpture, *The Burning Bush* [fig. 19]. This intricate and exquisite work may be seen to offer a double visual pun. The bronze itself rises and twists and turns in a manner that recalls the gnarly extrusions of some extraordinary thicket—the sort one might imagine obscuring the path to Sleeping Beauty's palace for a hundred years. Yet the tips of all of these "branches" arrive at delicate pointed tips that suggest flames. So the bush that Moses turned aside to see, that "burned with fire but was not consumed" (Exod 3:2)—the bush that proved to be the moment defining his rite of passage from anonymous middle-aged shepherd of his father-in-law's flocks to his stentorian senior adult years of staring down the Pharaoh and leading the recalcitrant Israelites through the wilderness, all the while communing with God—as well as the flame that could not consume that bush are both contained within the bronze.

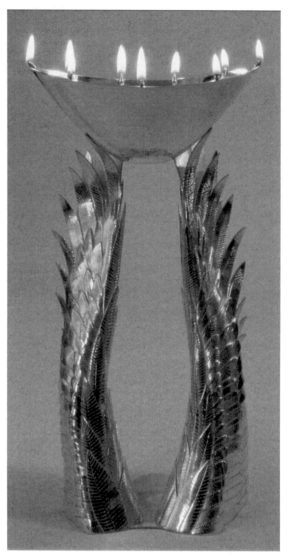

Fig 18: Cynthia Schlemlein. *"Zoe*: Hanukkah
Lamp." Sterling silver. 1997.

But in fact the bronze sculpture bears nine candles—so it is at the same
time a ("nonkosher")[27] *hanukkiyah*, a holder for the flames that pertain to the
Hanukkah story. This is to say that the beginning of the narrative that will
lead to Sinai, the eventual reshaping of the Israelites from desert tribes to a
kingdom that will spiritually center itself in a Temple that will be destroyed as
that kingdom self-destructs and that will be rebuilt, and in the many centuries'
aftermath of that destruction and rebuilding, the remnant of those tribes-
become-kingdom will throw off a religious oppressor and rededicate the

Fig 19: Bea Mitchell, "The Burning Bush." 1994. Bronze.

Temple menorah—this entire narrative, over a millennium long, is contained within the bronze of Mitchell's work. And the memory of that defining narrative is carried by her into the present day within this metal meeting point between art and ritual object.

## FOUR: THE LIFE CYCLE BETWEEN ART AND OBJECT

In one sense we come full circle back to the specifics of the life cycle and in another revise the ongoing conversation regarding "fine art" versus "ritual object" in turning to Malcah Zeldis's 1984 oil-on-board painting, *Jewish Wedding (Me and Leonard)* [fig. 20]. The self-taught artist—her work would be

Fig 20: Malcah Zeldis, "Jewish Wedding (Me and Leonard)." 1984.
Oil on board.

labeled "primitive" or "naïve," if one were seeking to define her style within the standard canons of art historical discussion—has embraced a kind of God's-eye view. The couple hovers, dreamlike, iconlike, large—larger than any one else in the tableau, for this is pre-Renaissance significance perspective, in which importance to the theme and not distance from the viewer generates comparative sizes of figures within the image. Dancing couples swirl around them, punctuating the expanse of Barbie-doll pink floor. Celebrants dine around a bright sky-blue table. Across the upper background register, the artist extends basic Jewish wedding elements, from the *huppah* [wedding canopy] to the band to the cake. This is not a ceremonial object but the image of an idealized ceremony.

Indeed, within its idealized imagery there is something stiffly and formally odd about the bride and groom, beyond their eye-catching size: they are there but not there as others raucously celebrate on their behalf. The work offers a range of diverse and real elements, but it turns out that it is less a record of a real event than a visual wish for it: dream, memory (Zeldis was married, but that marriage ended years ago), and reality converge within that wish: "I get my boyfriend to marry me in my paintings," she has commented.[28] So, as with life in general and as with the Jewish experience across history and geography in particular, the further that we follow into life-cycle rites of passage, the stronger seems the possibility for shadows to appear within the celebratory light.

One gains a particularly poignant sense of the mixture of shadow and light in considering that most fundamental and traditional of customs associated with the Jewish bride as she prepares for her wedding: the *mikvah* [ritual bath]. While the intention of the *mikvah* is to purify her before her wedding night and to underscore the purity with which she enters her marriage (and the groom, too, might immerse himself in a *mikvah*), there is more to the ritual of immersion than this, both in its premarital significance and in its other-than-premarital use. Shari Rothfarb addresses this in a moving 1999 video installation—thus incidentally offering an example of the expanding range of media encompassed by contemporary "Jewish art" both in general and as it encounters rites of passage—called *Water Rites* [fig. 21]. From a ceiling-installed video projector, the artist projects twenty-seven comments regarding the significance of the *mikvah*—the pool of ritual purification into which Jewish women have immersed themselves for endless generations, not

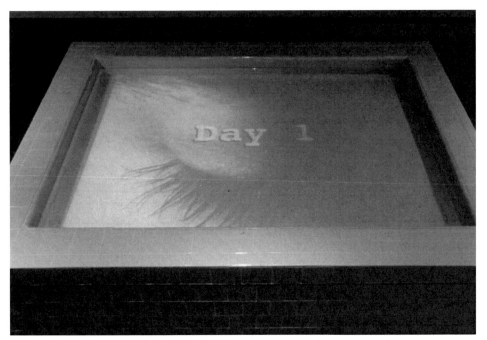

Fig 21: Shari Rothfarb. "Water Rites." 1999. Video projection on water.

only before getting married, but most often before the Sabbath and also after menses—into a tiled, *mikvah*-like pool of water.

This last, postmenstrual immersion, precisely because it is a ritual immersion [called *niddah*] and not merely a physical act of bathing, reflects in part on the supposition that menstrual blood is unclean—thereby offering a shadow component to the bright light of Jewish marriage. For traditional laws govern the times when a Jewish man and wife may and may not indulge in sexual relations, based around this supposition of ritual uncleanliness that afflicts the wife every month but does not afflict the husband—even though that same blood is associated with the bringing forth of life that is made possible by those sexual relations, which are commanded by God in the renowned biblical imperative to "be fruitful and multiply."

But Rothfarb does not allow this particular shadow to consume the complex mottling of her work. Shimmering within the shallow waters of the pool into which they are projected is a time- and spacewide array of images of *mikvaot*, including footage of ancient and modern *mikvaot* from Massada, Jerusalem, and the Galilee. And the quotations are not just commentaries but narratives, including one, for example, that speaks of a group of women who insisted to their Nazi executioners that they be allowed to immerse themselves properly, cleansing themselves before crossing the border from life—that is, before being shot to death. Here the *mikvah* becomes a symbol of a spiritual light that would not be dimmed by the most intense of darknesses. Landscapes of lush and provocative imagery form a backdrop for the speakers of the artist's words that summarize her project of "transgressing the boundaries of time and space to reflect the many different experiences and points of view about Mikvah."[29]

In a unique combination of word and image, stasis and motion, stillness and dynamism, Rothfarb's work suggests a range of understandings, from onerous to uplifting, of this rite of passage within the Jewish tradition.[30]

On the other hand, Canadian artist Devorah Neumark's 2000 work, *Harrei At Mutteret . . . Harrei At Mikoodeshet. . .*, adds a new conceptual and visual twist to the dark edges of the beginning and potential end of Jewish married life—wedding and divorce—but with irony and wit. *Harrei At Mutteret* [Behold you are released] are words of divorce, echoing the words spoken by the groom, as he places a ring around the bride's finger: *Harrei At Mikoodeshet [lee]* [Behold you are sanctified (unto me)]. Neumark's installation follows women through the passage between marriage and nonmarriage, a metaphor for the passage between entitlement and nonentitlement [fig. 22]. Framed transparencies of historic illustrations by unknown (presumably Jewish)

Fig 22: Deborah Neumark, "Harrei At Muteret." 2000.
Mixed media installation.

and well-known artists (not Jewish, like Rembrandt; and Jewish, like Moritz Oppenheim) depict the joy of the Jewish wedding. There are ten of these photo boxes, as if we are observing a women's *minyan*; each is surmounted by a wine goblet. The breaking of the wine glass at the culmination of the Jewish wedding ceremony (wine being the most traditional of Jewish symbols of joy) is intended to recall, even in the midst of happiness, the destruction of the Temple.

Seven of the goblets (the number of blessings recited at the wedding and the number of times the bride traditionally walks around the groom) are inscribed with the Hebrew words of release. Scores of goblets complete the installation, stacked and pulling from the wall in a semicircle. The shattered forms of some recall simultaneously the relative ease of divorce (when compared to the Christian tradition) in Judaism and its difficulty, indeed impossibility, if the husband should not desire it. While a wife can, under defined conditions, demand a divorce, the husband may refuse. If Judaism is a historically marginalized minority within Christendom, women are a historically limited majority within Judaism, particularly as defined by the beginning and even more so the ending of a marriage.

Differently, within the ever-widening circle of modes both of addressing the rituals of Jewish life and festival cycles and of expressing that address artistically, one might consider the "postmodern wedding" that took place in Toronto, Canada, on October 12, 2003, between Canadian media artist Melissa Shiff and Louis Kaplan. The wedding took place during Sukkot and was planned as a complexly choreographed work of art—part video, part performance piece; thus the ceremony was embedded in art and art was embedded in the ceremony. In naming the ceremony *Louis and Melissa's Chuppah in the Succah*,[31] Shiff and Kaplan also interwove the individual, life-cycle rite of passage with the communal, festival-cycle rite of passage.

In 2006 an exhibition of the project of the wedding was on view in the Jewish Museum in Prague—thus what began as a video, wedding ceremony, and performance piece became a video and installation of the wedding ceremony as performance piece, installed on the bimah of the Spanish-Portuguese synagogue that is part of the museum complex.[32] The title of the "exhibition" was in fact "Reframing Ritual: Postmodern Jewish Wedding. *Featuring Melissa Schiff as the Bride and Louis Kaplan as the Groom.*" As Shiff wrote in the catalogue of the exhibition, "It was a blurring of the lines between the intimacy of the contemporary wedding as a life-cycle ritual that is normally designed for family and friends alone and the acknowledgment that what we were doing in terms of reinventing the rite and mediating ritual would have a larger audience outside of the private and personal domains. This moved the ceremony away from the intimate and into spaces of self-reflexivity and meta-commentary about Jewish ritual in general."[33]

The wedding couple reconceived the *huppah* in terms of both form and function.[34] They tilted it at a forty-five-degree angle; from the perspective of the audience/congregation, it became a large movie screen onto which a range of images was projected at strategic moments during the ceremony. These included intersplicings, for example, of two classic Yiddish films,[35] for which Shiff rewrote the intertitles from one. The scene from the second shows men marching around the pulpit on Sukkot carrying the *lulav* and *etrog*—the four species of the fall harvest festival.[36] They then reshaped that processional, asking four close friends to march down the aisle with the same four fruits and to tie them to the four posts of the *huppah*, thus making explicit an equation between *huppah* and *sukkah*.

As the bride and groom marched down the aisle, video visuals of passages each had selected from the Torah were projected onto their bodies; arriving at the bimah, they turned to face their family and friends as "the Hebrew text washed over us as we faced the projection,"[37] while non-Torah texts, also chosen by the bride and groom, were projected onto the *huppah*. The projections onto themselves literalized the idea of taking the Torah onto and into themselves in this celebration of joining themselves together and to the "House of

Israel"—thus transforming the idea traditionally conveyed through the words recited as the centerpiece of the ring ceremony. This may also be seen as yet another oblique response to the question of where the Jewish artist fits into the history of Western, Christian art: as some denominations of Christians (and once upon a time, all of them) take Christ—the ultimate intermediator between divinity and humanity—into themselves through the Eucharist, Shiff and Kaplan imprinted the word of the ultimate Jewish intermediator between God and ourselves onto and thus into themselves [fig. 23].

The traditional seven circlings of bride around groom became 3.5 circles around each other, as passages from the Song of Songs that they selected circled around each other on the video screen/*huppah* beyond them—against a rich background of *sukkah* imagery, thus further merging the *huppah* and the *sukkah*. Moreover, the idea that consistently pervades Jewish celebration—that the past and present/future become blurred; that our memory is a constant means of connecting the living and the dead—that is conveyed in the Sukkot notion of *ushpizin*,[38] and that can have a personalized echo in the modernist idea of welcoming the souls of the dead to the wedding ceremony,[39] was expressed by a series of projections of images and names of deceased family members onto the *huppah*/screen. Thus, the past in the form of family members watched over the present and the future as these images hovered over the bride and groom [fig. 24].

On that screen, too, passages from the Torah that offer a patriarchal and arguably misogynistic image of how to be in the world[40] were transformed though the use of the After Effects software program into free-floating poetry, through the elimination and reorganization of words. For "[i]f we do not rewrite Biblical scriptures and invent new rituals with the help of the tools of the Electric Age, then we will still be stuck in the Stone Age."[41] Thus the Shiff-Kaplan wedding project, aside from crossing the various separating lines between art and not craft, but the ritual that craft has traditionally served, and also between different "categories" of celebration and passage in the Jewish tradition, sought to examine some of the shadows endemic to this central life-cycle celebration and to turn them to light.

## FIVE: THE ONGOING BLURRING OF DEFINITIONAL LINES

One might argue that the traditional sense of imbalance explored by Rothfarb and Neumark and addressed by Shiff extends from birth to the birth and the death of a marriage to the Jewish ceremonies pertaining to death in general. The centerpiece of such ceremonies is the recitation of the *Kaddish* [sanctification].[42] What originated as a statement of affirmation—of one's

Fig 23: Melissa Shiff, "Reframing Ritual: Post- Modern Jewish wedding" (detail). 2003. Video projection onto body.

Fig 24: Melissa Shiff, "Reframing Ritual: Post- Modern Jewish wedding" (detail). 2003. Video projection onto *huppah/sukkah*.

faith in the greatness and goodness of God—evolved as a "mourner's prayer" precisely because it is at a time of mourning for a loved one that we might be inclined to feel anger against God and therefore are required to affirm our faith. But only sons are expected—or permitted—within the Orthodox tradition to recite the *Kaddish* as part of a formal *minyan* of mourners for his father. Hence, an imbalance.

It is perhaps less this issue than her fascination with writing in general and Hebrew calligraphy in particular—and her interest in focusing on writing in a rhythmic and repetitive manner—that led New York artist Jane Logemann to do her ink, oil, and varnish-on-muslin *Kaddish* series in 1995. The series offers a subset of Logemann's work wherein rows of letters and words are washed over with subtle pigments. These may be viewed as abstractions (particularly if one does not read the Hebrew—or Arabic, Japanese, Russian, and other writing systems that she sometimes uses), while at the same time they may be read (literally) in terms of their content and message.[43] The word has become the image: the ongoing repetition of a word runs together so that its beginning and end points are not apparent, and so the visual result is simply as if the letters and not the words are repeated endlessly. This suggests the patterns of sound-and-syllable repetition prescribed for the mystic in some kabbalistic systems,[44] and it also recalls contemporary music (Philip Glass,

for instance), ancient Byzantine mosaics, Islamic art, and some of the wall
paintings of Sol Lewitt.

In each work within Logemann's ten-part *Kaddish* series, the text
of the *Kaddish* is repeated, in Aramaic letters that sandwich a Latin-letter
transliteration, all within a circular frame [fig. 25]. The circle, without
beginning or end, bespeaks the notion of continuum that is essential to the
idea of the *Kaddish* both as a mourner's prayer and as the affirmation of faith,
which was its inception. Logemann's rendition is in turn framed by a repeating
Hebrew alphabet—each line a letter—from beginning [*aleph*] to end [*taf*] and
then beginning again and continuing until the rectilinear space that frames the
circular frame of the *Kaddish* runs out. The sense, then, that it continues—not
only that the letters repeat themselves, but that the lines of letters and the
entire alphabet repeat ad infinitum, beyond the picture frame—is paramount.

Fig 25: Jane Logemann, "Kaddish 5." 1995. Ink,
oil, varnish on muslin. From *Kaddish* series.

Moreover, across the ten-image series, the circle within the rectangle shifts upward and downward within the picture plane, as the color—whitish to grey, which is almost white toward grey and then grey, which is almost black to blackish—modulates in harmony with the shifting of the circular form within the series frames.

The ten parts of the series, circles ascending and descending, correspond to the ten ascents and descents of the *hekhalot* that define the relationship between heaven and earth in pre-kabbalistic *merkavah* mysticism.[45] They correspond to the Ten Commandments that are the heart of the Torah received at Sinai. The concentrated, repetitive focus on the ultimate statement of prayerful connection to God corresponds to the devotional ethos of Jewish mysticism, and the rhythmic, graduated color and form shifts point to contemporary minimalism in visual art—but also to music and dance, as within Logemann's larger body of work.

The notion of art and artifact that pertains to the cycle of mourning is very differently reflected in the small bronze sculptures of Soviet-born Seattle artist Simon Kogan. His 1993 eight-inch-high *Yahrzeit Lamp* offers an oil wick within a small bowl (into which he has inscribed the word "Amen" in Hebrew letters), from which a flat backstop slab arises that culminates in—the flat, bronze wall simply metamorphoses as—the head of a bearded figure, bent over, inclined toward the flame in the bowl below. The figure is hooded, his brow furrowed in prayer. His hands protrude directly from the wall, pressed together, palm to palm, finger to finger. The latter are configured with the two central digits of each hand held together, the index and pinky finger separated from the others, the thumbs pressed up into the beard, against the chin, yielding the familiar configuration of the Hebrew letter *shin* [fig. 26].

That letter, standing for the power-protective Name of God, *shaddai*, is used on *mezuzot*, both those worn around the neck and even more commonly on those attached to the doorposts of Jewish homes. Its form is the one assumed by the hand configuration of those who administer the threefold priestly benediction that God instructed Aaron and his sons to offer to the Israelites in the wilderness, which is repeated at the conclusion of services by leaders in many contemporary congregations.[46] Thus, Kogan's memorial lamp bears within its sculpted form the notion of a divine, protective blessing accorded to the soul of the deceased to complement—in a kind of conceptual chiasm—the affirmation of faith in God's protective and loving power being articulated by the mourner as he or she recites the *Kaddish* on the anniversary of his or her loved one's death.

In the same year, Kogan sculpted another small bronze sculpture, in which from a small base rises an irregular and rough-hewn slice of torn and

Fig 26: Simon Kogan, "Yahrzeit Lamp." 1993. Bronze.

twisted geometrically shaped material. At its uppermost reaches, an old man's head, reminiscent of but not identical to that on the *Yahrzeit* lamp, protrudes. The face is long, the eyes beads of fierce focus, the beard lush and matted, its thick tangles bulging and then dripping downward in an increasingly narrow configuration. That lower, whispier part of the beard seems almost to fall through the square, windowlike opening in the bronze slab from which the head extrudes—and at the same time suggests not a beard falling but both a tangle of human bodies falling and a flame rising up from the bottom of the opening to envelop both the bodies and ultimately the face. The windowlike opening itself suggests a passage between worlds—that of the living and that of the dead [fig. 27].

This twelve-inch-tall work is entitled *Don't Forget*, and it is intended as a memorial for the six million Jews who perished during the Holocaust. For our purposes we may recognize three issues engaged by it—and by both Kogan works. Once more an artist has blurred the line between creating an object for ceremonial use and creating a work of art for display. Once more an artist has blurred the line between an individual, life-cycle event and its visual concomitants and a communal, festival-cycle event. And thirdly, the principle of constant expansion and reshaping to which the Jewish festival calendar has been subject throughout history (expanding the articulation of a given festival or expanding the number of festivals that Jews celebrate), a principle that has

Fig 27: Simon Kogan, "Don't Forget."
1993. Bronze.

never been more accelerated than in the last few generations, is demonstrated. For *Yom HaShoah*—Holocaust Memorial Day—became part of the calendar in Israel six years after that horrific event, in 1951. It was formally and programmatically embraced in the Diaspora only thirty years later.[47]

*Yom HaShoah* was originally keyed to coincide with *Yom Ha'Atzma'ut* [Israeli Independence Day]—preceding it by eight days. Not only was *Yom Ha'Atzma'ut* obviously itself a new addition to the Jewish calendar in the second half of the twentieth century, but the timing of the two holidays, eight days apart, recalls the eight-day-long celebration of Hanukkah—and the idea of cleansing and rededicating the Temple after a disaster—on the one hand, and the idea of welcoming a new child into the community in a formally way, through *Brit Milah* [circumcision] or, more recently, baby-naming, on the eighth day after birth, on the other. In tandem, the two holidays offer symbolic statements of death and rebirth.

This sort of interpenetration of celebrations and commemorations is expressed if we backtrack for a moment to J. Barry Zeiger's *Seder Table*. The details of his non-ritual-object installation, with its trees bursting through the table overrun with broken crockery, and his Israeli-flag-reminiscent windows, coalesce for us as not merely Passover-related but intended, in part, as a post-Holocaust statement of paradoxic unremediable destruction and yet rebirth. The trees have been shorn of leaves that cannot come back, but they soar nonetheless toward those windows and their color and shape symbolism.

Moreover, Zeiger's *Seder Table* is typically accompanied as an installation by a second, related piece, *Resistance*, in which he has filled an entire light-ringed, broken-paned window in its frame with bleached bones and colorful beads [fig. 28]. On the right corner of the sill sits a blood-red pomegranate, a symbol of fertility, of physical continuity. Because of the pomegranate's myriad seeds, and in the Jewish tradition offering a particular association with spiritual and intellectual continuity, the rows of seeds have for centuries been likened to rows of Torah-studying students. In juxtaposition with his *Seder Table*, the artist underscores his intention of encompassing Passover, Shoah commemoration, and the fact of the rebirth of an independent Jewish state in one overarching art installation.

One may turn the matter of the Holocaust in a number of directions as it pertains to the making of art. Thus, for example, Iowa-born Robert Lipnick, in growing up as the son of a rabbi and learning about the Shoah, determined not only that he would become an artist—specifically, a crafter of ceramic art—but also that he would devote himself largely to ceremonial objects in order to help fill in the large hole in Jewish material culture left by the destructions and depradations effected by the Nazis and their associates.

Fig 28: Jay Barry Zeiger, "Resistance." 1997-
2001. Mixed media found objects installation.

Thus, for example, his early 1990s *Hanukkiyah* (one of many) is both a
ritual object to be used for that holiday and, in effect, a Holocaust memorial
sculpture [fig. 29]. The latter role is most obviously conveyed by the sort of
brightly colored visual vocabulary with which this work, like most of Lipnick's
work, is decorated. Thus, against a black background that is glowing rather

Fig 29: Robert Lipnick, "Hanukkiyah." Ca 1992.
Glazed ceramic.

than mournful are symbols recalling the sweep of biblical and Israelite-Judaean-Jewish history.

Torah scrolls encompass the entirety of Jewish history. The forms of ancient clay containers suggest the biblical past, as pyramids allude to the experience of the Israelites in and coming out of Egypt, and an ark alludes to the story of Noah as well as to that of the Shoah—those who were drowned by it and those who managed somehow to survive it. The dove swoops toward the center of the bulging composition. This is the symbol of peace and of

Noah's search and discovery of dry land—but that moment recounted in Genesis 8:8-12 may be seen to intersect the post-Holocaust return and rebirth of the People Israel in *Eretz Yisrael* [the Land of Israel]. Scattered leaves, still robust and green, are strewn from top to bottom of the piece: like the Jews attacked by the Nazis and their allies, they have been torn from the tree but refuse to go brown and die. And in the midst of it all, a little white house with a red roof stands there, silent yet eloquent: it symbolizes the home in which the artist grew up and heard the narrative that helped drive him to create just this sort of object in just this style. It weds the personal to the communal.

Thus in different ways Kogan, Zeiger, and Lipnick have addressed the culminating traumatic rite of Jewish passage, each intersecting it with different other passages, communal (Passover, Hanukkah), individual (*Yahrzeit*), and personal (red-roofed childhood). One might argue that Sarah Belchetz-Swenson's early 1970s *Revisions* series served as one of the starting points for this growing range of ways of addressing the Holocaust—and of the idea of that experience as a rite that, however horrifying, in the end became another passage for the Jewish people and not a terminus. Her work also offers a beginning of the act of commemoration by thinking simultaneously about past and future, in an artistic analogy to the shaping of *Yom HaShoah* in relationship to *Yom Ha'Atzma'ut*. For in her series, the Egyptian-born Connecticut artist inserted the images of her own two young children[48] playing, resting, sleeping, flourishing onto, into, and around details, floor plans, or elevations of timber synagogues of which, before the Holocaust, there were hundreds scattered among the *shtetl*s of Poland, Ukraine, Russia, and, above all, Lithuania—and of which only a handful remain today.

Thus, for example, the image of her kids playing hide-and-seek—the older (Zoe), leaning, hiding, against a tree trunk; the younger (Saskia), running, searching—is framed within the floor plan of the Wolpa synagogue [fig. 30]. The past contained within the rich architectural history of these structures, intermediated by the powerful idea of a well-rooted, heaven-reaching tree, interweaves with the healthy future of healthy Jewish children in a new land, playing the children's games that every American kids plays on a summer evening. The past, largely obliterated by the Holocaust, nonetheless survives to meet the future. Moreover, for the purposes of our discussion, the timber synagogues with their unique yet individualized styles raise the definitional question of what the criteria are for defining synagogue architecture as "Jewish"—style, symbols, identity of the architect, purpose of the edifice?

Conversely, the work of Israeli photographer Margalit Mannor overlaps the other historical shoe dropping—the creation of the State of Israel—with the historical, conceptual, and definitional debate about what the State should

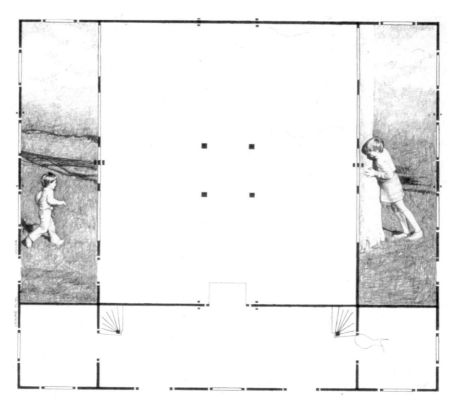

Fig 30: Sara Belchetz-Swenson. "Wolpa Synagogue/Hide-and-Seek."
1971. Pencil on paper. From *Revisions* series.

be. This was a debate that began over a century ago, when in the incipient Zionist movement, the Theodore Herzl, and Ahad Ha'Am views clashed regarding whether the Zionist goal should be political or cultural/spiritual, whether what was needed was an independent Jewish state—anywhere—or nothing geographically less than a return to the Jewish homeland, regardless of under whose governance, the Ottoman Turks, the British, or the Jews themselves.

One can see that issue as continuing through the rite of passage that created the State by 1948-1949, and the transformation of the issue, in part, into the question of whether and in precisely what manner Israel is "The Jewish State," given its governmental complexity. Israel is a secular democracy in which Christians, Muslims, Hindus, Bahais, and others are citizens, which at the same time operates along specifically Jewish lines with regard to the automatic citizenship accorded Jews through the "Law of Return" and with regard to the keeping of the Sabbath and the holidays according to the Jewish calendar, to name two obvious instances.[49]  Moreover, the continuation of the question of the state's identity is also expressed by those Israelis who ask whether or not the state as it currently operates is fulfilling the Zionist dream of a century ago—and if so, which version of the dream—and to what extent the state does or does not operate according to traditional Jewish principles.

Mannor's visual address of this issue is woven of various issues—her celebration of *Yom Ha'Atzma'ut*, as it were, by both rejoicing and questioning (and is not questioning the preeminent Jewish art?)—and is reflected in a series of works from 1997-1998. A few years earlier, she had stumbled upon a series of several dozen old black-and-white postcards from the 1920s—with images of the Zionist dream in evolution, intended to be sent to friends and family throughout the Diaspora regarding what was developing there. She has taken one or more of these postcards and superimposes it/them as an insert onto and into a large, color image that she has photographed, usually of the same site depicted in the postcard(s).

Thus, for example, an old image of a busy corner in Tel Aviv, marked by the typical Bauhaus-style architecture of that time—three or four-story-high rectilinear buildings rising from rounded pillar "stilts" and busy traffic—rests against and within the 30" x 40" image of a tall, elegant building beyond which there soars a virtual skyscraper, only part of which can even fit into the image [fig. 31]. With some of these double images, the intention seems to be to express pride in what has grown out of the seeds of eighty years ago and the Fourth and early Fifth *Aliyah* periods.[50] In others the intention is clearly to question or even perhaps to bemoan developments that have transformed a certain cultural innocence into a cynically sophisticated reality—and for some (perhaps this one) the message seems deliberately ambiguous: one can cheer or lament the implications of the skyscraper, depending upon one's perspective.

Israel is, in the Jewish world of today, one of the two primary pillars of Jewish life, culture, and thought, and the United States is the other. And if we twist the subject of *Yom Ha'Atzma'ut* one turn further in returning to the United States, we can come full circle to where we began with issues of definition, identity, and memory within the question of how today's Jews celebrate, commemorate, and commiserate. New York artist Marilyn Cohen's unique work—she tears, stains, and layers pieces of paper to create stunningly nuanced collage works that address any number of issues—has offered, among other things, portraits of fifty-two American Jewish families who arrived at various times to each of the fifty states and portraits of extraordinary Jewish women of valor—or a triptych of a "posed and seated" range of historical and mythical women, from Amelia Earhart to Wonder Woman, who share with women artists across history a tendency to be insufficiently recognized for their accomplishments.

Fig 31: Margalit Mannor, "H.G. No. 990." 1997-1998.
Color print.

Cohen's torn papers, reconstituted as images in layers, serve as a metaphor for the artistic art of re-visioning and for the historiographic act of remembering, as well as for the historical experience for families and peoples of piling experience onto experience.  One of her emphatically American pieces is her 1995 *Independence Day* [fig. 32].  For our purposes, this work combines these standard elements of Cohen's work with the issue of an

Fig 32: Marilyn Cohen, "Independence Day." 1995.
Watercolor-soaked torn paper collage.

expanding Jewish calendar of celebration and, in the case of Jews in America, identity. Thus, her image of this particular American Jewish family is a not atypical visual narrative of having once been immigrants but having become "American" in part by the experience remembered in the words inscribed around the periphery of the beach blanket/towel—"life was once a day at the beach"—and in part by the embrace of American Independence Day on the calendar of annual celebrations.

Thus, the secular *Yom Ha'Atzma'ut* and even the secular national *Yom*

*HaShoah* that define Israeli Jews both as Israelis and as Jews-by-nationality is echoed by the secular Independence Day that is part of the identity of American Jews who feel themselves Jews by religion or custom and tradition and who feel themselves no different from their American Christian (or Muslim, or Hindu, or Bahai) neighbors. The calendar of celebration—and in Marilyn Cohen's case, the visual address of this piece of that calendar—can include Independence Day and Memorial Day, Labor Day and Thanksgiving Day—and for some, even Christmas Day—as distinctly as and as discretely separate from Yom Kippur, Hanukkah, Passover, Shavuot, and Sukkot.

*        *        *        *        *

Let us complete the coming full circle of our discussion by reference to an incomplete circle of stone, for that is the material basis for Maryland artist Sy Gresser's 1998 *Menorah (Tribal Faces)* [fig. 33]. Gresser's work is an incomplete circle of steatite into which he has carved a stylized seven-branched menorah—no actual candles, no actual candelabrum, just the distinct and formalized low-relief impression of the centerpiece of Temple ritual. It is that image, in various iterations, that one finds most ubiquitous in the two millennia since the time of the Second Temple's destruction and the history

Fig 33: Sy Gresser. "Menorah (Tribal Faces)." 1998. Carved steatite.

of what one might call "Jewish" art. As a symbol, it not only recalls the Temple, traditionally suggesting the hope for its restoration in the messianic future, but its seven-ness also recalls the commandment to keep the seventh day holy—that most "Jewish" among the Ten Commandments[51]—enunciated by God through Moses at that people-forming rite of passage at the foot of Mt. Sinai, as the Israelites moved from Egypt toward the Promised Land and from slavery to freedom. It thus connotes both the promise of redemption and the responsibilities of the Covenant.

Around the menorah image crowds a series of faces that ask who and what we are, extending from the personal to the universal by way of certain Jewish qua tribal specifics. The faces represent different races and ethnic types (Jews offer no specific racial or ethnic typology, in spite of those who would assert otherwise, but at least one of those depicted here represents the artist's grandfather), held together by the most consistent symbol in two millennia of Jewish art. The faces—one eye open, the other closed—have both outer and inner vision as they are literally connected to each other in a circle (universal symbol of perfection and completeness) that, in its incompleteness, suggests that there remains work for us to do to in fulfilling the responsibility of *tikkun olam*—"repairing a[n imperfect] world," in partnership with the God to whom all of these ever-constant, ever-evolving ceremonies of celebration, commemoration, and commiseration have been directed for millennia, and to whom there has been such an explosively varied visual response in the contemporary Jewish world.

## NOTES

[1] As a convenience, I am using Kaplan's *Judaism as a Civilization*, first published in 1934, as the starting point for this category assertion.

[2] There was even a sense of hierarchy among the fine arts: Michelangelo is said to have understood architecture to be the loftiest of the arts, followed by sculpture and then by painting.

[3] It is certainly arguable for that matter that Schatz and Bezalel did create "Jewish national art." Certainly Early Bezalel made use of particular symbols, such as the seven-branched candelabrum, the Star of David, the rising sun (the dawning of the new Jewish nationalist era); focused on particular subjects, such as heroic biblical and contemporary Jewish figures (e.g., Abraham, Moses, Theodore Herzl, Herzl as Moses); focused on both natural landscape and architectural imagery that was endemic to Eretz Yisrael; used a distinctive, art nouveau-reminiscent style; and emphasized particular materials for both arts and crafts, such as copper (evocative of Solomon's legendary mines), olivewood from the Galilee, stone quarried from the Negev desert, and so on. But whether these aspects of "Jewish national art" add up to "Jewish art" is a slightly different question.

[4] Interestingly, at least two aspects of style with regard to both secular and sacred objects produced at Bezalel reflect the fact that, in the Muslim world, Jews were almost exclusively the craftspeople in metals—the opposite of the condition throughout Christendom. Thus, so-called Damascene work that embedded brass with copper and sometime silver or even, rarely, gold in dynamic, low-relief interweave patterns, whether for sword blades or *Megillat Esther* cases, was exclusively the product of Jewish craftsmen in Damascus. Schatz sent a handful of his master craftsmen there to learn this technique, and a substantial influx of already-skilled Yemenite silversmiths was trained in the (for them) new technique of metal beading.

[5] Moreover, in the context of the post-Holocaust world and the theological question asked by many Jews (and non-Jews)—where was the all-powerful, all-good God while more than a million Jewish children were being destroyed?—Newman may be seen to be providing an answer: God was absent (for those for whom God was absent, who lost their faith in the face of the Nazi atrocities) and yet present (for those who survived because of their conviction that God was watching over them).

[6] This information was derived from a conversation with the artist in spring 2009.

[7] Snyder has done an entire series called *Life Cycle*. In the interests of space I am discussing only one work, but the general sense of all of them points in a similar direction, albeit with interestingly varied details, with respect to colors, texture, and dominant female figure (for the central figure is usually less ambiguous than in the work under discussion).

[8] In case this is not inherently clear, I mean the following: untrammeled rejoicing over the birth of a boy, an heir, with a more compromised joy over the birth of a girl; the official bringing into the Community of Israel for a boy (circumcision) but not for a girl; the formal assumption of moral adulthood for a boy (Bar Mitzvah) but not for a girl—and the studying that he undertakes but she does not, together with the prayers that he recites (including thanking God for having been made a man and not a woman) but she does not; the primary ceremonial focus on the groom, rather than the bride— he recites the words of consummation when he places the ring on her finger and she does not; should there be (God forbid!) a divorce, only he may initiate and articulate it with a *get* [bill of divorce], not she; at death, both will be formally mourned by their sons through the recitation of the *Kaddish*, during *shiva*, at *shlosheem*, and year by year at *yartzeit*—and not by their daughters. While it should certainly be noted both that other Abrahamic and non-Abrahamic traditions are as gender-imbalanced or often even more so in their traditional forms; and also that there is nonetheless a distinct and not unhappy role for women within traditional Judaism; nonetheless, from a nontraditional perspective, these life-cycle imbalances can only be seen as profound and, for a woman, spell out a distinct ambiguity with regard to where she fits into the House of Israel.

[9] Chelm is, in fact, a fictional *shtetl*, the tales about which inevitably focus on the "wisdom" of its lame-brained leaders. Those leaders, of course, are male—we rarely hear about the *women* of Chelm—so Tango's overall subversion in the first place is that her comic-book-like series is all about the women and the issues and concerns of their lives.

[10] The reference to "sainthood" is marvelously tongue-in-cheek. Fraydl, the daughter who converted and is therefore "dead," will still be regarded as Jewish by Nazi racial

ideology and therefore capable of being sent to the gas chamber to physically and not just metaphorically die. But as a Catholic, she can achieve sainthood, which as a Jew she cannot: Jews do not have saints as Catholics do, only *tzadiks*—but are not *tzadikeem* virtually the same as saints?—all of which alludes to the question engaged by the Catholic Church in the 1980s as to whether Edith Stein, a converted Jew who died at Auschwitz, should be canonized.

[11] The Hebrew form is ambiguously a noun or an adjective, but unambiguously given in the feminine form, thus referring to female modesty, not to male or to male and female modesty.

[12] Modigliani (1884-1920) was an early twentieth century Italian Jewish artist who was one of the leading figures of the so-called *Ecole de Paris* [Paris School].

[13] To be absolutely precise, at the time the first chair was being made, Kahn and his wife did not yet know whether their first child would be male or female. They ended up with two girls and one boy. But the point is that all three chairs were made identically, without gender-prejudiced variations.

[14] *Mamzer* is the singular; *mamzereem* would be the plural.

[15] This is the same process, but the nuantial opposite, of a euphemism, a benign term used in lieu of a term found offensive: our sensitive ears prefer "John" to "toilet" or even "bathroom," and in the "John" we prefer to refer to going "#1" or "#2" to—well, the reader knows. . . .

[16] Strictly speaking, a "booth"—which is what *sukkah* means; thus Sukkot is the "[Feast of] Booths."

[17] The Hebrew verbal root *H-G-D* means "tell," so the liturgy and narrative text that guides the Seder is a book of "telling."

[18] For example, the notion of combining the matzah [unleavened bread] with the *maror* [bitter herbs] later begets the inclusion into that sandwich of the *haroset* [sweet herbs] in the early rabbinic period. The opening of the door for Elijah was introduced in the medieval period. In the 1970s, a fourth matzah was added to the traditional three to assure that Jews in free countries would not forget their co-religionists experiencing oppression in the Soviet Union.

[19] One might say that, whereas Elijah is traditionally viewed as the forerunner of the messiah, Miriam is the symbol of sustaining the entire people of Israel in life until the messianic moment arrives.

[20] Thus one recites, "You abound in blessings, oh Lord, creator of the universe, who sustains us with living water. May we, like the Children of Israel leaving Egypt, be protected and nurtured and kept alive in the wilderness, and may you give us the wisdom to understand that the journey itself holds the promise of redemption."

[21] Based on Leviticus 23:15-16.

[22] The counting down of the twenty-four days leading to Christmas seems to have begun with the German Lutherans in the nineteenth century. The earliest known handmade Advent calendar dates from 1851; the earliest printed one was produced either in Hamburg in 1902 or 1903 or by a Swabian named Gerhard Lang, in 1908. But that controversy is beyond our discussion. The first *omer* counters appear to date from the twentieth century.

[23] By this I mean that Christians and Muslims would certainly embrace the importance of the other nine, but where the Sabbath is concerned, Christians shifted away from the seventh day to Sunday, and Muslims came to treat Friday as the most important day of the week. So, with the exception of the occasional anomaly, like the Seventh Day Adventists, Judaism is the only Abrahamic tradition that observes that commandment as articulated in Exodus 20 and Deuteronomy 5.

[24] Any American Jewish community large enough to produce a Jewish weekly will deliver that paper on Thursday and indicate, on its front page, what precisely is the candle-lighting time that Friday.

[25] *Havdalah* means separation—so this is the most emphatic of Jewish celebrations that distinguishes one given time from another.

[26] And for that matter, the first "star" is as often as not a planet, usually, but not always, Venus.

[27] Because the candles are not all on the same level.

[28] This was expressed in a conversation with the author during the summer of 1991.

[29] From the artist's statement for the 2000-2001 exhibition *Jewish Artists: On the Edge*, which showed at The Marion Center and the College of Santa Fe, Santa Fe, and Yeshiva University Museum, New York, curated by Ori Z. Soltes and by J. Barry Zeiger, and quoted in the catalogue of the same name (Santa Fe: Sherman Asher, 2005), 77.

[30] In fact, there have been several interesting turns with regard to the *mikvah* in the last decade or so, particularly in the Reform movement. First of all, there has simply been a trend back to using the *mikvah*, which had been largely abandoned because of its perceived sexist connotations. Second, that return has been facilitated by the wider range of ways in which *mikvaot* are being used to mark both life-cycle and other kinds of events, both joyful and grief-related—from immersions before a Bar or Bat Mitzvah to marking a divorce or the death of a loved one to expressing gratitude for recovery from a serious illness. Thirdly, not only are both genders marking occasions with *mikvah* immersions, in some cases *mikvaot* are being used by groups made up of both genders to mark some event. See, Sue Fishkoff, "Reimagining the Mikveh," *Reform Judaism* (Online, Fall 2008).

[31] I am using their chosen transliteration spellings for *huppah* and *sukkah* here.

[32] With apologies for my pedantry, the Sephardic term is *tevah*, but I am using bimah as the more familiar term for the likely readership of this article.

[33] Melissa Shiff, *Reframing Ritual: Postmodern Jewish Wedding* (Prague: Jewish Museum of Prague—Spanish Synagogue, 2006), 1.

[34] There are no precise rabbinic requirements regarding the size, configuration, or disposition of the *huppah*.

[35] Sidney Goldin's 1923 *Ost/West* and Michal Waszynski's 1937 *The Dybbuk*.

[36] The lulav consists of three elements: palm fronds flanked by myrtle and willow branches.

[37] Shiff, *Reframing Ritual*, 3.

[38] This is when one invites the spirits, as it were, of the patriarchs and matriarchs into the *sukkah*.

[39] As discussed in chapter 7 of Rabbi Arthur Waskow and Rabbi Phyllis Berman, *A Time for Every Purpose Under Heaven: The Jewish Life–Spiral as a Spiritual Path* (New York: Farrar Straus and Giroux, 2002).

[40] Specifically, Deuteronomy 22:12, 20-21

[41] Shiff, *Reframing Ritual*, 7.

[42] The word is an Aramaic sibling—and the *Kaddish* is recited in Aramaic—of the Hebrew words *Kiddush* [referring to the blessing over the wine] and *Kedushah* [referring to a series of prayers before the Holy Ark that focus on God and the relationship between God and ourselves mediated by the Torah].

[43] For instance, she did a *Ten Plagues* series in which each of the colors tries to suggest the particular plague (red for blood, green for frogs, etc.) and the Hebrew word for that plague repeats and repeats across the picture plane.

[44] In which the sense of the words is lost within the abstract mental and aural patterns that carry the mystic toward union with the hiddenness of God.

[45] According to *merkavah* [Throne-chariot] mysticism, there are ten *hekhalot* [chambers, houses] through which one must ascend/descend in order to achieve intimate contact with God's most hidden recesses. *Merkavah* mysticism flourished between the first and tenth centuries; its concept of the *hekhalot* may be seen to lead into the idea of ten *sephirot* so essential to Kabbalah.

[46] The blessing is articulated in Numbers 6:23-27 and reads in part, "May the Lord bless you and keep you; may the Lord make His face to shine up you and be gracious unto you; may the Lord lift up His face upon you and grant you peace."

[47] The Israeli Knesset [Parliament], led by Prime Minister David Ben-Gurion and President Yitzhak Ben-Tzvi, officially created *Yom HaShoah*—or properly speaking, *Yom haZikaron laShoah velaG'vurah* [Day of Holocaust and Heroism Remembrance]—as a day both to mourn for and memorialize the fallen and to remember with pride the resistance against the Nazis. It was intended to be a national, secular commemoration, as opposed per se, to the religious celebration that the Orthodox Israeli rabbinate had established two years earlier. The rabbinate had designated the already-extant winter fast of the tenth of Tevet as the day; the Israeli Knesset decreed the 27th of Nisan as the day. The rabbinate observed that the month of Nisan (during which Passover occurs) is traditionally a month of joy, during which fasting and other traditional acts of mourning are forbidden by rabbinic law. Many ultra-Orthodox Israelis ignore *Yom HaShoah* completely, including their prayers for those killed during the Holocaust in traditional days of mourning, such as the midsummer Ninth of Av [*Tisha b'Av*], during which the destruction of the Temple has been mourned for centuries, or such as the Tenth of Tevet. Parts of the American Conservative Jewish movement formally defined a program for *Yom HaShoah* in 1981 and further articulated it in 1984—but not all Conservative Jews abide by the fast that others undertake, agreeing with the Orthodox view that no fasts should be held during the month of Nisan. Others, like their Orthodox co-religionists in Israel, observe the traditional *Tisha b'Av* and Tenth of Tevet fasts as inclusive of Holocaust memorial mourning.

[48] At that time, of course! (Zoe was then ten and Saskia was three.) They are by now both grown up: the future has become the present.

[49] This is, by the way, not particularly different from how the United States operates as a secular democracy that nonetheless operates in certain respects according to the Christian calendar—Sunday as the rest day where, in some states, one cannot, for example, purchase alcoholic beverages, to say nothing of the ubiquity of the Christmas celebration. Much of this has changed in the past two generations, but some of it remains in place in many locations.

[50] The periods of immigration [*aliyah*; "going up"] to *Eretz Yisrael* are schematized as the First *Aliyah*, 1882-1903; the Second; 1904-1914; the Third (after World War I), 1919-1923; the Fourth, 1924-1929; and the Fifth, 1929-1939. These last two coincided with the virtual closing of the doors of immigration to the United States and the rise of Nazism in Germany, respectively. They yielded largely middle-class families and, in the case of the Fifth *Aliyah*, a good number of artists, notably those associated with the Bauhaus School in Germany.

[51] See above, section three.

# A Need for New Rituals?  American Judaism and the Holocaust

## Oliver Leaman

"Der Ritus des rabbinischen Judentums wirkt nicht und verwandelt nichts."
[The ritual of rabbinic Judaism is ineffective and changes nothing.]
—Gershom Scholem[1]

Ever since the Holocaust, there has been a huge debate about its significance in Jewish life and ritual.  Is it an unprecedented event that requires some dramatic change to how things are done, or at least some specific ceremony to commemorate it, or is it merely one disaster among many, and so the existing rituals are sufficient to deal with it?  This question also brings into discussion what makes a ritual effective, something that Gershom Scholem suggests is a problem for Rabbinic Judaism.  The account presented here is the result of several years of research into how different Jewish communities responded to the Holocaust, with some reflections on what the rituals they employed meant for them.  I concentrate on Judaism in North America since the Holocaust is so omnipresent in Europe, being the site of the event itself, meaning that perhaps it plays a different role in the lives of European Jews.  In many ways the role of ritual in religion and its relationship with grief is a constant theme. I will argue that it is by no means obvious what ought to be said about this sort of relationship or how religion ought to embody it in ritual.  On the other hand, a reflection on the experience of different Jewish communities will bring out some of the relevant features of the topic and give us some indication of what we can realistically expect religions to achieve here.

## RITUAL AND CHANGE

Ritual in religion sometimes is very sensitive to changing circumstances and events, and sometimes it is not.  This is a particularly lively issue in Judaism, which has versions of ritual that self-consciously seek to change in line with changing events and versions that do not.  Those forms of Judaism that can be roughly classified as "Orthodox" tend to believe that the ritual as it has developed over long periods in the past is sufficient for our purposes today, and thus the ritual need not be changed or indeed ought not to be altered for any reason.  On the other side are those forms of worship loosely called

"Reform," whose name is accurate in suggesting the need for reform of the existing ritual to make it more appropriate to modern circumstances. This is not the place to revisit the hoary arguments between these two groups, but the arguments between these groups are relevant to the issue of how the Holocaust can and should be embodied in modern forms of ritual.

There is a marked contrast between what might be called Orthodox and Reform approaches to the Holocaust. That contrast looks very straightforward. The Orthodox ignore the Holocaust for ritual purposes in the sense that they change nothing to acknowledge its existence. For them the Holocaust is just another disaster in a long line of earlier disasters, and perhaps there will be future disasters to come also. Here we need to distinguish between what might be called modern Orthodox Jews, who do accept some additional Holocaust rituals, but not the changing of any existing ritual to take account of it, and those Orthodox Jews who regard even this accommodation to modernity to be unacceptable. The Reform are in favor of ritually marking the Holocaust in some way, and so many of their synagogues have some pictorial display commemorating it, and the various prayer books often include some direct reference to it. This marking can be accomplished by using familiar prayers like the memorial prayer and referring directly to the Holocaust, in particular on Yom Kippur. There is also the inclusion of direct new prayers to deal with the Holocaust, including in some *siddurim* [prayer books] even Yiddish prayers representing songs of the Jewish partisans, German poems about the Shoah, and so on. These are often presented as alternatives to the normal service, and it is not clear how often they are actually used or whether their role is simply to give the congregation something to read and think about when the normal service is going on. I have personally never heard this additional material being employed, and when I asked I never got much of an answer as to how frequently it is used. But these compositions are there in the siddur and are available, suggesting that they are thought to be significant.

## RITUAL AND MELANCHOLY

It would be wrong to think that the absence of the Shoah from the Orthodox service means that it is ignored, since this is very far from the truth. It would also be wrong to assert that the ubiquity of the Shoah in the Reform service means that it is important for religious reasons for Reform Jews. In interviews carried out with a variety of different Orthodox communities, it is clear that the Shoah is ever-present in people's minds. Here we might enter psychological territory and refer to Sigmund Freud's essay "Mourning and Melancholia" to suggest that the absence of direct reference to the Shoah in Orthodox ritual has prevented the Orthodox from appropriately dealing with the event. Since they do not have a specific mourning ritual for it, they persist in melancholy with respect to it. The Reform, by contrast, have adequately represented it in their liturgy, and so for them it is not such a significant continuing issue. Yet it is a continuing issue for the Reform, and the Holocaust plays a big role in the continuing desire to preserve Jewish ways of life amidst the assimilationist possibilities of modern society, the fact that we should not give Adolph Hitler any posthumous victories, what Emil Fackenheim called the 614th commandment. This is not really a religious issue but a defiant gesture in the face of an awkward history, it might be argued, and yet in the Reform as in the Orthodox the desire to continue a Jewish form of existence despite the Nazis is significant as a motivation for religious allegiance. That suggests that the presence of ritual in Reform Judaism has not done anything much different from its absence in Orthodoxy, in that mourning has not prevented melancholy and the sort of decision-making that stems from it.

The Orthodox often suggest that it is hardly worth investigating Reform ritual because there is so little of it and so few Reform Jews go to synagogue. On the other hand, Reform Jews may retort that it is hardly worth investigating Orthodox ritual because there is so much of it and because Orthodox Jews could not possibly be thinking about why they are doing what they do, since there is so much to do and say. It is certainly true that it is far from clear how ritual works in any religion, and in particular in Judaism, especially given the very diverse groups who employ it. We need to acknowledge that "Holy days, rituals, liturgies—all are like musical notation which, in themselves, cannot convey the nuances and textures of live performance."[2] This is something we need to bear very much in mind, since having a ritual is fairly meaningless unless it is embedded in some wider system of practice, while not having a ritual may nonetheless mean that the event that is absent from ritual is very far from absent in reality.

## RITUAL AND CONTEXT

So the ritual needs to be linked to its actual performance before we can really understand it, and that certainly makes sense. What is that context? For both the Orthodox and the Reform, it is one where the Shoah is actually a frequent topic of reference. Interestingly, although theologically the Orthodox often have the neatest resolution of the Shoah—it is generally *umipnei hata'einu* [on account of our sins]—they have the most unresolved difficulties with overcoming it as a community. It is constantly referred to as a rationale for doing things, having lots of children, valuing places in Eastern Europe, maintaining steadfastly a certain religious behavior, and not deviating from a routine; some of this procedure fits in with what Freud and his followers would call abnormal behavior. The Orthodox react to a tragedy in a way that does not resolve the tragedy for them, leading them to redouble their stylized reactions. For the Reform, the Shoah represents a phenomenon difficult to define, and yet the feeling generally was that it is adequately dealt with in the ritual. (This is not a question one can really ask the Orthodoxy because the adequacy of the ritual is taken to be a given.) Reform Jews want so many different things from ritual that asking a number of them about the role of the Shoah in it and what it should be resulted in a vast variety of opinions. Here again we should remember Josef Yerushalmi's comment and take account of the general context within which the ritual takes place, since it is this context that gives the ritual its meaning and relevance. Context will be shown to have a considerable significance in what follows.

Marshall Sklare identifies five criteria for ritual retention:
1. the ability to remain distinct without being separate, different but not too different,
2. it does not demand social isolation or the adoption of a unique life-style,
3. it accords with the religious culture of the wider community,
4. it is centered around children,
5. it is annual or infrequent.[3]

Sklare's criteria explain why in the United States, for example, more Jews participate in Passover and Chanukah ceremonies than are affiliated with synagogues or temples. Developing new Holocaust rituals does not really fit into these criteria, and this fact perhaps accounts for the rather shaky appearance of Holocaust rituals, where they do appear. The Holocaust is much more developed as a theme in ritual in the Reform. It is also much more a part of the iconography of the building itself in which religious activities take place. In Reform congregations the Shoah is often linked closely to other genocides, a link that is less the case in Orthodox congregations.

Such is the situation at the official level of what is in the *siddurim*, the interior design of houses of worship, and the sorts of ceremonies that take place in the different Jewish communities. In my research I was interested also in what Yerushalmi calls the "context," since like him I think this concept is as significant as or even more significant than what is officially part of the service or a building. Interestingly, with context, the situation is reversed. Whereas officially the Reform movement pays more attention to the Holocaust, unofficially Orthodox Jews reflect more on it and its implications for them and the Jewish world as a whole. Whereas Reform Jews spend a certain amount of time as part of the service and linked activities discussing the Holocaust, Orthodox Jews in fact discuss it much more, albeit in less formal settings, and they seem to regard it as closer to them as a phenomenon. Finally, although Reform Jews discuss the Shoah more as part of their ritual, they have less fixed ideas about it than the Orthodox have. The reasons for this difference are worth discussing, and they perhaps have something to tell us about how rituals in religion actually operate.

## IDENTIFYING CONTEXT

Let us take the issue of informal discussions about the Holocaust, including the issues of why it happened and what it means to us today. A large number of Orthodox Jews refer to the Holocaust as a major motivation for their commitment to Judaism generally and to Orthodox Judaism specifically. The suspicion of assimilation, the virtues of separation, the need to reestablish Eastern European styles of Judaism were all suggested as implications of the Shoah, albeit usually in informal discussion, not as part of any ritual. It is clear that for many young Orthodox Jews, who probably have no contact with any Holocaust survivors, the significance of this distant event has not diminished with time. Some of my informants were surprised when I suggested that the Holocaust might be regarded as something that happened a long time ago and so not be that important, since so much that they regard as important happened much longer ago, of course. Yet most of my informants were satisfied with the treatment of the Holocaust in the traditional ritual, feeling that there was no need to innovate or to enter it in new ways into the prayer book, since there are already many mournful occasions on which it can be commemorated. An additional Holocaust Day was not regarded as that helpful, since it suggests the need to add to the ritual repertoire when there is no lack of opportunities to commemorate it alongside the regular ritual.

For Reform Jews the Shoah is much harder to pin down, and there was general support for its inclusion in the service through new rituals and prayers. The existence of a Holocaust Day was regarded as important and indeed vital to show appropriate respect for the catastrophe. Given the ethical character of Reform Judaism, the Holocaust was often linked with other genocides and made part of the political program of the individual, and individuals adopted a generally redemptive attitude toward it. This attitude was not something mysterious or challenging but provided an opportunity for action and linking up with non-Jews in order to promote social justice. In informal discussion, Reform Jews offered a vast variety of reasons for the Holocaust, and they very much supported its inclusion in the ritual through specific new prayers and rites.

It is not difficult to see why the discussions went in these distinct directions, since Orthodox Jews tend to be suspicious of assimilation and so would not emphasize working with non-Jews to commemorate the Shoah, while Reform Jews are happier to work with others and would see fighting genocide as a common ethical aim that can easily be shared with other communities.

However, the discussions that I participated in actually went in rather unexpected directions. The Orthodox, who theologically should have been more limited in their responses to the Shoah, were in fact all over the place, united only in believing it to be a hugely significant event for them. The Reform were less interested, some even referring to how long ago it took place; moreover, the institutionalization of it in the ritual was sometimes referred to as putting the Shoah in its place, as it were, where it could be taken out and examined but where it would not dominate. It might even be said that Reform Jews take a rather optimistic attitude to things, and so the Shoah does not fit in that well if they regard it as a disaster where the basic distinctions between Jew and non-Jew became the rationale for murder and dispossession. Hence, Reform Jews generally do not understand the Shoah in this way; rather, it is a less dramatic and more manageable period of moral decay that has in other ways been repeated subsequently, and thus it needs to be resisted today as in the past in a general sense.

One thing that will be noted here is that these views are linked with some of the leading theological views today but are far from fully developed or well argued like those views. This is what one would expect; at the level of popular theology, views will never be fully articulated and may have many gaps in reasoning, but they are important despite these gaps for their representation of a wide range of thinking on the issue by the ordinary affiliated Jews in the United States. There are at least two issues here that need to be addressed. The more general one is how we know that a new ritual is required. What are the criteria for the existing rituals no longer doing the job, as it were, of what we want to do in religion, which Scholem refers to in the epigraph to this essay? The less general but still rather abstract issue is how a religion should commemorate a traumatic event such as the Shoah.

## RITUAL AND MEANING

One of the things worth noting about the Jewish liturgy is that it is often not closely connected with what it is being used for. For example, the prayer for the dead, the *Kaddish*, does not actually say anything about death directly, and when one reads it, it is difficult to see why it is the prayer for the dead.

Many mourners find the *Kaddish* highly satisfying as part of the ritual, since it is firmly part of the tradition of marking a death, and the requirement for a *minyan* [quorum] to be present, however that is defined, also brings in an aspect of solidarity. The prayer itself, though, does not address the topic of death; it is the context here that does all the work. Some contemporary Jews find the existing repertoire of prayers unsatisfactory, and the Reform movement regularly changes its prayer book, very usefully for those interested in how attitudes change in different periods, since those changes are very much present in the different prayer books that come and go. An intriguing modern phenomenon is the reinvention of older rituals and the rediscovery of former rituals to fill in a perceived gap in what exists today. So, for example, there has been a revival of *tekhines* [supplications], a genre of devotional prayers recited and written principally by women who did not know much Hebrew. Many of these are designed for outside of the synagogue, which is where many women feel perhaps they have more of a role. People often say that these prayers are private and direct, reflect personal experience, and address God directly. Yet it has to be said that much of the "official" liturgy shares this quality, although much of it certainly does not. One thinks in particular of the Psalms that are traditionally recited at a time when someone close has died. Many of the Psalms have a very personal flavor to them, and it is easy to think of the author seeing himself in a close relationship with God, which is discussed in the psalm, or trying to re-establish such a relationship that he feels has been lost. But here, as with all ritual, what is important is not the nature of the ritual itself—in this case the particular prayers—but the context within which it takes place, and if it is felt that the existing rituals are too impersonal and public, then there is a need for new rituals that are regarded as more satisfactory. The question we should perhaps raise is not what is lacking in the current rituals, and what fills the gap with the new ones, but what is perceived to be missing and what is perceived to be an answer to what is missing.

When we come to consider the Holocaust, this issue of perception is crucial. The discussions within Jewish theology about the nature of the event are significant here, since it relates to how it should be embodied directly, if at all, in ritual. If the Shoah is seen as a unique and extraordinary event, then there is perhaps more reason to think that it should be part of some specific ritual. If it is seen as just one disaster in a long line of earlier disasters, then nothing new is required, although the fact that it is relatively recent might call for some direct reference to it alongside existing rituals, the position largely of what might be called the Modern Orthodox. For those who regard the Shoah as exceptional, not to have a specific ritual suggests that this very unusual status is being denied. A gap in what is required is then perceived and needs to be filled. These sorts of debates are very prevalent when the issue is how to cope with trauma, whether one should note in a dramatic way the traumatic event and then get over it, or whether one should put it within the context of many such previous events and deal with it in that way.

This issue is much debated today in Israel, where domestic terrorism has during some periods been so damaging to life and limb. When a bomb blows up a bus, should the site be marked in some way, should the road be closed for a long period, and then periodically should there be a service of some kind at the site of the bombing? Or should the bodies be removed, as completely as possible, the parts of the bus carted away, and everything get back to normal as quickly as possible, which is the strategy that is largely carried out right now? The point of the former approach is to mark in some way the terrible events that have taken place, thereby helping us come to terms with them. The point of the latter approach is to show that we can cope with the disaster and it will not prevent us from getting on with our ordinary lives, which is certainly important in any conflict situation in which the enemy tries to sap the confidence of the civilian population.

This has nothing specifically to do with religion, or ethnicity, and certainly nothing specifically about Jews. In many different civilizations some people are not happy with the ordinary grieving rituals available to them, and they invent or follow others. For example, when someone is killed on the roads in Europe and North America, most people have the person buried or cremated and that is it. Others, however, place flowers or religious symbols, perhaps together with photographs and letters to the deceased, by the roadside where the death occurred. Some people place similar things on trees in woods that were visited by the dead person, perhaps on the birthday, maybe with birthday cards and tributes, and so on. Of course, there are also a variety of rituals that have grown up at the graveside, sometimes resulting in problems for those administering the sites, where perhaps the parents of a dead child wish to leave a teddy bear on the grave and only flowers are allowed, or where they want to leave artificial flowers and only real flowers are acceptable. We tend to think that the growth of new rituals is something new, as it obviously is since otherwise they would not be new; we also tend to think such new rituals reflect the decline in traditional authority in society and perhaps a decline in the authority of the existing religious structures. This is particularly the case when we look at new rituals for women, for gay people, and for others who have been traditionally excluded from the religious community.

But this is far from the truth: even far back in religious history there are accounts of people doing unapproved different things in particular in connection with the dead, and on the basis of these practices religious legislation was developed to rule on what is legitimate behavior and what is not. So in Islam, for example, there are many *hadith* [Traditions of the Prophet and his Companions] that report on what may be done at the graveside, by whom it may be done, when it may be done, and so on, and these stipulations are often reflections on a variety of different practices that the Prophet observed or that those who followed him thought he might have observed. One of the chief motives of the radical theologies of Ibn Taymiyya and Ibn al-Wahhab that have formed the basis of Saudi society today was the behavior of people at gravesides, or indeed the very existence of gravesides at which people come continually to pray. Ibn Taymiyya was in fact imprisoned and tortured in Cairo for disapproving of the popular practice of praying at the graveside. Throughout Islamic history a vast number of practices grew up in connection with how to commemorate the dead, how to mark a traumatic event, and what religion has to teach us here. So although many of the new rituals that we observe today are new to us, they are probably merely versions of alternative ceremonies that were performed in the past, with varying degrees of official sanction, since the normal ways of doing things were felt to be unsatisfactory for one reason or another.

## THE SUCCESS OF RITUAL

When I started conducting research on the varieties of ways of reacting to the Holocaust in Jewish ritual, I wondered whether the Reform movement had dealt with it better by introducing a variety of new ceremonies to acknowledge the event. This is a popular psychological move, to suggest that after a traumatic event a period of grieving takes place, and if it is "successful" then the mourners move on and are much more capable of coping with the aftermath of the event than those without some way of properly marking the event. The Orthodox, who talk about the Holocaust at length and in ways that suggest that it is an event that is always with them, are like people who have not managed to transcend the traumatic event, and as a result they are constantly revisiting it. This resembles a situation of having an organic illness that one group takes the appropriate medicine for and so recovers, while another group does not take the medicine and so hangs onto the disease; although it may get a bit better, some of its effects linger on and on. This analogy is a neat solution to the different approaches that diverse groups take to the Holocaust, but we should be careful about accepting it. It is far less acceptable now to insist on just one healthy way to grieve. It used to be thought that one criterion of success here is managing to carry on and carry out one's normal functions, but this is not much of a criterion, since both the Reform and the

Orthodox seem to have no difficulty in continuing to do things despite the Holocaust. With his enthusiasm for the secular, Freud would have no time for the constant reminding of the Orthodox community of past disasters in a way intended to make them sad again and again, although it has to be said that the sadness is supposed to be mitigated by the sense that God has a plan or by some other feeling of meaning behind the events of the past and indeed the present. In the Talmud *Pesachim* 116b, we are told *matchil bigenut umesayem beshevach,* a phrase often repeated by the Orthodox when discussing the Shoah, since it refers to something "beginning in shame, ending in glory." The fact that the Orthodox feel that they can put the Shoah into some sort of wider theoretical context, at the very least as an act that plays a role in a divinely organized world, might be contrasted with the Reform attitude that a wide variety of explanations for it exist and none, if any, of these make any direct reference to God. It might then be suggested that the Orthodox grieve more successfully than the Reform because their constant repetition of tragic events is carried out within a context where such events have a meaning. So perhaps it is the latter who have difficulties coping with the events, despite their ersatz rituals and generally optimistic view of Jewish history.

In vindication of this line of argument, interviewing Reform Jews about the Holocaust tends to result in different responses than those provided by the Orthodox. The general rationale of *tikkun olam* [repairing the world] does not make much headway when the Shoah is concerned, since there seems to have been a distinct lack of such a spirit in the past and it is not at all clear how its existence today might prevent another similar disaster or what role it might have played then in preventing it. This does bring out a phenomenon in grief-coping strategies that has often been noted by observers, and that is that some people are very effective in channeling their grief into something else. For example, when a child dies, the father will often become very active in some campaign against the disease that killed the child. In this way people often feel that their grief has found a reasonable escape valve. If, though, the reaction to the death is just that it is inexplicable, then grief may be more protracted and difficult to resolve. Here we are coming close to an unlikely suggestion, which is that the Reform Jews, who see the world as a rational space in which moral action should be carried out to improve the lot of humanity, find it difficult to account for a period of extreme savagery, while the Orthodox, who see the world far more as a site of mystery and divine activity, find it easier. The explanation is not just that the Orthodox line is simpler, the Reform subtler and thus more complex. It might be said that the Reform approach is unsatisfactory in itself since it fails to do justice to the phenomenon of human wickedness, something that the *tikkun olam* principle tends to avoid. The approach may be to say that, if the world were a better place, then events like the Shoah would not take place, but such a position is rather weak as a call to action because very few observers could possibly blame the actions of the Jews at the time for their eventual fate.

So do the rituals of the Reform surrounding the Shoah represent a Lady-Macbeth-washing-her-hands sort of ritual, where action is taken and repeated because it is felt that it never succeeds in reconciling the individual to what has occurred in the past? Lady Macbeth kept on washing her hands because she kept on seeing blood on them, appropriately since she had murdered Duncan. The more she washes, the more it will need to be done, since it is always going to be unsuccessful. So the greater number of rituals of the Reform Jews may reflect the fact that they all fail to reconcile the community to the Shoah. Over time rituals seem to have increased, and the institutions supporting them, like Holocaust monuments and museums, Holocaust days and so on, have increased in tandem. Yet it is not at all obvious that this explosion of attention has really contributed a great deal to reconciling the Jewish community to the Holocaust, at least in terms of the Reform section of that community. It might of course be said that this is a rather ambitious aim, and not one that we normally think of when we analyze rituals and the institutions that exist around them. One of the aims of such institutions at least is to relate a message about the Holocaust to society as a whole, which is surely being done relatively effectively given the attention that is paid to the Holocaust in much of Western society.

Yet we might also wonder whether the role of a ritual is really to reconcile its practitioners to an event in the past, especially when that past is so recent, as it is in the case of the Holocaust. Perhaps it is entirely appropriate that we should feel that the sufferings that existed in the Holocaust remain issues that we still have to deal with, and the rituals we establish with respect to this fact do not have as their main purpose making us feel all right about what happened. Of course, some Jews manage to take very personally events that occurred a long time ago, but this is much more plausible for Orthodox than for Reform Jews. It is said that Napoleon was impressed by the Tisha B'Av ceremony during which Jews sit on the ground and read the book of Lamentations by the light of a candle. What impressed him was not so much the ritual but the fact that it commemorated something that happened a long time ago. If the mark of a successful ritual is helping people get over a past tragic event, then does the Tisha B'Av ritual do this? It does in the sense of putting the destruction of the Temple in Jerusalem within some sort of context, but not in the sense of making those observing the ritual feel that they have gotten over the sadness of the event. This brings out the problematic nature of regarding rituals commemorating tragedies as though they are part of coping mechanisms. They are such coping mechanisms in the sense that they put the tragedy in some sort of context, but they are not in the sense that we transcend the tragedy. That whole notion of getting over it is rather offensive, and it suggests that a disaster is rather like being sick, something to be dealt with and promptly put into the background. Neither the Reform nor the Orthodox Jews react to the ritual in this banal way, one hopes, although it might be claimed that the theology of the latter makes such a simplistic response more rather than less likely.

## ASSESSING RITUAL

We need to spend some time thinking about what the ritual is actually for, and this is often dealt with in a more sophisticated way in the Bible than in the psychological literature. For instance, the Jews are told both to blot out the name of Amalek, their great enemy on their journey through the desert to Israel, and also never to forget him (Deut 25:17). This might well be taken to be a reflection on the significance of a traumatic experience: it is something that cannot really be forgotten, but it can be put in its place by its significance being grasped and installed in some form of ritual, perhaps not directly connected to it. Freud tends to ignore the possibility of a middle position between mourning, where mourners detach themselves from the lost and beloved object through some grasp of reality, and melancholia, where mourners continue to cling to the lost love in what he calls a "wishful psychosis."[4] What religion tends to suggest is that there is a middle position where the missed object is remembered and reflected upon, while at the same time such remembrance and reflection does not prevent us from carrying out our normal tasks. This middle position is often ignored today in the United States in connection with the post-traumatic stress disorder (PTSD) that affects many of the troops in military conflict situations. There is a tendency for military personnel who are suffering nightmares, depression, or general anxiety to be diagnosed as having PTSD. This is not just a medical issue but very much a moral and conceptual one also. The important feature of PTSD is that memories are inescapable and prevent the individual from successfully incorporating his or her past into his or her future, and so those memories are traumatic. Yet there are clearly degrees of this phenomenon. At a lower level, such memories are not an obstacle to normal life, while at an advanced level they clearly are. One might even wonder whether someone who has gone through remarkable events involving death and violence should be able to just forget about it and not use it in his or her future life.

One of the social roles of religion that ritual embodies is a way of establishing what I have called a middle position, where grief is experienced but not in a disabling way, where it does not skew the future experiences of the individual but does shape them to a degree. This balance is always going to be unstable, in the sense that some religious observers may be so influenced by a past event that they use it as a justification for some act of violence, for example, while others may find it almost disappear from their consciousness because the ritual connected to it effectively dissolves it. From a religious, and indeed moral, point of view, neither of these alternatives is acceptable. What is ideal is that the event is noted and commemorated and that ordinary life is resumed, albeit not necessarily in just the same way as before. Perhaps Freud's antipathy to religion explains his inability to see any sort of role for its rituals in moderating melancholia and marking grief. Perhaps his influence has meant that PTSD is regarded as so prevalent today, in that any remaining psychological sadness due to involvement in a conflict zone is often classified as an illness, a grief that has not been transcended, as opposed to a perfectly natural indication of a life event that requires some time to work through.

One of the nice, neat conclusions that we cannot adopt is that one religious approach to an event like the Shoah is "better" than another approach, although we have seen how the psychological literature does tend to operate in this value-laden manner. The rituals developed by the Reform movement have not really succeeded in resolving the issue for the Reform, but then we do not really understand what it is for a ritual to resolve an issue satisfactorily. The constant repetition of the Shoah in the social context of Orthodox Judaism perhaps expresses more their strong interest in and links with anything Jewish than with this event in particular, but I suggested that the Shoah does pervade the living experience of many Orthodox communities, even if theologically they do not acknowledge it as a central problem within their belief system. I have challenged the view that this shows that they need a new ritual, and I have shown that how rituals work and what they are supposed to do if they do work are problematic. When researching this rather specific topic, I expected to end up with some results that would shed some light on these questions, but I am not sure that I have. More worryingly, in studying rituals, we need to do more than just describe them and explain how they are supposed to operate, as we have seen here. We need to put the ritual within an appropriate context, one that is often much wider than we might expect, including informal discussions between people looking after children, decisions about what cars to buy, how to name children, and so on. Particular people may see this same ritual entirely differently, as Patricia Curran shows when she examines the culture of nuns from different generations in convents.[5] If we are going to be able to judge the successes of ritual use, we shall have to use a theory of the context within which that ritual operates, and as we have seen, we are still a long way from that today.

## NOTES

[1] Gershom Scholem, *Zur Kabbala und ihrer Symbolik* (Zurich: Rhein-Verlag, 1960), 163. The translation from the German is my own.

[2] Yosef Yerushalmi, *Zakhor: Jewish History and Jewish Memory* (Seattle: University of Washington Press, 1982), 43.

[3] Marshall Sklare and Joseph Greenblum, *Jewish Identity on the Suburban Frontier: A Study of Group Survival in the Open Society* (Chicago: University of Chicago Press, 1979).

[4] Sigmund Freud, "Mourning and Melancholia," in *The Standard Edition of the Compete Psychological Works of Sigmund Freud* (vol. 14; trans. J. Strachey; London: Hogarth, 1957), 243.

[5] Patricia Curran, *Grace before Meals: Food Ritual and Body Discipline in Convent Culture* (Champaign: University of Illinois Press, 1989).

## FOR FURTHER READING

Glennys Howarth and Oliver Leaman, eds., *Death and Dying* (London: Routledge, 2001).

Aliza Lavie, *A Jewish Woman's Prayer Book* (New York: Spiegel & Grau, 2008).

Oliver Leaman, *Death and Loss* (London: Cassell, 1995).

Oliver Leaman, *Evil and Suffering in Jewish Philosophy* (Cambridge: Cambridge University Press, 1997).

Richard McNally, "Progress and Controversy in the Study of Post-traumatic Stress Disorder," *Annual Review of Psychology* 54 (2003): 229-52.

Michael Morgan, ed., *"The 614th Commandment": The Jewish Thought of Emil Fackenheim* (Detroit: Wayne State University Press, 1987).

Fanny Neuda, *Hours of Devotion* (trans. and int. Dinah Berland; New York: Random House, 2007).

Gerald Rosen and Scott Lilienfeld, "Post-traumatic Stress Disorder: an Empirical Evaluation of Core Assumptions," *Clinical Psychology Review* 28:5 (2008): 837-68.

Ben Shephard, *A War of Nerves: Soldiers and Psychiatrists in the Twentieth Century* (Cambridge: Harvard University Press, 2001).

Jonathan Tropper, *How to Talk to a Widower* (London: Orion, 2007).

# Karaism: An Alternate Form of Jewish Celebration

## Daniel J. Lasker

## INTRODUCTION

This volume and the conference on which it is based are themselves celebrations of the diversity of contemporary Jewish celebration: new rituals, new rites of passage, new inclusion of historically marginalized Jewish groups, and new ways of looking at the tradition. Yet, with all the emphasis on the contemporary, we sometimes lose sight of the diversity of Jewish life in the past, as if until the modern period, all Jews were God-fearing and *halakhah*-observing. This accepted wisdom is widely believed despite all the evidence to the contrary in rabbinic discussions of the status of the nonobservant or the not sufficiently observant. In the premodern period, loyalty to traditional Jewish law may have been the theoretical norm, and what we now call secularism may not have been an option, but then, as now, not everyone who thinks he or she should observe the law, or whose neighbors think he or she should observe it, actually does so. The Jewish calendar provides a number of opportunities during which repentance is one of the major themes, especially during the High Holy Days; if people did not sin, why such an emphasis on repentance?[1]

When looking at Jewish diversity in the present and in the past, we generally consider varieties of Rabbinic Judaism. Although Sephardim [Jews from Mediterranean lands] and Ashkenazim [Jews from Eastern Europe] had different practices concerning liturgy, dietary restrictions, or laws of purity, somehow they still were able to share the same *Shulhan Arukh* as the ultimate legal authority, with Sephardim bound by the words of the author, Rabbi Joseph Karo, and Ashkenazim by the comments of the glossator, Rabbi Moses Isserles. When members of modern Jewish denominations ask how much of the traditional prayer book should be maintained and which prayers should be modified in terms of modern sensitivies, they are still using the rabbinic prayer book as the standard from which they are deviating.

Some recent adjustments might have been made in the calendar, such as Reform Judaism's dispensing with the second day of holidays in the Diaspora, but the general outline of the calendar is still determined by the rules finalized over a thousand years ago in the rabbinic academies of Babylonia (present-day Iraq). Not all Jews believe the dietary laws are binding, but if they wish to observe them, they know the basic outlines of the prohibited species, the norms of ritual slaughter, and the prohibition of milk and meat. Most Jews today might not accept the *Shulhan Arukh* as authoritative, but if one wants to know what the traditional standard is, it is to that book that one turns. In other words, normally when we think about Jewish diversity, we are thinking of diversity within Rabbinic Judaism, the Judaism that is based on the idea of an Oral Torah given by God to Moses on Mt. Sinai and later encapsulated approximately 1,500 years ago in the Talmud.[2]

Rabbinic Judaism, however, has historically not been the only form of Judaism. However we reconstruct the religion of biblical Israel, it seems to have been significantly different than the Judaism of rabbinic literature, not to mention from modern Judaism. During the Second Temple period, any number of Judaisms competed for the hearts and minds of the Jewish populace; historical circumstances seem to have determined that Pharisaism, the precursor of Rabbinic Judaism, survived the destruction of the Temple and became dominant. Even with the canonization of the Talmud, the rabbinic pursuit of hegemony was never totally unchallenged; the greatest challenge came in the form of Karaite Judaism, an alternate variety of Judaism whose methods of Jewish celebration will be the topic of this essay.

Who are the Karaites? Simply put, they are Jews who do not accept the authority of the Talmud. Their rejection of the rabbinic Oral Torah has resulted in the development of a different Judaism with its own unique ritual practices, although in theological matters, they are remarkably close to Rabbanites, the followers of Rabbinic Judaism. Despite the accepted wisdom, and despite their name, which is most likely derived from the Hebrew *miqra* [scriptures], Karaites are not scriptural literalists; many of their own interpretations of the Bible and its legal requirements are as nonliteral as the Rabbanite ones.

Most histories of Judaism state that Karaism began in the late eighth century CE as a result of the personal pique of Anan ben David, a disgruntled office seeker who was passed over as a candidate to be exilarch, the head of the Jewish community in Babylonia. Today, we know that Anan's group, the Ananites, were not Karaites, but later Karaites did retroactively claim Anan as one of their own. The first Jews to call themselves Karaites lived only in the ninth century, but Karaism claims to be the original form of Judaism; it is Rabbinic Judaism that, they maintain, is an innovation from the Second Temple period. The discoveries of the Cairo Geniza (1897) and the Dead Sea Scrolls (1947) have led to the possibility of a connection between Medieval Karaism and Second Temple groups, but the evidence is not clear cut. Karaism developed fully only in the tenth and eleventh centuries during a

"Golden Age" in the Land of Israel. This was the period of greatest Karaite influence, but the idea that Karaites were ever a numerical threat to Rabbinic Judaism seems to be misplaced.

With the decline of the community in the Land of Israel in the wake of the Crusades, the next great Karaite center was in Byzantium (present-day Turkey); from there, Karaite communities were established in the Crimean Peninsula and in such Eastern European locations as Troki in Lithuania, Halicz in Galicia, and Lutsk in present-day Ukraine. When the Russian empire took over lands of Jewish habitation at the end of the eighteenth century, Karaites in these areas looked for ways to avoid discriminatory anti-Jewish legislation; eventually, they declared themselves a separate, non-Jewish ethnic group, a tactic that was vital for their survival during the Holocaust but that has alienated the few surviving Crimean and Eastern European Karaites from the Jewish people. At the same time, however, the ancient Egyptian Karaite community remained fully identified with the Jewish people, and today's Israeli Karaite community, numbering approximately 25,000 individuals, is mostly of Egyptian origin. Most of the few thousand American Karaites, centered in the Bay Area of California, are also originally from Egypt.[3]

## CALENDAR AND HOLIDAYS

This cursory historical survey must suffice to introduce the main topic of this article—namely, a review of some of the ways in which the Karaite celebration of Judaism differs from the standard Rabbanite patterns and an explanation of some of the reasons behind this divergence. We may begin with something simple: the calendar. The Bible gives no instructions as to how the calendar is to be calculated, and there seem to have been a number of competing calendrical systems in ancient Israel. Indeed, one of the major differences among the various rival forms of Second Temple Judaism was how to calculate the calendar. The calendar that survived—the luni-solar one used by Rabbinic Judaism—is now calculated in advance, but originally it was determined by actual observation of astrological and agricultural data. By the tenth century CE, when classical Karaism was in its formative stage, the calculated rabbinic calendar was fully developed and it no longer relied upon observation of natural phenomenon.

Karaites, for their part, argued that the ancient procedure of determining the calendar should be maintained. New months would begin only when the new moon was sighted, and a leap year would be proclaimed only if the ripening spring barley crop [the *aviv*] in the Land of Israel was not seen during the month before Passover. Eventually, when Karaites found themselves at a distance from the Land of Israel and an observed calendar became unwieldy,[4] they agreed that a calculated calendar could be used. They adopted, however, a slightly different calculation from the Rabbanite one; thus, the two calendars, although similar, are not synchronized, and the Karaite holidays usually fall a day or two after the Rabbanite ones.

Without going into the technical details of calendation, even a brief glance at the Karaite calendar will show some of its unique characteristics.[5] In 5769 (2008-2009), the first day of Rosh Ha-Shana [the New Year] in the Rabbanite calendar was on Tuesday, September 30 (a Tuesday Rosh Ha-Shana is not a very common occurrence; it was occasioned by the beginning of the previous Passover on a Saturday night). Most Jews, even in Israel, where biblical holidays are usually only one day, observed two days of Rosh Ha-Shana, Tuesday and Wednesday. Yom Kippur was on Thursday of the following week.

In the Karaite calendar, however, the first of Tishrei was on Wednesday, October 1, not on Tuesday; it is called *Yom Teru'ah* and not Rosh Ha-Shana, and it lasted only one day.[6] Furthermore, since the Karaite first of Tishrei was on Wednesday, the tenth of Tishrei, Yom Kippur, was on a Friday—that is, right before the Sabbath, which, as many Jews know, is not possible in the Rabbanite calendar. Why the differences?

First of all, the reason why the first day of Rosh Ha-Shana cannot come on a Wednesday in the Rabbanite calendar is specifically to prevent Yom Kippur from falling on a Friday, with its multiple complications. Leviticus 23:4 reads: "These are the appointed feasts of the Lord, the holy convocations, which [*otam*] you shall proclaim in their appointed season." The Rabbis noticed that the word *otam*, referring to the holidays, could as easily be vocalized *atem*, "you," understanding that the human element was paramount in determining when the holidays would occur. That included the possibility of making sure the holidays did not fall on undesired days of the week, which was accomplished by the use of certain "postponements."[7] Karaites, however, emphasize the part of the verse that states "in their appointed season"; it does not read "in their appointed seasons unless it is inconvenient." Thus, most holidays can fall on any day of the week in the Karaite calendar.

Second, the Torah never calls the first of Tishrei the New Year, Rosh Ha-Shana; after all, in the biblical calendar, the first month is the month of Passover in the spring. The Bible calls the first day of the seventh month *yom teru'ah*, which Rabbanites understand to mean "the day of blowing the shofar." The Karaites, maintaining the biblical name, say that nothing is mentioned about a shofar; *yom teru'ah* means a day of calling out loudly to God. Therefore, they do not blow the shofar as part of their holiday observance.

The third difference was the fact that the Karaite *Yom Teru'ah* is only one day long; again, the Bible is the source. The two days of the rabbinic Rosh Ha-Shana go back to the doubt as to when the holiday occurs, a doubt that existed in the Land of Israel as well as in the Diaspora (other one-day biblical holidays, such as Passover, became two days in the Diaspora but remained one day in Israel). Thus, a one-day Rosh Ha-Shana, or Yom Teru'ah according to the Karaite name.

As noted, generally Karaite holidays can fall on any day of the week. There is one major exception to this rule: Shavuot [Pentecost] can fall only on a Sunday. In a manner reminiscent of some Second Temple Jewish groups, Karaites interpret Leviticus 23:15, *mi-mahorat ha-shabbat* [on the morrow of the Sabbath], to mean that the *omer* offering of barley always begins on a Saturday night and Shavuot occurs fifty days later on Saturday night/Sunday (on different dates of the month), rather than the rabbinic fifty days after the beginning of Passover, always on the same date.[8]

The Karaite Sabbath celebrations are different from the Rabbanite ones as well. The Torah (Exod 35:3) forbids the use of fire on the Sabbath, but according to rabbinic law, lighting candles or preparing an oven before the Sabbath is permissible; indeed, late Friday afternoon candle lighting is obligatory, and the typical Rabbanite Jewish food for the Sabbath is the long-cooking *chulent* [or stew]. Anan ben David, however, taught that if a fire was found lit on the Sabbath, it should be extinguished rather than allowed to remain burning. For centuries, Karaites sat in dark, unheated homes and ate cold food on the Sabbath. As of the fifteenth century, a Karaite reform permitted lighting candles before the Sabbath, but it was not obligatory and no blessing is recited. Heating food and houses was still forbidden.[9] Karaite law also forbids sexual relations on the Sabbath, in contrast with the rabbinic endorsement of such activity.

Going back to the calendar and the other holidays, there are some additional divergences with Rabbanite practice. Karaites do not observe Hanukkah (at least not as a religious holiday), since it is postbiblical. The biblical holiday of Purim is celebrated in the first Adar of a leap year, not the second. Some of the fast days are on different dates; for instance, the fast known as Tish'a be-Av, the ninth of Av, is celebrated twice—on the seventh and on the tenth of that month. The four species of Sukkot (the palm, the myrtle, the willow, and the citron) are not used in the synagogue; at most they might decorate the sukkah. It has often been noted that a sure sign of schism is the adoption of a sectarian calendar; this has certainly been the case with the Karaites.

## SYNAGOGUE AND LITURGY

A Karaite synagogue is very different from a Rabbanite one—true, there is a *bimah* [raised platform] in front with an *aron qodesh* [holy ark], and there is a separate women's section, but there are no chairs, only rugs on the floors.[10] The worshippers remove their shoes before entering the synagogue, and at various points in the service they practice full prostration. Some of the prayers are accompanied by other motions, such as raising the arms in supplication. There are other differences as well: the threads of the Karaite prayer shawl, the *tallit*, are knotted and twisted differently than on the Rabbanite *tallit*; the Karaites do not use phylacteries (the *tefillin*) or parchments on the doorposts (the *mezuzot*) at all, giving a nonliteral interpretation of the injunctions in Deuteronomy. Karaites do put up a mezuzah-like item on their doorposts, but it is in the shape of the Ten Commandments and does not include biblical selections written on parchment.

Most remarkable of all in the Karaite synagogue is the order of prayers; their prayer book is not at all familiar to most Jews. It is not a reworking of the Rabbanite prayer book but a totally different text, based mainly on biblical passages (thus, it is missing the central Rabbanite prayer, the *shemonah esreh*, the "eighteen blessings"). Everything is said out loud, sometimes responsively with a leader, and the service can last for many hours (much like in a Sephardic synagogue). Each man who participates in the Torah reading must read his own section.

The Karaites have no concept of a prayer quorum (the Rabbanite *minyan* of ten). Any number of Karaites can pray together with no distinction between men, women, or minors.[11] There is also no concept of different obligations for a minor as compared to an adult; as soon as Karaite children can fast, the expectation is that they will do so on the fast days, like Yom Kippur. Karaite tradition, therefore, has no place for a Bar or Bat Mitzvah celebration marking the transition to legal adulthood. Nevertheless, modern Karaites do make note of this rite of passage.[12]

## FOOD

The Bible specifies which animals are permissible to be eaten and which are forbidden, as well as prohibiting the eating of blood and the cooking of a goat in its mother's milk. Rabbanites have understood this latter prohibition to include cooking, eating, or deriving benefit from any meat (including fowl but not fish) with any milk. Karaites did not accept that interpretation, and, thus, they have no separate dishes, silverware, sinks, or tablecloths for these two categories. They do not wait between eating milk and meat or vice versa.

The only concession the Karaites make to the separation of milk and meat is a prohibition of two items from the same species at the same meal. A beef burger with cow's cheese would be forbidden; with goat's cheese, it is allowed.

Certain Karaite dietary restrictions are actually stricter than Rabbanite ones. They forbid the eating of what is called the fat-tail, which rabbinic law allows. After the ritual slaughter (which is mandated in both Karaite and Rabbanite law even though it is not explicitly required in the Torah), the Karaites check the animal's body parts in a manner that is different than the rabbinic requirement. And the blessing recited over slaughtering an animal refers to the permission to slaughter, not to the obligation as in the rabbinic blessing. Thus, a Karaite cannot legitimately eat food that is kosher according to rabbinic standards.

## PERSONAL STATUS

There is one more important aspect of Karaite law that separates them from Rabbanites, and that is in the realm of marriage and personal relations. Karaite law tends to be much stricter in terms of incest; for instance, early Karaism forbade most relations between a husband's relatives and his wife's relatives, eventually making marriage in a relatively small group almost impossible. An eleventh century reform modified those prohibitions, allowing greater flexibility in marriage partners. Nevertheless, to this day, the Karaites prohibit relations that the Rabbanites allow. Thus, on the basis of the analogy with the biblically prohibited aunt-nephew relations, uncle-niece relations are also not allowed. In rabbinic tradition, not only is uncle-niece marriage allowed, but it is even considered praiseworthy.[13]

The Karaite marriage and divorce procedures are similar enough to the Rabbanite ones to look familiar, but they are sufficiently divergent as to make intermarriage between the groups a legal problem. In general, Sephardic, especially Egyptian, rabbis have been more accepting of Karaite-Rabbanite marriage, when the Karaite partner agrees to accept rabbinic law, than Ashkenazic rabbis. There may also be sociological considerations behind the divergent practices, since Karaites in Islamic countries tended to identify as part of the Jewish community whereas relations between Rabbanites and Karaites in Christian countries were usually not as close. In any event, the difficulty of Karaite-Rabbanite marriage leads to interesting developments in the State of Israel, where Jewish marriage and divorce are controlled by the Orthodox rabbinic rabbinate.[14]

## MODERN KARAITE ASSIMILATION

The discussion up to now has described what might be called traditional, classical Karaism.[15] Yet, just as many modern Rabbanite Jews no longer observe Jewish law fully, the same is true for Karaites. The spread out nature of the Bay Area community makes walking to the synagogue impossible, even for the acting rabbi.[16] Assimilation can be seen in the Israeli community as well. A number of years ago I attended the ritual circumcision of the son of the national secretary of the Israeli Karaites, held in a catering hall in Ashdod, one of their centers. The catering hall had a certificate from the local rabbinic rabbinate testifying to its kosher status. When queried about this, one of the Karaite rabbis said it was okay; for those who cared, there was a fish alternative. Only the Karaite rabbis eschewed the meat.

In addition to the inroads of modernity, Israeli Karaites have another reason to loosen the chains of their religious traditions. In Israel, many Rabbanite Jewish practices are not just religious rites but national celebrations as well. Thus, Hanukkah is a national holiday, celebrating an ancient Jewish military victory, not merely commemorating the putative miracle of the oil that lasted eight days. It is hard for an Israeli Karaite to ignore the national aspects of Hanukkah, even though this postbiblical holiday is not in the Karaite calendar.

Other factors also discourage Karaite observance. The Israeli calendar follows the Rabbanite yearly cycle; schools, factories, and many businesses are closed on the holidays according to the Rabbanite calculation; they are often open on the days on which the Karaites celebrate. No Rabbanite child has to choose between going to synagogue for the holiday or going to school; this is not the case for Karaites. The Israeli army provides kosher food for all soldiers but not special food to meet Karaite needs. Israeli chaplains are Rabbanite rabbis; Karaite soldiers have no religious guidance inside the army.

## CONCLUSION

This article has given a little taste of the alternate form of Judaism called Karaism and its distinctive celebration of Judaism. Despite inroads of secularization and acculturation, present-day Karaites have succeeded in maintaining their own separate identity and rituals, continuing a tradition of at least 1,200 years. Their unique forms of celebrating Judaism are part of the story of their survival over the centuries.

## NOTES

[1] See, for example, Ephraim Kanarfogel, "Rabbinic Attitudes toward Nonobservance in

the Medieval Period," in *Jewish Tradition and the Non-Traditional Jew* (ed. Jacob J. Schacter; Northvale: J. Aronson, 1992), 3-35.

[2] One of the major historical disagreements among the various denominations of Rabbinic Judaism is the extent to which either the Written or the Oral Torah is considered divine or divinely inspired, a question that then has an impact on possibilities of innovation and change. Nevertheless, these discussions assume that the Bible, the Talmud, and subsequent rabbinic literature are the molders of the Jewish tradition.

[3] Meira Polliack, ed., *Karaite Judaism: A Guide to its History and Literary Sources* (Leiden/Boston: Brill, 2003), contains articles from different points of view describing Karaite history and accomplishments. For further background, see Zvi Ankori, *Karaites in Byzantium* (New York: Columbia University Press, 1959); Fred Astren, *Karaite Judaism and Historical Understanding* (Columbia: University of South Carolina Press, 2004); Philip Birnbaum, ed., *Karaite Studies* (New York: Hermon Press, 1971); Daniel Frank, *Search Scripture Well: Karaite Exegetes and the Origins of the Jewish Bible Commentary in the Islamic East* (Leiden/Boston: Brill, 2004); Daniel J. Lasker, *From Judah Hadassi to Elijah Bashyatchi: Studies in Late Medieval Karaite Philosophy* (Leiden/Boston: Brill, 2008); Leon Nemoy, *Karaite Anthology* (New Haven: Yale University Press, 1952); Naphtali Wieder, *The Judean Scrolls and Karaism* (London: Horovitz, 1962), reprinted with additions (Jerusalem: Ben-Zvi Institute, 2005).

[4] Notice how in the Islamic world the end of Ramadan and the feast of Id al-Fitr can come on different days in different countries, and until the new moon is sighted, one does not know for sure when Ramadan ends and the new month begins.

[5] I will be using the calendar issued by the Religious Council of Universal Karaite Judaism, Ramlah, 5769 (2008-2009).

[6] In fall, 2008, the Web site http://www.karaite-korner.org/holiday_dates.shtml posted that *Yom Teru'ah* fell on Thursday, October 2, and Yom Kippur on Saturday, October 11; this Web site is run by Nehemiah Gordon, an Israeli who is a former American Rabbanite Jew, who has become a Karaite but does not always agree with the Israeli Karaite leadership. The Web site is a good source in English for Karaite beliefs and practices.

[7] Rosh Ha-Shana cannot fall on a Sunday, Wednesday, or Friday; Passover cannot fall on a Monday, Wednesday, or Friday. These postponements prevent Yom Kippur on a Friday or a Sunday (i.e., two consecutive Sabbath days) and Hoshana Rabba on a Saturday (since the holiday is marked by breaking of willow branches, forbidden on the Sabbath). For a brief description of the Rabbanite Jewish calendar, see Arnold A. Lasker and Daniel J. Lasker, "Behold, A Moon is Born! How the Jewish Calendar Works," *Conservative Judaism* 41:4 (Summer, 1989): 5-19.

[8] For references to the non-Pharisaic practice, see Mishnah Hagigah 2:4; Menahot 10:3.

[9] It is hard to see how Lithuanian Karaites survived the winter there without some sort of heating on the Sabbath.

[10] Some Karaite synagogues, including the one in Beer Sheva, have taken to putting up folding chairs in the back for elderly participants whom they wish to spare physical exertion, but this is not in accord with authentic Karaite tradition.

[11] Women sit in a separate area of the synagogue, and Karaites deny entry to the

synagogue to menstruating and postparturient women. Nevertheless, in the Beer
Sheva synagogue at least, some of the Psalms are led by women from their section,
and children are also able to lead the recitation of certain prayers. In classical Karaism,
women did not play a ritual role in the synagogues.
[12] A number of years ago someone sent me a clipping from the San Francisco Jewish
newspaper about a Karaite youngster who was given the choice between a Karaite and
a Rabbanite Bar Mitzvah. According to the newspaper, the boy chose the Karaite Bar
Mitzvah in order to maintain the family tradition. Apparently, it would be difficult, if
not impossible, to deny Karaite youths what has turned into the ultimate Jewish rite of
passage, even if it is not part of their tradition. Hence, Bar and now Bat Mitzvah have
become Karaite ceremonies in Israel and as well as in the United States.
[13] The biblical prohibition of aunt-nephew relations is found in Leviticus 18:12-13;
20:19; for a positive rabbinic statement about uncle-niece marriage, see B. Yevamot 62b.

Fig 1: Karaite Synagogue Interior - Ashdod. Note the
absence of chairs or benches. This feature is typical of
practically all Karaite synagogues in all countries of the
world; a few chairs for the elderly may be found at the
entrance in the area called *moshav zeqeinim.*
Photo by Mikhail Kizilov

[14] The summary by Michael Corinaldi, *The Personal Status of the Karaites* (Jerusalem: R. Mas, 1984) (Hebrew), is somewhat dated but still very useful.

[15] A number of aspects of Karaite law have not been surveyed here—for instance, ritual purity and impurity including laws of menstrual separation, as well as Karaite understandings of civil and criminal law and agricultural laws pertaining to the Land of Israel.

[16] A description of this community is available in Ruth Tsoffar, *The Stains of Culture: An Ethno-Reading of Karaite Jewish Women* (Detroit: Wayne State University Press, 2006).

Fig 2: Mezuzah - Ashdod Synagogue. A Karaite "mezuzah" placed at the gate leading to the entrance to the Ashdod synagogue. Karaite "mezuzot" are usually metal symbolic images of the Tablets of Law—and not parchments with biblical passages (Deut 6:4-9, 11:13-21) used by the Rabbanites. Karaites normally treat their mezuzot as Rabbanites treat theirs, e.g., kissing them upon entering a building. Photo by Mikhail Kizilov

Fig 3: Karaite Synagogue Exterior - Cairo. The Musa Dari Karaite synagogue in the center of Cairo is named after the most famous medieval Karaite poet, Musa Dari. At the moment it is forsaken by the community and is in the hands of Egyptian authorities; until recently there was a small library with Karaite books, photos, and manuscripts in the small building in front of the synagogue. Photo by Mikhail Kizilov

Fig 4: Karaite Kenassa - Chufut Kale (Crimea). Eastern European Karaites, who speak a Turkic dialect, called their synagogues "kenassa," a word of mixed Semitic origin (similar to the Hebrew *beit keneset*). The mountainous fortress of Chufut Kale was the main seat of the Crimean Karaites until the mid-nineteenth century. Note the unusual Oriental design of the building. Photo by Mikhail Kizilov

Fig 5: Karaite *Kapporet* - Halicz. The *kapporet* is a valence or short curtain hung on the Ark of the Law above the long curtain [*parokhet*]. This nineteenth century *kapporet*, with gold embroidery, originally was used in the Karaite synagogue in Halicz (now in Ukraine), formerly the site of the main Karaite community in Galicia. It was donated by Hanna, the wife of Rabbi Levi. Photo by Ivan Yurchenko

Fig 6: Karaite residents at the entrance to Karaite synagogue –
Jerusalem, 1921. The people in this photograph may have constituted
the entire Karaite community in Jerusalem in 1921. The man with a
beard in the middle is the *hazzan* [head] of the community; the man
standing to the right of him is the Crimean Karaite E. Sinani, later
also elected as the *hazzan*. After 1948, the community dwindled to
two persons only. Photo by J. Prik. Published in the Polish Karaite
periodical *Myśl Karaimska* Vol. 2, nos. 3-4 (1930-1931): 28-b.

Fig 7: Karaite Mug. The catchphrase "by the book" indicates the
widespread belief that Karaites are literalists who do everything
strictly according to the simple meaning of the biblical text. In
reality, they have their own exegetical stances which are often nonliteral; these alternate interpretations of biblical verses are the reason
for a legal system that is different than that of Rabbanite Jews.
Published with permission from Tim and Deb Arndt

# Without a *Minyan*: Creating a Jewish Life in a Small Midwestern Town

Daniel Mandell, Barbara Smith-Mandell, and Jerrold Hirsch

Throughout Jewish history, Jews have tended to live in community with other Jews. There are many reasons for this, but an important logistical reason is that although the basic unit of participation in Judaism is the family, a *minyan*—ten adult Jews—is required for many rituals and community celebrations, like reading from the Torah scroll. We do not have to have a rabbi or a cantor to lead a service, but most Jews, even those who are fairly well educated in the religion, cannot lead a service unless most of the participants are fully conversant in the prayers. And since the service is designed with the assumption that there will be a *minyan*, it does not lend itself very well to a setting that includes significantly fewer Jews than a *minyan*. Since hospitality is an important aspect of Jewish holidays, Jews tend to seek other Jews with whom to celebrate, enhancing our celebrations in many ways. Living in community gives Jews opportunities for worship, celebration, and support that are not available in areas without a significant Jewish population.

During the second half of the twentieth century, Jews have become a part of mainstream America, welcome in board rooms and private clubs. Part of that trend has been the growing percentage of Jews living in American metropolitan areas. Many Jewish communities in small towns in the Midwest and the South have shrunk or disappeared altogether as the children of immigrants find success as urban or suburban professionals. Another part of that trend is the increasing acculturation, rising intermarriage, and other developments that concern Jewish leaders, organizations, and parents. Many pages of many reports and many academic papers and conferences have been generated in dissecting and arguing about this trend in modern Jewish life.

But barely noticed and almost never written about are Jews living in small rural communities, often in very small numbers, who lack the institutions, organizations, and other support mechanisms that exist in and near cities. Indeed, the number of Jews living in small towns may be increasing. This is not only because at this stage in American Jewish history more Jews feel they do not need the security of a Jewish community, but also because through their work they are more and more integrated into American life, which often takes them to places they would not have expected to live in, places where there are few Jews. A significant and perhaps growing issue is how Jewish families and their children will manage in this isolation and (by extension) how or if Jewish institutions will cope with this aspect of modern life in the United States. In part to start a discussion of these concerns, the Mandell family—Dan, Barbara, and their two sons, David and Joshua (with the help of another Jew in Kirksville, Jerry Hirsch)—offers this account of their life in Kirksville, a small isolated town in rural northeast Missouri.

## OUR STORY

In July 1999, we moved to Kirksville so that Dan could take a tenure-track teaching position at Truman State University. At the time Truman was completing its transition from a regional teaching college to a highly selective statewide liberal arts college that was winning recognition from various national college-ranking services. For Dan, this was a great opportunity—and after seven years of wandering in the wilderness from one temporary position to another (and two years teaching secondary schools), it was the only opportunity to continue working as a scholar.

When Dan interviewed at Truman State University, the department and administration made sure he knew that he would not be the only Jew on the faculty and introduced him to another Jewish faculty member. But we were still apprehensive about this move because we knew Kirksville had no organized Jewish community. With a population of 17,000, Kirksville is the largest town in northeast Missouri. It is big enough to have a movie theater, some decent restaurants, and a Wal-Mart Supercenter. There is a public pool, a nice public library, a lot of small city parks, and a state park nearby. We were warned that we would probably miss the shopping and other conveniences of a larger community, but our only real concern was that the nearest synagogues were in Columbia, Missouri, ninety miles to the south, and in Quincy, Illinois, ninety miles to the east. The folks at Truman were helpful and supportive; we got acquainted and quickly found out that there were about three Jewish faculty members at Truman—and that was about all for the entire town. We were also living in the Bible Belt, something that was a new experience for us.

Our concerns about how we would manage in Kirksville were in large part shaped by what we had left. For a decade we had been part of a large and close-knit Jewish community in the Boston suburb of Sudbury, including many academics and artists, embracing and studying Judaism and seeking ways to make its traditions more contemporary. Shabbat was the centerpiece of our week and was truly a day of rest and rejuvenation with the community. We began with Torah study over bagels and cream cheese, with fifty or more participants drawing on history, psychology, language, and other elements to glean as much as possible from the week's *parasha* [Torah portion]. This was followed by services that would last two or three hours. There were no pews, no one sat on the *bimah* [raised platform], everyone participated in everything (including taking turns reading from the Torah scroll), and children played on the floor at the back of the room while their parents participated in the service. After services, there would be a *kiddish* luncheon where we lingered, sometimes for hours, as we ate and schmoozed. Even "minor" holidays were important community events: the Tu B'Shvat Seder packed the sanctuary; dancing, singing, and music overflowed the building on Simchat Torah; and only freezing temperatures put a damper on Sukkot's progressive dinner where we visited sukkahs at half a dozen homes before ending up at the synagogue, Beth El, for desserts [fig. 1].

Fig 1: Many families with young children attended services on a typical Shabbat morning at Congregation Beth El in Sudbury, Massachusetts.

Even in the Boston area, we were part of a minority, but there were lots of minority groups and most people seemed to know the basics and to respect the cultures of their neighbors. Being part of an active and vital Jewish community meant that the rhythm of our lives was largely dictated by the Jewish calendar. Before moving to Kirksville, we had lived for a year in the Chicago suburb of Carpentersville, where Dan taught at a private secondary school. We had not found another congregation like Beth El, but our lives did not change that much. In both Massachusetts and Illinois, most of the people we interacted with on a day-to-day basis were not Jewish and work schedules were still based on Christian holidays, but we never felt alone. Obviously, things in Kirksville would be very different.

We were quickly exposed to one of the more disquieting aspects of being Jews in a small midwestern town: the strange and occasionally tense conversations with non-Jews. A day or two after we moved in, a neighbor stopped by with a plate of cookies and told us to stop by if we needed anything. Two days later, Barbara needed some local information, so she went to the house of the cookie lady. She invited Barbara in, asked how the unpacking was going, and began chatting. After Barbara had jotted down the information she needed, cookie lady leaned toward her and whispered, as if sharing an especially good piece of gossip, "So I heard you're Jewish." Several times, when discussing with colleagues or acquaintances about how to meet people outside of the college, including other children to play with our sons, aged one and four and one-half, people suggested joining a church—including some who knew we were Jewish. One person said, "Well you live in Kirksville now, so can't you just go to church like everyone else?"

Many similar encounters gave us the clear message that we were somehow strange but could easily fit in if we tried. The prevailing culture in Kirksville is much more homogenous than other places we have lived, and that culture is ruled by the rhythms and assumptions of Christianity. Much of the social activity (especially in the summer) revolves around churches. Almost all social activities and sports are on Friday nights and Saturday mornings, and few people have any awareness of Jewish holidays. One of the few other Jews in town told us that when she told someone she did not celebrate Christmas, she was asked, "So when do you celebrate Christ's birth?" Somehow people thought even after they found we were Jewish that we could and should still attend a church [fig. 2].

Barbara in particular was confronted with this lack of comprehension because she was a stay-at-home mom for the first five years in Kirksville and interacted primarily with people outside the university community, while Dan from the beginning spent most of the day in the more cosmopolitan university. These conversations shaped subsequent relationships—or lack thereof. Because we do not attend a church and have experienced tensions in relationships with some of the townspeople we have dealt with in Boy Scouts and a few other organizations, we have very little social life outside of our Truman State University friendships. As a result, while in many ways we have adjusted to life in Kirksville, even after a decade we still feel like outsiders.

Fig 2: The churches in Kirksville are the center of social life
and there are strong communal connections among churches.

Our biggest problem—really, the boys' problems (although they may not
remember)—came in public school. David as the elder was first, and to some
extent he seems to have blazed a trail for his young brother. Kindergarten
was the most trying. In early December, the teacher started to incorporate
Christmas themes into art projects, songs, reading and writing assignments—
everything—and later there were special assemblies and decorations. But she
had no sense of how to deal with the inevitable issues that might arise for
a non-Christian student. When David became upset at having to attend yet
another Christmas assembly, she treated it as a discipline issue. We pointed
out that she should not force him to attend but should provide an alternate
activity, like reading in the library. So the next day, when there was (another)
Christmas concert, she sent him to the principal's office rather than the
library—as if he had violated some rule and was being punished. Things got
better over the years, and by third grade the teachers were aware enough to
offer secular alternatives to Christmas crafts.

Joshua has generally had better experiences with teachers, although both
boys are occasionally harassed by classmates from fundamentalist households
who seem to take great joy in explaining how they are going to hell, and

both boys are bothered by T-shirts with evangelical messages and the fact that classmates can bring Bibles to school, while they are expected to keep quiet about their religion. For both, throughout elementary school every year we had to explain to teachers and administrators (the same ones as the year before!) why our children would miss school on certain days and had to remind them that these were excused absences. Sometimes it took more than a gentle reminder. And we battled with the principal over whether Joshua should be eligible for the annual attendance award since the only school days he missed were for Yom Kippur and Rosh Hashanah. As a result of such stresses, both boys for years became defensive when, for example, a store clerk would wish us "Merry Christmas," and both are also adamantly opposed to public observance of any religion.

Some of these problems followed our boys to extracurricular activities and clubs. After David missed a soccer practice during first grade because of Yom Kippur, the coach kept him out of the next game as a penalty. Of course all of the soccer (and baseball) games were on Saturdays, while nothing was done on Sundays. Boy Scouts was another stressful situation. Forget the close connections with the hosting church and the fact that opening prayers were never really nonsectarian: adult leader training was scheduled on High Holy Days three years in a row, and the Scout summer camp near Kansas City (despite the presence of Jewish Scout troops in that city) seemed unable to deal with the need to avoid pork and shellfish, although they did manage to get a Chabad rabbi to visit—on Sunday morning. More generally, how much do Jewish children miss socially because they are not members of any of the numerous Christian youth groups in town?

Of course, most of our friends, acquaintances, and others we deal with regularly are not Jewish, and that is to be expected. But there is an inevitable moment in any developing relationship when religion comes up and we mention that we are Jewish and try to be observant. Sometimes we find that the person has never met a Jew and does not know what that means. In this area, new acquaintances often ask where you attend church, which forces us to decide whether to finesse the question, sound vague, or say simply that we are Jewish. To a large extent our decision depends on the situation, and over time, we have become better at saying we are Jewish and keeping the conversation short. Another aspect of settling in is how David and Joshua have become better at handling the very public celebrations of Christmas, although the "What is Santa getting you?" question continues to be a problem for the younger Joshua.

Missouri is part of the Bible Belt, and there are many fundamentalist and evangelical Protestant churches in Kirksville. So there is a general attitude of respect for religion, and for many people, this includes a respect for religions other than their own. Often, when someone finds out we are Jewish, they are interested and want to know more. But just as often, we encounter people who have a view of Judaism that is at best distorted and at worst simply wrong. Some know only what they learned in church Bible school about the Old Testament and think our beliefs and rituals have not really changed since biblical times. While they do not seriously believe that we still sacrifice animals, there are quite a few who think our goal is to return to those practices. Most believe that we are still waiting for the messiah—that is, the Christian definition of a messiah—because we just do not quite get it about a certain Galilean carpenter. And many think we will have a significant role to play in the End of Days. They are focused on beliefs and see what we are and do through that lens, so they are more interested in Jewish beliefs than ritual and are baffled by the way Jews tend to be distinguished by level of observance rather than minutia of theology.

For example, at our first Seder in Kirksville, one of our two guests was a reporter from *Rural Missouri* magazine who had asked to attend because he was writing a story on Jews in rural areas. He hung out in the kitchen while we cooked, asked lots of questions, and took a few pictures. Then he asked how we could be sure we had gotten all of the *chametz* [leavened products] out of the house. When we told him that we did our best and then recited a blessing in which we "disowned" any we had been unable to find, he responded that this just reinforced the idea that Jews were overly legalistic. We tried to explain that we saw it as taking the laws seriously, while recognizing the realities and limitations of real life. Somehow this led to contrasting the Jewish view with the Christian view of the laws in the Torah, and he told us that the problem for those of us who are still Jews was that nobody had really explained Christianity to us properly. We were taken aback, but since then, we have heard similar things, though not from guests at our table.

## JEWISH COMMUNITY IN KIRKSVILLE

Many people also have interesting ideas about the Jewish population in this area. While most say that we are the only Jews they have ever met, a surprising number are nevertheless convinced that there are lots of Jews in town and there must be a synagogue. An equal number tell us they are pretty sure there are not any other Jews in town, at least none who were openly Jewish. And in a number of cases, people have told us about friends who have a Jewish parent or grandparent, but they have attended this or that church for years. Despite the common assumption that Judaism, like Christianity, is based on personal belief, they still classify those people as at least partly Jewish and see them as slightly different. And one woman we met, whose grandmother was born Jewish but never practiced the religion, was sure that she knew more about our religion than we did because she had heard a few stories.

The actual Jewish population in Kirksville is fluid and hard to identify, partly because students at the university and medical school generally maintain religious ties to their home community rather than establishing new ties in Kirksville. Of course, more importantly, the lack of an organized community means that we are sort of invisible. For the first couple of years, each time we met someone Jewish, they said, "I thought I was the only one in town." They are not, but there is only a handful of Jews who celebrate holidays—which takes much more of an effort in Kirksville than in places where there are Jewish communities.

If we lived in a town with a Jewish community, it would be easy to meet other Jews. Here in Kirksville such meetings are rare flukes—and one has to pursue every opportunity. Once Barbara was in the grocery store and heard a woman (who turned out to be a medical student) asking whether the store carried matzah, so she followed her and introduced herself. Another time, the mother of a student was behind her in the checkout line and noticed her *Magen David* [Star of David] necklace. The woman struck up a conversation and introduced herself. We ended up becoming friendly and saw her several times while her son was at school in Kirksville. Once when Barbara and a friend were at a local coffee shop, a visiting doctor overheard them discussing Torah and introduced himself. Another visiting doctor showed up for our Tu B'Shvat Seder one year because someone at the medical school told him about us. We are not sure who told him and it was nice to have him, but it was interesting that the assumption was that anybody and everybody could just show up. But then again, our house has often been referred to as the center of Jewish life in Kirksville.

The most significant Jewish community in Kirksville has been the Hillel at Truman State University. Hillel students have had a major role in our lives, helping us fill our living room for holiday gatherings and planning and putting on Shabbat dinners and other events on campus. But that group did not exist when we first arrived. Many years ago, when more Jewish families lived in small towns in the Midwest, a local Jewish businessman bought a house where a small group of Jewish students could live and hold events, and he paid for a rabbinical student to come on High Holy Days. But by the late 1990s, the businessman, the house, and apparently most if not all of the Jewish families in the area had been gone for many years. We found a small, informal group of Jews (about five) and no trace of a Jewish student group on campus.

In the spring of 1999, a Jewish student approached Dan to help organize a Hillel, and the following year a small but fairly active group of students got involved: they obtained university recognition and national affiliation for the group [fig. 3]. Since then, Truman Hillel has grown and become well known on campus for their Shabbat dinners, annual Hebrew learn-a-thons, film series, and other events. The Jewish students are part of the sixty percent of Truman students who come from the St. Louis and Kansas City suburbs. Despite Truman's status as a highly selective liberal arts college, few actively Jewish students choose to come to Truman. Although their number has increased slightly over the past decade, from perhaps ten to about forty (with fifteen to twenty quite active), Jewish students with the kind of academic records that would allow them to attend Truman generally choose instead to go somewhere with a flourishing Jewish student life.

Since it became a formal organization in 2000, Hillel at Truman has organized various events and activities, depending on the needs and interests of the students involved.

o Since 2001, Hillel has held annual Chanukah parties, occasionally featuring events for the entire university community.

o Since 2001, Hillel has organized a week-long Yom Hashoah commemoration, including movies, speakers, and memorial services on campus.

o Since 2003, Hillel has sponsored for the university community an annual one night "Hebrew-athon," taught by a rabbi from St. Louis, which in 2006 had to turn down many students who wished to attend.

o In the 2006/07 academic year, Hillel has sponsored evenings of Israeli folk dancing nights.

o From fall 2002 through spring 2006, Hillel students held weekly kiddush and havdalah services on campus.

o In November 2005, Hillel participated in Shabbat Across America, including a community Shabbat dinner and services led by a rabbinical student from New York.

o In October 2004, Hillel sponsored a week of events on the Israeli-Palestinian conflict, including movies and a panel discussion-debate.

o In spring 2004, Hillel students held a fund-raising pizza dinner that was extremely successful and drew large numbers of students.

o In February 2004, a delegation of Hillel students from Truman attended the AIPAC Midwestern Israel Summit in Chicago.

o In the 2002/03 academic year, Hillel held a monthly Jewish film and discussion series that drew many students.

o After 9/11, Hillel students held a Yizkor service for the victims of the attacks on the World Trade Towers, and in 2006 held an anniversary memorial service.

*Hillel-community Chanukah party, 2003*

**OTHER RESOURCES**
Community holiday celebrations, including Tu B'shvat, Pesach, and Chanukah, involving students from Truman and AT Stil University, faculty, and area residents.

Judaic courses at Truman:
Judaism
Hebrew (Biblical), 1 and 2
Hebrew Scriptures
The Holocaust in History, Identity, and Memory
Vichy France and the Jews
(more under development)

**of TRUMAN STATE UNIVERSITY**

Fig 3: Truman Hillel has created a brochure to promote
the group and its activities.

Every few months, Dan receives an e-mail from a parent of a prospective student asking whether there is a Jewish community in Kirksville and Jewish students at Truman; some are probably wondering whether their daughter or son will be able meet a nice Jewish boy or girl here. Some say they are concerned that Truman might be dominated by Christian evangelicals who will target their children or that they will be the objects of other forms of antisemitism. While he can truthfully reassure them that antisemitism and other forms of harassment are not a big problem, he finds it more awkward to tell concerned parents about the lack of a Jewish community in Kirksville while still touting Truman Hillel's activities. He is helping Truman recruit Jewish students, trying to tap into the large pool of potential students in St. Louis and Kansas City that so far the school has had little success in attracting. Dan has also helped to make Jewish students feel more at home at the university—for example, by persuading food services to get matzah during Pesach.

More Jewish students at Truman would benefit our efforts to build a community in Kirksville. They play a very important role at the university and in Kirksville. And of course, Hillel students regularly attend celebrations with our family, giving us the community we would otherwise lack. Perhaps most importantly, Hillel events draw many non-Jews and therefore educate the university community about Jewish rituals, holidays, and history [fig. 4]. As Hillel has become more established, more Jews seem willing to be "out of the closet."

Fig 4: At Passover, Truman Hillel hosts a table in the Student Union Building to educate the community about Jewish traditions.

## JEWISH LIFE IN KIRKSVILLE

Most of our Jewish life in Kirksville has been within our household. One important observance that we have maintained is keeping a kosher kitchen. We began keeping kosher fairly early in our marriage and continue to do so, with separate sets of dishes for milk and meat and separate things for Passover. We have a third set of cheap plastic dishes for the other Jewish food group—Chinese takeout—but we still avoid pork and shellfish and do not combine milk and meat. There are two grocery stores in town—Wal-Mart and Hy-Vee—and the latter is willing to special order food and has been more likely to stock some kosher and Passover foods. For a while we bought kosher chicken there because they were willing to store a case and allowed us to pick up a few boxes at a time. But this stopped after the manager ended up with a case of frozen kosher turkeys when we asked him if he could get us one for Thanksgiving—they got annoyed when we said we did not need one for Christmas. But generally the unavailability of kosher meat in Kirksville (aside from Empire kosher hot dogs) is for us not a problem because our older son is vegetarian, the younger one mostly so, and we generally eat fish or tofu products.

We usually buy a few prepared kosher foods at a store in Columbia, where our synagogue is located. This is particularly important at Passover, but over the past decade the Columbia store has stocked fewer Pesach items and less of each type. Starting several years ago, Hy-Vee started carrying a limited but vital selection of Passover food, apparently in part because Truman food services began regularly buying from them large amounts of matzah for Jewish students. For less-common items, like whole-wheat matzah and cereal kosher l'pesach, we have managed in different ways. For several years we had Dan's mother in Tucson ship it to us; two years ago Dan happened to be driving back from the St. Louis airport just before the holiday and stopped at a store; and last year he was in Chicago for a conference and filled up a suitcase that he carried back on the train.

For people who keep kosher, eating out is a challenge almost anywhere. When dining in restaurants, we look for dishes that are either vegetarian or kosher by ingredient—meaning they could have been kosher if they had been made in a kosher kitchen. When we ask about ingredients, it is often easier to mention lactose intolerance or shellfish allergies or to say we are vegetarian—otherwise, we have to explain at great length why we cannot mix meat and milk or must avoid shrimp. Most people know that Jews do not eat pork but think that is the only element in keeping kosher, and we would rather not discuss religious rules in every conversation. Moreover, we have noticed that many people in the Kirksville area do not know what "vegetarian" means and apparently think it refers only to avoiding red meat (i.e., beef). At various times, we have been told that pork egg rolls, a dish containing shellfish, and a cream sauce containing bacon bits were all vegetarian.

One of the more fascinating and challenging aspects of our experiences in Kirksville is that fundamental theological differences have shaped our experiences and particularly our problems in ways we did not anticipate. We somewhat expected that we would spend a lot of time explaining ourselves and our religion to other people in town because we would be the only observant or at least knowledgeable Jews they have met. What we did not expect is that many assumed that because they are Christians they already know a lot about Judaism because, as they say, Christianity replaced Judaism. Unfortunately, most of what they think they know is wrong. For example, we are not sitting around waiting for the messiah to come. We are not going to recoil in shock and bewilderment if they tell us we are going to hell because we do not believe the right thing.

These may sound like abstract and distant theological minutia that should not affect day-to-day life, but somehow they do, at least in this part of the United States. If you think religion is based on personal beliefs and that the individual's relationship with God is central to your practice, then you approach the whole subject of religion differently than when you see religion as a set of behaviors that are practiced within a communal setting and that the community's relationship with God is central. We begin with the assumption that religious pluralism is normal and good. But many people we meet who claim they have no problem with religious pluralism still insist that their religion has The Truth—which means that they feel it their duty to tell you that Truth. This tends to make us want to roll our eyes and is not something we experienced before we moved to Kirksville. So we are often a bit nervous whenever the subject of religion comes up because we are afraid someone is going to ask us why we do not accept Jesus as our personal savior or ask "but you still celebrate Christmas, don't you?" or try to tell us that the problem is that we just do not understand Christianity properly.

All of this underlies our basic dilemma. While much in Judaism is centered in the family, an active community is vital to observance. And while other aspects of life are very nice in Kirksville, unfortunately that particular (and very significant) part seems unlikely to change in the near future.

## HOLIDAYS IN THE WILDERNESS

Our tradition tells us that, more than Jews keeping the Sabbath, the Sabbath has kept the Jewish people. This became very apparent in our experience in Kirksville, in which bit by bit we have stopped doing the Shabbat things that used to be so important to us. When we first moved to Kirksville, we knew that the long distance from the synagogue was going to affect how we celebrated Shabbat. During our first year, we were able to participate in a Torah study group that met on Saturday mornings, led by the wife of a medical student, with ourselves and two other faculty members. Unfortunately, the group dissolved when the medical student graduated and moved away; the others were not interested enough to keep it going, and both drifted away from Jewish practices soon after. After that, we were pretty much on our own.

We did join Congregation Beth Shalom in Columbia, ninety miles and nearly two hours away, and every few weeks we went there for services. In a weird, contradictory way, the long travel times made Shabbat once again a daylong event even though it violated the basic point of it being a day of rest. Initially we went for Friday night services and drove home afterward, even though this meant that Shabbat dinner was sandwiches or fast food eaten in the car and we could not light the Shabbat candles. After services, we would stay around and chat for a little while, but the children, then preschool aged, were tired and we needed to head home. We eventually shifted to attending Saturday morning services, which allowed us to have a relaxing Shabbat dinner with candle lighting and challah—but shifted the burden of traveling to another day and made for a very long day for the boys. To attend services in Columbia meant packing up toys, books, snacks, and often lunch and spending almost four hours in the car. If the weather was nice, we would go to a park or something in the afternoon, but few people attended services and no other families were bringing children, so we were unable to make the kind of connections that would make the day enjoyable for both parents and children.

For several years regular attendance at Beth Shalom helped us keep the "fence" up that makes Shabbat special and holy. But it bothered us that so few members of that community came to services—some Saturdays they did not even make a *minyan*. No children of our sons' ages attended services, so the boys spent most of the time outside the building or reading in another room, which made it seem less meaningful as a family. Because we lived so far away, we felt more like celebrities than members of the community; we were unable to attend other types of events, which were held during the week, and while we made some friends we never felt that we had really become part of the community.

If the week had been particularly busy, if the weather or the roads were bad, or if we were just too tired for the long drive, we did not go. For a couple of years, the boys played soccer, which meant not going to services at all during soccer season, and for a while, Boy Scout activities often interfered with Shabbat. If we lived in a community with a synagogue, these activities would not have meant the whole family missing services altogether. We could have left services early to get to a soccer game, or the adults could have taken turns attending Scout activities with the boys. Dan's job has also, at times, interfered with our ability to observe the Sabbath. Truman always scheduled recruiting activities and parents "meet and greet" events for Saturday mornings. While Dan could and for several years did decline to take part in these events, he also recognized that if the university was to attract more Jewish students, he needed to meet potential students and parents.

Ironically, we really got out of the habit of going regularly to Beth Shalom when our sons began Hebrew school in 2001; since we had to take them down there on Sundays, also going on Friday night or Saturday was too tiring and too expensive. And then the rabbi and congregation decided to reduce the length of Yom Shabbat services to about the time that it took to drive there, which meant that we were traveling for twice as long as the time we actually spent "shabbating." We still went once or twice a month, but then the price of gasoline began zooming upward. Last summer (2008) we went only once, only rarely went during the school year, and have not been to services yet this summer.

In other ways the town, the neighborhood, and our jobs have exerted pressures that have worn away at Shabbat. For example, while we do not live in a particularly noisy neighborhood, people around us mow their lawns on Saturday and on Sunday do quiet things. After Barbara went back to work, we sometimes needed to do some errands or housework on Saturday that previously she would have gotten done during the week, and since many places are not open on Sundays, some errands had to be done on Saturday. Other pressures have increased as the boys have gotten older. One factor was that they wanted to do regular things like watch TV and play computer games, and we had nothing interesting to offer them instead. For a long time we just said no, but we had to compromise. We did not want them to see Shabbat as a day of boredom and deprivation, and we had no alternatives.

We decided that when we cannot do specifically Shabbat things, like praying, studying, and socializing with a Jewish community, then we should try to do family activities together, and this has often included TV, computers, and other traditionally non-Shabbat-like things. With the public library open on Saturday afternoons and closed on Sundays, going to the library seemed like an appropriate compromise activity for Shabbat. But recently, Dan's research and writing projects seem to be calling him to spend more time with them, so that some Saturday mornings he will go downstairs to his study and write. In the afternoon, he will often go bicycling with a friend whose need for company has increased as his wife's health has worsened. That too seems like an appropriate thing to do on Shabbat—at least more so than many other activities. But if we lived close to a synagogue, we could take turns going to services or Torah study if the whole family cannot or did not want to and would at least have the opportunity to socialize with others who are also observing the Sabbath. At this point, we often feel that we are no longer keeping Shabbat but are only remembering it—and sometimes it seems we are barely doing that.

We always attend High Holy Days at Beth Shalom, though that also has had its challenges. We found it strange the first year, when we found that the congregation borrowed the larger Baptist Church in Columbia; the few crosses that could not be removed or covered up bothered us, although we did get used to the building after a few years. We always stayed the night in Columbia rather than go back and forth from Kirksville: initially in a hotel, then in the farmhouse that the congregation had purchased, and more recently (as the boys have grown) in the more comfortable hotels. This is a major expense and requires extensive preparation, packing, managing meals, arranging pet care, and other concerns that would be irrelevant if we lived in the same town as our synagogue.

While we are not completely happy with our synagogue, we realize it is doing the best it can. It has grown over the years since we moved to Kirksville, bought its own land and recently built a sanctuary, and has a fairly active program even as other Jewish communities in Missouri are dying. During the past five years, several synagogues in central Missouri and northern Arkansas have closed and given their ritual objects and remembrance boards to Beth Shalom. This is part of the larger story of American Jews as the grandchildren and great-grandchildren of those who had lived in rural communities, especially in the Midwest, have moved to the cities to attend universities and become professionals. Those going in the other direction are relatively few, but given the circumstances of Jews in America, it may be growing.

So at this point, our Jewish life is largely in Kirksville, and other than Shabbat it is centered in the holidays we celebrate with others: Chanukah, Tu B'shvat, Pesach, and Sukkot. Right from the beginning, we found that we needed (and wanted) to have non-Jewish friends participate in our festivals. Part of this was the simple desire to share, but more critically, without them we would rarely have more than our family and a few others at the celebration. As time went on, Truman began attracting more Jewish students, and they

Fig 5: Our friend Jen and her son Christian
light Hanukkah candles with us.

attended many holiday events. Still, the participation of non-Jewish friends
was and still is very important to us. In a very substantial way, the regular
participation of non-Jewish friends in our celebrations is our community in
Kirksville [fig. 5].

We usually have a latke party for Chanukah and invite everyone to bring
their *hanukiot* [Chanukah menorahs] and to play dreidel; at this festival we
occasionally get a few families with children. At Tu Bsh'vat we have a Seder
that Barbara wrote with some Beth El friends years ago, and usually several
friends participate with us. And at Sukkot we build a large sukkah and host
at least one large potluck dinner [fig. 6]. But Pesach has been perhaps the
most important celebration for us—which fits into the general trend among
American Jews. We use our own *Haggadah* [book for Passover Seder], which
we put together from various sources, designed to keep all of the essential
elements and incorporate some new ones while relying heavily on English
translations. Over time, the number of participants has grown, cresting at
about thirty-five, although we reduced it last year to only twenty-five. To
keep kosher l'Pesach, we do all the cooking, although those who can manage
bring raw ingredients, and some friends and students come to help with the
cooking. We have also twice received grants from Hillel-Soref to help defray

Fig 6: At Sukkot, non-Jewish friends join us
for a potluck dinner in our sukkah.

Fig 7: Truman students create a family for us at Passover.

costs since many attending are Truman or medical school students who cannot get home for the holiday [fig. 7]. One medical student attended all of our holiday celebrations for three years, and at his last Seder he made a little speech thanking us for providing him with a Jewish community. But it goes both ways: we were grateful to him for giving us what we needed—people with whom to celebrate over the years. Students are a wonderful and critical part of our Jewish community, but unfortunately as soon as we really get to know them they graduate and leave town.

We love having a big crowd for the Seder, and we are grateful to all those who come and celebrate with us. It would not seem like a holiday without our friends and our community. But because people know we host a big Seder and are happy to invite people who just want to learn, sometimes we look around the room and realize that we will need to explain the Seder as we are going through it because most of the people in the room are not Jewish and this is their first Seder. We may talk late into the evening, but that is not because we are debating the serious spiritual and philosophical issues raised in the Seder ceremony but because we are explaining the Seder, the holiday, and our entire religion to those who are there to learn. The first night Seder often ends up being so much work that we do nothing special for the other nights of Pesach, and we miss being able to just participate in a Seder without having to do all the work. We worry that our children's Jewish education and their experience of the holidays are skewed by the constant emphasis on educating non-Jews about our exotic customs. We wish they could live somewhere where they did not always have to explain themselves and were not so often the first Jewish persons someone had ever met.

## OPENLY JEWISH IN THE BIBLE BELT

Right from the beginning of our lives in Kirksville, we have been some of a very few "public" Jews in the area. There are many interesting aspects of being the only identifiable Jewish household in the town. For example, putting the Chanukah menorah in the window of our living room is traditional, but here it takes on special resonance [fig. 8]. Several years ago, the boys insisted that we get an electric menorah that attaches to our big picture window that can be seen from the street, and every year since then they make sure that is up and lit every night. Perhaps the best symbol of our life in Kirksville is that, five years ago, we purchased a sticker for the rear of our car: it is a fish, on the outside like those various Christian fish that so many cars in town sport, but inside that outline it has the word "GEFILTE" [fig. 9].

As a result of being open about our religion, a regular aspect of our lives

Fig 8: Each family member has a favorite hanukiah [Chanukah menorah], and we light them all.

Fig 9: It's easy to see which car is ours in the Wal-Mart parking lot.

in Kirksville has become educating others about Jewish culture and traditions, especially holidays. When the boys were younger, Barbara was regularly invited to talk to their classes about Chanukah. One time she and David even made and cooked latkes in the classroom. Friends in Truman's religion department who teach Judaism or world religions invite her to talk to their classes about Jewish culture and traditions. She finds that it can be fun and is happy to do it, but we are sometimes disconcerted when people with whom we have no connection ask us to do things for them. For example, the high school world cultures class has a section on Judaism, and one year a woman called us out of the blue to ask if her daughter could borrow some menorahs to show for her project on Chanukah. Another time a student asked Barbara to provide recipes for traditional Passover foods for his project—due the next day.

Some requests have been more intrusive. One time Barbara got a call from a teacher at a high school located an hour away, who asked her to talk to his class on a particular date and time. When she said she could not, he became irritated and told her that when he called a mosque in Kansas City they had agreed to send a person who worked there, and so he felt Barbara (who has a very different full-time job) should be equally available. In the end, it turned out that she had to go to Kansas City, so she agreed to stop in Brookfield and talk to his class on a different day. While even that was inconvenient, Barbara was concerned that if she did not go, the teacher would assume that all Jews were aloof and selfish.

Some of our more interesting experiences have been at Pesach. One year a Mormon discussion group asked Dan to come talk to them about Passover. Unfortunately, they asked him to come the first night of Passover. They picked another evening, and it was an interesting experience; but he is still not sure they actually believed him when he told them that most Jews are not eagerly anticipating that the messiah will come rebuild the Temple in our time. About five years ago, an acquaintance whose church was holding a Christian version of the Seder asked Barbara to provide recipes and matzah. She made this request two days before Passover; we were busy with our own preparations, we had purchased what little matzah we had in Columbia, and at the time none was available in Kirksville. Two years ago, a Christian student group asked us to provide a Seder plate and other objects for their Christian Seder, which they were holding during Passover, when we needed to be using them ourselves. But it was better than the previous year, when they advertised and held an "authentic Jewish Seder" without talking to the Hillel students or us.

It is not that we mind being asked to educate others about our religion and culture, but apparently to some people, that is our only reason for being here. We would not have minded if they wanted to interview one of us, but in some cases, we felt that they were not interested in us as individuals; instead, they saw us as "official" Jewish representatives or (even worse) they just wanted our stuff. We do see educating others as something we should do, but it totally changes the focus of our own holiday preparations and celebrations to have to spend so much time dealing with other people's needs.

## RELIGIOUS EDUCATION

Religious education is an important part of Jewish observance, but when the synagogue is so far away, decisions about religious school end up affecting the rest of our life. When we moved to Kirksville, Joshua was one and David was four and one-half. We assumed that much of their religious education would be what they do at home on a regular basis, but we have also sought to get them a more standard Hebrew and religious training. About 2001, we began taking them down to Columbia every Sunday for religious school. The experience was not always a good one—after sitting in a car for almost two hours, the boys did not want to sit still and pay attention in a class. And needing to drive to Columbia every Sunday meant that we really did not want to drive down on Saturdays for services.

Then three years ago, a student sent Dan an e-mail telling him she was about to start at Truman and asking whether there was a synagogue and religious school in Kirksville, as she had been teaching in a congregation outside St. Louis and hoped to continue. There is no synagogue, he told her, but have we got a couple of boys for you! She began tutoring both boys but soon found it best to focus on Joshua while helping Barbara with the curriculum for David. This worked very well: last December, David became a Bar Mitzvah in Columbia [fig. 10]. We studied at home with the assistance of a tutor from the congregation who worked with us via e-mail. David read his portion flawlessly after giving an amazing *drash* [commentary]. Unfortunately, most of the Kirksville contingent was unable to make it because of an ice storm that closed the roads. The student working with Joshua has begun Truman's Master of Arts in Education program, and so she should be here long enough to help him prepare for his Bar Mitzvah ceremony.

## THE CHILDREN SPEAK (WITH JERRY HIRSCH)

One way of gaining a telling perspective on Jewish life in a small midwestern rural town in the late 1990s and early twenty-first century is to look at questions of identity, of being a minority, and of antisemitism from the perspective of children who are growing up in this world. For that reason I conducted oral

Fig 10: David became a Bar Mitzvah in Columbia after studying
at home with mom and occasional coaching sessions with
a creative tutor in Columbia.

history interviews with Joshua, age ten, and David, age thirteen. These were open-ended interviews, not questionnaire-driven sessions. The interviews took place in October 2008, during the presidential campaign, an event both boys tried to integrate into their American and Jewish identities.

A sense that they were Jewish and that made them different permeated the interviews with the Mandell children. Clearly their primary Jewish community was their family, where they learned about and practiced Judaism and being Jewish [fig. 11]. Between them and a larger gentile (overwhelmingly Protestant) community, there was no cushion of having other Jews who understood them and their experiences, and most importantly there were no other Jewish children for whom living a Jewish life was important.

These two children have very strong positive feelings about being Jewish and equally strong negative feelings about the experience of difference in a community where as Jewish children they are virtually alone. Each child recalled antisemitic incidents vividly: Joshua talks about how hard it is to be Jewish in Kirksville, "without everybody teasing you all the time." Asked to describe this teasing, he responded: "it's like whenever something bad

Fig 11: David and Joshua enjoy taking turns holding
the havdallah candle at the end of every Shabbat.

happens they're like, it must be another Jewish conspiracy. In other words, they're real jerks." David is unlikely to ever forget "finding that the swastika has been carved into the desk. And wondering what will it take for them to replace the desk. What will it take, a huge four letter word scrawled across the entire thing?" He tries to take a large perspective on the students who do this: "they're ignorant. Most people don't know what a Jew believes." From the interviews, it is apparent that the boys do not in response play down there Jewish identity. Just the opposite is true. And they maintain a strong sense of the injustice of antisemitism that helps them link their Jewish and American identities. Asked about good things about Kirksville, Joshua declares, "there aren't religious laws forcing us to believe one thing."

In his ideal world, "it would be against city law to mock someone because of their religion." He perhaps at times fantasizes a world in which the tables would be turned and you would, as he says, "need a license to not keep kosher"—but he also immediately concludes, "no, that would be kind of rude." Reflecting on the harsh treatment he occasionally receives from other children, he weaves together both the abstract principles of religious freedom and kind manners. David would like to live in a "more accepting community." He would like not to be asked so often, "Do you celebrate Christmas?" and

"Are there Chanukah figures like those in Christmas stories?" Jews, he points out, "want separation of church and state."

Aside from overt antisemitic incidents, Joshua and David have experienced on a regular basis the incomprehension, insensitivity, and ignorance of a community where Jews are virtually unknown. This is not limited to just other children, nor is it limited to just some adults. The issue of difference has made itself manifest in the institution in which they have spent a good part of their lives—public schools. They have a clear sense that not only other children but also public school educators make too little effort to accommodate difference and, indeed, often do not think they should have to do that. David comments that, at every stage of his schooling, "when everyone else was getting perfect attendance . . . I wasn't." Some of these educators have no sense that it is wrong to call being absent for Yom Kippur an unexcused absence, while ignoring the fact that since Christmas is an official school holiday the majority is accommodated so that there is no issue of an unexcused absence. David recalls that "on the High Holidays we've had to deal with the schools counting them as unexcused absences." He sees the issue of difference and majority privilege and insensitivity clearly: "they still said that because it's the majority that is Christian, they don't have to count Jewish holidays as excused absences." David makes it clear that he thinks these school officials are "pretty dumb" and that in his view their policy is "unconstitutional."

David in particular resented that some teachers insist that they know more about Judaism than he does: "My teacher even thinks a Jew has to believe in God, which isn't true; if you are Orthodox, yes, but if you're Reform or something, not really." This is but one example, but it stands out for David because right now he considers himself "an atheistic Jew." But aside from defending his own views, he is clearly irritated that non-Jews, even some of his teachers, presume to know all about Judaism and attach too little value to his experience and knowledge. This insensitivity at times carries over into incomprehension about why assignments that posit children living in a Christian family are wrong for Jewish children. Nor did he think he should have gotten "in trouble" when he said "the Easter bunny didn't exist." David makes clear that he has little patience with adults who ask if he has "a Chanukah figure," presumably like they have Christmas figures.

My sense that neither child thinks about being Jewish as only a burden is confirmed by their strong identification with the Jewish life and practice of their parents, their sense that antisemitism is not only painful but wrong, and their creative response to their situation. David not only talks about celebrating Shabbat in his family but also regrets "we haven't been able to make our own challah. Usually we have to settle with twisted bread rolls."

He mentions that he liked making challah. At Passover, Joshua likes looking "for the *Afikoman* [hidden piece of matzah] over and over and over and over and over and over and over." His answer to the question, "Who asks the four questions?" is hardly matter of fact and quite revealing: "Me always, because *I'm like the youngest Jewish person in town* probably besides someone else who isn't actually old enough to ask the four questions" (emphasis added). As important as they find Jewish family celebrations, including both those just with their parents and those where guests are invited to the house, Joshua and David are well aware that to go to a synagogue, for example, for Sabbath services or for Yom Kippur, "they have to," as Joshua puts it, "go to Columbia every single time." Joshua, as is David, is ambivalent about this because of the hour-and-a-half drive each way. On the other hand, David points out that he does like the open discussion on Shabbat of the Torah portion and recalls interesting sermons by the rabbi, such as one on the environment.

In response to a world, in this case, a school, saturated with Christmas stories, these two boys have created and developed their own stories about the Chanukah slug. It is important to see the stories as more than a form of self-defense, although David recalls, "someone asked me if I had a Chanukah figure and I said, yes, we have the Chanukah slug." And surely there is some fun, transgression, and aggression, when David told the other children that instead of milk and cookies, "we leave [the Chanukah slug] beer." Both boys, as one would expect, like the presents that come with Chanukah, the latkes (the cat, Pumpkin, getting sick eating latkes is part of family lore), the menorahs, and the candles. Joshua is very enthusiastic about how "my brother tells funny stories about the Chanukah character he made up called the Chanukah slug." He clearly enjoyed retelling how "the Chanukah slug, it is has a Star of David on its back and carries all the presents and [my brother David] says the reason that Chanukah is eight days long is because the slug takes so long to deliver the presents." How elaborate this story cycle is is not entirely clear, but as the boys point out, one year Chanukah "lost one day because the Chanukah slug had an implant that made him faster." What clearly comes across in this story cycle is how much both boys enjoy telling and performing these stories. Their own creativity is a source of pleasure for them. In addition, the performance affirms bonds of community for them that defy and/or counter a less sympathetic outside world with its Christmas characters.

Both boys also claim that being for Obama over McCain is in line with Jewish tradition and values. Both boys intensely dislike Sarah Palin's evangelicalism, although they do not use that word, and her attitude toward the environment in general and toward hunting moose in particular. (Joshua and David try to be vegetarians and also see that as compatible with their

Jewish identity.) The point here is not whether they are right about politics but that they integrate their being Jewish into the fabric of their lives as Americans. David declares, "Obama is more sympathetic to Jewish values," does not favor the rich over the poor, and, more than McCain and Palin, stands for "separation of church and state." And he makes assumptions about what it might mean to have a minority status in the United States: "Well for one thing [Obama's] a minority and we can identify more with that than McCain and because McCain is bland." If, by calling McCain "bland," David meant that, unlike minorities, the majority does not have a distinctive culture, he would be echoing a thought common among both those perceived as the majority and those seen as minority groups in the United States. This widespread perception, although it is probably wrong, affects how Americans think about each other.

There is no denying that growing up Jewish in a small town like Kirksville is difficult for Joshua and David. And while they convey a sense of meeting the challenges and embracing their Jewish identity, the story is not all one of triumph. The question of whether they would like to live where there was a larger Jewish community and synagogue elicited a sort of "yes" response and a protest that the idea was too abstract, something they had never experienced. And while it is difficult to talk about what was not said in the interviews, it is possible to make some inferences. Being Jewish for these two boys is rarely routine. Some adult Jews are concerned about the shallowness of merely going through the routines of Jewish observance without contemplating their meaning. But there is a positive side to routine; it is the familiar that makes us feel that we are with others in our community, that we are at home. For Joshua and David, being Jewish is all too rarely familiar and reassuring. The nearest synagogue in Columbia is an hour and a half away, and the boys find the trip a burden. Joshua points out that if "there were more Jewish people [in Kirksville] then someone would start a synagogue." And as it turns out, going to Columbia has not, in fact, created for them a community of Jewish children who would find them not different or odd for being Jews, but part of their community. They do not see the community of people who come to the Mandell house for Jewish holidays, such as Passover, as their community. Joshua off the top of his head imagines that anyone who is Jewish who comes to the Seder must be coming from Columbia—which is not the case, as he knows when he stops and thinks about it a bit longer—because he can hardly think of Kirksville and Jews outside of his family. Nor, as David points out, are most of the people who come over people he feels are part of a familiar community: "I look forward to Passover. And I look forward to some people coming over. About half the people, I don't know so, you know." Much of the time he says, "I keep to myself." A sense of difference and aloneness is not inherently a negative experience, but when coupled with a sense of isolation, it is clearly difficult. Perhaps even David's Jewish atheism is tied to his lack of a Jewish peer group. Perhaps it is a reaction to the fact that the only people in Kirkville his own age who talk effusively about believing in God are evangelical Christians.

When I started this interview project, I assumed I would hear a lot from Joshua and David about both antisemitism in Kirksville and about the richness of the Jewish life their family practices. I did, indeed, hear about these things. I anticipated to some extent that the absence of a Jewish community in Kirksville would be important. Adult that I am, I did not think enough about what it must be like to not have a peer group of Jewish children where much could be taken for granted, where there was little need for explanation, where one could relax and just be someone who was Jewish. A self-conscious identity has in various ways been a positive part of their lives; but unlike Jewish children in communities with other Jewish children, they do not get to experience many moments of Jewish identity as shared and accepted, a "natural"-seeming part of daily cultural life.

## JEWS IN OTHER SMALL TOWNS

Our situation in Kirksville is important to us, of course, but does it have any larger significance or connections to larger developments among American Jews? Lee Shai Weissbach, historian and author of *Jewish Life in Small-Town America: A History* (2005), found that most Jews in rural and small-town America before 1950 owned and operated small stores. Many were "well integrated into local society and came to play prominent roles in public life," although widespread Christian prejudices and stereotypes of Jews generated anxiety and a sense of social separation. There was usually only a single synagogue in the community and few other opportunities for Jewish education and culture. Maintaining Orthodoxy was especially difficult, and "observing the traditional prohibition against work on the Sabbath was particularly hard and often abandoned" because most rural Americans shopped on Saturday and Jewish merchants depended on that business.[1]

Peter Rose, in *Strangers in Their Midst* (1977), provides a more in-depth study of small-town Jews in the mid-twentieth century, based on a fairly extensive survey in 1958 of Jewish households in seventy-one communities in upstate New York and "several" in Pennsylvania. He predicted that those families that identified as Jews in these towns might actually have a more intense sense of identity than those in cities with Jewish neighborhoods, "for they could well find themselves in the position of representing 'their people' to the communities in which they lived." Most (96 percent) had come from a city rather than being born in the town. A slight majority was either in medicine (36 percent) or nonmedical professions (15 percent) such as lawyers, accountants, or engineers, all of which required skills lacking among locals who had not gone to college. The other major occupational category was merchants, with 20 percent of the small-town Jews surveyed.[2]

Rose found that these families had and often expressed the desire to be recognized by the Christian world—for example, by explaining their holidays by comparing them to Christian or secular ones and practicing only those that made sense in the American Christian context. What drew them to the small town was economic need; for example, that was the easiest place for a small peddler to become a merchant and for a refugee to practice medicine. But the cost "was often an overwhelming sense of alienation," a fear of "being swallowed up by that Christian world that had allowed them entry," and the constant fear that their children would become non-Jews—although in fact their children tended to more open and outspoken about their Jewish identity.[3] This seems a fair reflection of our situation in Kirksville. Rose also noted that his subjects would also need to either participate in small-town events and culture or be completely friendless. We are not sure in which category we belong: we are part of many university groups and activities, but our efforts to participate in town organizations were relatively tentative and have almost completely ceased.

Weissbach found that in the last few decades, small-town Jewish life has changed. Jewish-owned businesses have been replaced by chain stores, and Jewish children have pursued university educations and professional opportunities in cities. The numbers of Jews in small towns are growing, but most are professionals, educators, or retirees rather than entrepreneurs or merchants, and "they are seldom socially marginalized in small-town society."[4] Some sociologists who study contemporary Jewish population dynamics are fairly certain that the movement of Jewish professionals to small rural towns is an important development, even though the larger pattern in the twentieth century has been from rural to urban and suburban areas. Sergio DellaPergola, head of the A. Harman Institute of Contemporary Jewry at the Hebrew University of Jerusalem, notes that the movement of Jews from cities to rural areas

> is not a mass movement, but it is an increasingly visible part of American Jewry. The reason is obviously the national spread of socioeconomic opportunities, and the occupational skills of Jews who are generally highly educated. There are two opposite trends at work

here. Usually large metropolitan areas offer more opportunities of the kind congenial to Jewish population training and skills. . . . But there is also the opposite. . . . Many universities and research facilities that are attractive to Jewish manpower are located on purpose out of the main metropolitan areas. Many of the old minor communities in the US have declined because they were located in locales mainly based on basic resources processing and on manufacturing, and these places had little to offer to Jews. The new locations offer more sophisticated employment in the tertiary services, higher education and the like and are attractive to Jews. In addition, the overall acculturation of Jews in America tends to create a sort of major convergence in geographical terms between Jews and the total (white) population.[5]

Facilitated by the Internet and other technologies that allow rapid communication and have to varying degrees eliminated the need to be near one's suppliers and clients, and driven by the rising costs of urban and suburban living, a noticeable number of high-tech companies and various professionals have since the 1980s been moving to rural areas, such as small towns in Idaho or in Iowa. Many Jewish professionals have become part of this movement.

## PRESERVING JEWISH LIFE IN RURAL AREAS

Since our situation is not unique but is rather part of a developing trend, our experiences raise the question of how Jews, individually and collectively, in parts or in the whole of the United States, can or should adapt to this development. We do have some recommendations that would enhance our Jewish lives and help others in very small rural communities expand their participation in Jewish rituals and celebrations. While there are important logistical difficulties for Jews in rural areas, the need for community through regular interactions with other Jews poses a much greater challenge, and it is a need that Jews in isolated areas cannot solve on our own.

• Create virtual communities through discussion groups, Facebook, or other technology that would link Jewish individuals and families in rural areas, creating a twenty-first century social web that would offer much of the support and assistance that other Jews find within their local synagogue or Jewish community center.

• Encourage and help urban Jewish federations to work with and reach out to Jewish individuals and families in rural towns within their region.

Through existing religious movements, have rabbis or rabbinical students visit such individuals and families on a regular basis. Perhaps the Chabad's experience would help in this effort.

• Encourage congregations that draw Jews from surrounding rural areas to make a special effort to integrate those individuals into the community socially and to consider scheduling changes that would increase opportunities for participation by Jews living at a distance.

•   Create opportunities at Jewish camps or other institutions for family vacation programs in parts of the country where Jews live in isolated communities.

When we moved to Kirksville, we knew that there were few Jews and no congregation here, that we would have difficulty getting kosher food, that we would probably be seen as somewhat different, and that to a large extent our household would need to be the center of our Jewish life. But we did not anticipate the effects, some subtle and others profound, that living in Kirksville would have on our lives and our family. In a community where social lives are centered on churches, we continue to feel like outsiders even after a decade. We struggle to balance our need to fit into the community with our desire to maintain our individual distinctiveness. A seemingly mundane but nagging example of that tension is that people get together to socialize on Friday nights; everyone mows their lawns on Saturday morning and afternoon; and schools, clubs, and teams have events on Saturday because Sunday is reserved for church and family.

Because we do not quite fit in but rather stand out as being different, we have become the Jewish representatives in Kirksville. We do not always feel like everything we do is seen as somehow reflecting on the Jewish people, nor are we conscious that people are judging us according to their preconceptions of Jews. But we do spend far more time and energy explaining our holidays, rituals, and aspects of our beliefs than we expected or desire. It can be almost laughable, like the time that, after ten minutes of us explaining how we celebrate Chanukah and not Christmas, someone asked "So, when DO you celebrate Christmas?" It can be somewhat annoying, as when others expect that we will loan them ritual objects or when we have to persuade the school administrations several years in a row that our children are allowed by law to be absent for High Holy Days without penalty. And it can be agonizing, as when our sons are told by classmates that they are going to hell.

Certainly there are many rewarding aspects of our situation. We have become the Jewish community center in town: the place where Jewish students year after year can come to observe holidays away from home and where non-Jews can learn about and participate in holidays. We have helped establish a strong Jewish organization at the university, and not infrequently we serve as a significant resource for the town. We are proud of our heritage and what we have been able to offer Kirksville. We think our situation has helped teach our sons empathy for those of other minority groups. But our situation places a burden on us to be available and to play host for every occasion rather than being able to just relax and enjoy ourselves from time to time. We desperately wish there were a few more permanent Jewish residents of Kirksville who also wished to celebrate Shabbat and other holidays—at least a *minyan*!

## NOTES

[1] Lee Shai Weissbach, "Jews in Rural America," in *The Encyclopedia of Rural America* (2 vols.; 2nd ed.; ed. Gary Goreham: New York: ABC Clio, forthcoming).

[2] Peter Rose with Liv Olson Pertzoff, *Strangers in Their Midst* (New York: Richwood, 1977), 1, 4, 64-65. Rose limited his study to communities with fewer than 10,000 residents in which ten or fewer Jewish families lived (2, 54). One of his students did a follow-up study in the mid-1970s of the adult children of those same families, which is the last chapter in the book.

[3] Samuel C. Heilman, review of *Strangers in their Midst, American Journal of Sociology* 84 (1979): 1307.

[4] Weissbach, "Jews in Rural America."

[5] Electronic correspondence to Daniel Mandell et al. from Sergio DellaPergola, Shlomo Argov Chair in Israel Diaspora Relations, The A. Harman Institute of Contemporary Jewry, Hebrew University of Jerusalem, October 16, 2008.

# Raising the Bar, Maximizing the Mitzvah: Jewish Rites of Passage for Children with Autism

## Steven Purzane

As an invested cantor from the Hebrew Union College School of Sacred Music, I began working with developmentally challenged youth about ten years ago. Initially they were primarily learning disabled, but over time I worked with children with Tourette's syndrome and Asperger's syndrome. I eventually came to focus almost exclusively on children diagnosed with autism.

In the early days of my work I was generally informed by the parents of their child's diagnosis, not necessarily because I wanted to know, but because anxious parents understandably wanted me to know what I was up against so that I would not have unrealistic expectations as to what their children could achieve Hebraically and Judaically. Given their difficulties with English subjects, including reading, very few of the children had expectations that they would be able to master Hebrew. I certainly did not want to turn the Bar or Bat Mitzvah into yet one more venue in which the children were fearful of judgment or failure. Nor, conversely, did I want to turn it into yet one more venue where the children were essentially given a "free pass"—that is, told overtly or covertly that because of their "shortcomings and deficiencies," everyone had nothing but the lowest possible expectations for them.

From the very beginning, and long before I had any real mastery of this subject, it was obvious to me that these children were far more capable than the diagnoses would indicate and those around them would expect. This capability was routinely confirmed as one after another demonstrated poise and competence during their Bar and Bat Mitzvah ceremonies, which were truly "off the charts."

Also from the beginning I could sense the devastating impact of several scarcely noticed but pervasive influences in their lives: constant focus on their shortcomings, coupled with endless feelings of failure based on little more than inability to handle the pressures of the standardized testing that was used to identify, quantify, and ultimately modify those shortcomings; and methodologies that were poorly attuned to apprehending and depicting the true essence of the child but remarkably good at reinforcing feelings of inadequacy and brokenness.

If the spiritually rich potential of this venerable Jewish rite of passage was truly going to be fulfilled, it would need to be an exquisitely crafted experience that carefully tapped into and strengthened parts of the children that were routinely overlooked, and very likely damaged, by many secular therapies and educational modalities.

To be sure, such transformative potential is an inherent, albeit increasingly unrealized, component of all *B'nei Mitzvah* ceremonies. But it soon became clear to me that for children who are rarely embraced by the Jewish community, rarely given opportunities to shine and show what they are made of, rarely experience being loved and accepted exactly as they are, this ancient Jewish ritual and the restorative elements it contains could potentially be the single most important experience of their young lives and, by extension, in the lives of their family and community.

That, however, was far from a "given," not an automatic feature of a special-needs Bar or Bat Mitzvah ceremony. Elevating it to that place would depend heavily on whether the teachers, tutors, and clergy held this as the goal or merely saw it as a one-day event for the special-needs child and those around him or her to feel proud and included.

Make no mistake: if that were all that happened, *Dayenu*, we would be grateful and sing praises to God for empowering us to provide such an experience. But as we know from the words we sing on Pesach, when we say *Dayenu*, we are really indicating how grateful we are that God not only took us out of Egypt but also gave us the Torah, the Sabbath, and a whole array of gifts and opportunities that went far beyond any one benefit.

So yes, a one-day event to feel proud and included unquestionably is grounds to sing *Dayenu* and *Halleiluyah*, but based on what I observed in the course of bringing dozens of special-needs children to Torah, it is paltry compared to the extraordinary life-affirming and life-transforming potential that this remarkable ceremony, and everything that precedes and follows, can represent to them.

In the beautiful and mystical prayer *L'cha Dodi*, written by poet and mystic Shlomo Alkabetz in the northern Israeli city of Safed, we encounter this *chochma*, this bit of wisdom, in the last line of the second verse: *Sof Maaseh B'machshava T'chila* [The end of the deed lives in the initial thought that creates it].

As applied to this discussion, that wisdom reminds us that the outcome of our efforts will emerge from the intention or the *Kavanah* that sparked the efforts in the first place. As valuable as this may be, so long as we see the goal of these services as driven by our Jewishly mandated obligation to provide equality and inclusivity, we will be placing considerable limits on the transformative and therapeutic impact on the children, dramatically reducing the likelihood that the benefits experienced on that extraordinary day will be an ongoing and positive influence in all aspects of their lives.

It seems cruel to lift them up in this way, with little concern as to how to sustain and maximize the experience (and I mean much more than a special-needs post-Bar Mitzvah class). At its core this represents a failure to substantively understand and address the child's true needs and potential, to embrace Judaism's real ability to nurture both of these, and to truly recognize our skills as religious leaders to bring all these positives together in a profound and permanent way—the very things the children and their families are hungering for but rarely getting from the outside world.

That this failure so frequently occurs lies, I believe, in how extraordinarily deferential we as a Jewish community have become to anyone and everyone with lots of letters after their name, lots of credentials, lots of bona fides. So when a parent of a special-needs child approaches us, we are inclined to refer them out to the proper "expert," usually a secular specialist who is truly "qualified" to deal with such things.

But that is not why parents approach us in the first place. They and their children generally have no shortage of such expert influences in their lives. They approach their religious leaders to provide them a vast array of services that are not in their lives: People to love, honor, and accept their children unconditionally. People to provide the pastoral care not found in the doctor's office. People to bring them beneath the sheltering wings of community that they are so desperately lacking. People to help them vanquish, once and for all, the devastating sense of isolation and exclusion that is a hallmark of special-needs families. The very thing that communities of faith and their leadership are historically well equipped to address, if only we understand our potential to do so not just for the mainstream but for everyone.

That we so regularly fail to do so, that we are so quick to "refer them out," is, I believe, a reflection of a mindset described in Exodus 13:33, when the spies returned from the land of Canaan to report on the inhabitants there. Upon their return they told their fellow Israelites "as we were grasshoppers in our own eyes, so we were grasshoppers in the eyes of the inhabitants of the land."

It is inconceivable that a seminary education (particularly one that includes virtually no course material to prepare us for the growing onslaught of special-needs children) might contain the requisite skills to effectively deal with such complex, daunting, and mysterious behaviors—symptoms and syndromes that even the best and most sophisticated medical scientists clearly do not understand.

How could we possibly expect that, equipped with little more than quaint and antiquated Jewish principles and practices, we could provide the core therapeutic benefits that these children and their families need and deserve— and that state-of-the-art clinicians and therapists seem so much better trained to deliver? In the words of Tevye, unheard of, absurd!

This mindset also reaches into the Orthodox community. Consider an article in *Jewish Week* titled "'Invisible Disability' Kids Are Being Left Out." It was written recently by Rabbi Dov Linzer, the rosh hayeshiva and dean of Yeshivat Chovevei Torah Rabbinical School, and his wife Devorah Zlochower, who teaches at Salanter Akiba Riverdale High School (SAR) (and she served as rosh beit midrash and director of full-time studies at Drisha Institute for many years). They are the parents of two children with Autism Spectrum Disorder (ASD).

Their observations are profound and disturbing, particularly as we are almost falling over one another to congratulate ourselves for the wonderfully inclusive services we as a community are providing after years of neglect. An entirely different picture continues to emerge, when we begin to actually talk to the parents of these children, who still feel perennially underserved, misunderstood, and largely unwelcomed by the Jewish community.

Here is some of what Linzer and Zlochower had to say in November 2009:

> Why are these disabilities "invisible?" When you see our children and others similarly diagnosed, you think they are "typical" children. These kids are often verbal and sometimes highly articulate; they are of average intelligence and even extremely bright, and their ability to maneuver physically, socially and emotionally in the real world seems unimpaired.
>
> In reality, these kids are dealing with a lot of complex issues. Many of these children find our loud, smelly, busy world overwhelming and may take refuge by shutting the rest of us out. Some seek out even more sensation and have difficulty modulating their voices, sitting still or remaining quiet. Many of them have trouble making and keeping friends despite an often passionate desire to do so. A need for order and control may make the regular, chaotic play of many children unappealing or scary.
>
> More profoundly, these disabilities are invisible because these children have become invisible in our community. Synagogues do not provide Shabbat programming for children who cannot handle the standard Shabbat groups or junior congregation. Day schools do not educate many of these children, and prayer services in synagogue are not welcoming places for these families.

While there have been a number of stories in the Jewish media recently about the rare programs that do exist, more often, families like ours hear that such programs are too expensive and serve too few children to make them viable. We in turn have pulled away from the community in our search to have our children's needs met.

We send our children to secular schools and camps that serve the special-needs population, we consult with psychologists, psychiatrists and neurologists rather than our rabbis, and we create community with each other, the folks who "get it." And we convince ourselves that we are doing just fine all by ourselves.

The truth is that we and our children need the support and acceptance of our community. We have asked for help in the past, but we have been told "no" so many times that by now we feel it is futile to ask. And we are angry—angry because our children survive by our advocating for them, and advocacy is not always pretty.

Our synagogues and our Jewish communal institutions need to become safe spaces where we can bring our children, confident that their behavior will be tolerated or, better yet, understood. Our children are entitled to learn and live their Jewish heritage, and they cannot fully do so if they continue to exist at the margins of the Jewish community.[1]

If these parents, so highly Jewishly educated, so deeply involved in Jewish life and community, feel "referred out," feel excluded, feel the need to access secular advisors rather than their clergy, it is truly mind-boggling how excluded and disconnected people of far lesser Jewish connection and resources feel.

But whatever the level of Jewish involvement, truly welcoming and inclusive offerings remain few and far between, neither accessible nor affordable for the overwhelming majority of Jewish special-needs children and their families. To the extent that they are offered at all, the programs are marginal extracurricular enrichment programs that pose no challenge to, nor raise any questions about, the predominantly secular regimens that dominate these children's lives. Nor do they seriously suggest any substantive manner in which our rich Jewish heritage could offer a full-bodied, robust, viable, holistic, and compassionate alternative to a status quo that is increasingly fiscally unsustainable and decreasingly effective in providing true quality of life.

Logically, the Jewish day schools would be the place where this more complete and healing Jewish experience could be provided. But for the most part, the parentally driven need to compete with the best and brightest college preparatory academies in their midst renders them disinclined to admit those who will divert scarce resources or reflect poorly on their record of academic achievement. It is the inevitable result of replacing quintessentially Jewish values with those of the marketplace.

All of this could easily be dismissed as interesting theory if there was no hard evidence that simple and profound Jewish principles and practices properly applied produce the kind of real-life transformative results described above. But family members describe exactly that outcome, talking about the remarkable increase in scholastic achievement, social skills, and sense of self-confidence directly attributable to the expanded "whole person" approach to their children, that was incorporated in every aspect of the *B'nei Mitzvah* experience.

Such testimony, coupled with other reports and direct observation, led the sociologist/anthropologist in me to ponder the specific structural elements that were producing such impact, often when nothing else was working.

I was eager to distill and apply these elements in a manner that would maximize such transformative impact for each and every special-needs Bar and Bat Mitzvah child. And perhaps most importantly I wanted to explore how such elements could be woven into a broad range of life-affirming, nurturing, and joyful therapeutic activities in no way limited to one faith tradition, one locale, or one rite.

The *B'nei Mitzvah* elements I isolated and successfully applied are not rocket science. They are things that we know work, that we routinely demand for ourselves and our neurotypical children, but that we do not routinely offer to children who have been diagnosed with developmental challenges. We obviously, and I believe falsely, believe that their challenges render them sufficiently different from the rest of the human species that they neither need, want, nor are capable of appreciating the basic offerings that we and our typical children simply take for granted. We must also consider that this attitude generates regimens and lifestyles so abnormal, so devoid of a proper balance of mind, body, and spirit, that they produce far more damage than the underlying problems they are designed to address. Rabbi Hillel said do not do unto others that which is hateful to you. Jesus said do unto others as you would have them do unto you. It would seem when it comes to this special-needs population we are heeding little of this ancient wisdom.

## ELEMENT 1: RELATIONSHIP

I believe the single most important therapeutic element that must be at the absolute core of every special-needs *B'nei Mitzvah* is the indispensable and life-sustaining experience of deep, personal relationship. It is the sense of being "gotten" at the deepest level. Social scientists have suggested that the lack of that experience is as damaging to our emotional and psychological well-being as oxygen deprivation is to the brain. Based on what I have directly observed, children and adults with developmental challenges rarely, if ever, have this experience.

To guarantee that this indispensable ingredient is consistently included and delivered means truly learning what it means to be an "observant Jew": one like Moshe Rabeinu [Moses, our teacher], who actually noticed that the bush burned unconsumed, while others might have simply walked on, or perhaps worse, in the parlance of modernity, grabbed a garden hose and extinguished the voice of God for the risk that it represented to life and property. It means learning to be an "observant Jew," empowered to see, celebrate, and support the vast array of interests, gifts, and potential that are part of all human beings, including those with developmental difficulties; it is an inherent part of being created *B'tzelem Elohim*, in God's image. Things like passion and compassion, enthusiasm and joy, love of music and animals. Things impossible to measure, lying well beyond standardized diagnostic and therapeutic procedure, perhaps more the stuff of art, philosophy, and religion than science, medicine, and psychology, but nonetheless real.

In the words of a sign that hung on the wall of Albert Einstein's Princeton office, "Not every thing that counts can be counted, not everything that can be counted counts."

If we honestly examine our own life experience, it is these intangibles, these "unmeasurables," that make us who we are, that make our lives worth living. We would also likely recall the vital role of a handful of people who believed in, reflected back, and helped nurture these elements, often before we even recognized them ourselves. It is said that faith is the belief in things unseen. In these instances our lives were transformed by someone in our midst "keeping faith" with our very best selves. Doing that requires time, patience, intuition, respect, deep love, and a willingness to persevere beyond external manifestations.

In the normal course of events, none of this is likely to occur once a diagnosis of developmental disability is delivered. The diagnostics focus on shortcomings, not strengths; diagnosticians have neither time nor training to identify these vital intangibles; and the hand-in-glove therapies that emerge are dis-integrative and designed to manage, modify, or medicate each area in which the child fails to measure up. While it is more than possible to impart and improve needed skills from a place of wholeness, it is not possible to arrive at wholeness by addressing in piecemeal fashion a raft of deficiencies. As we learn from the parable of the blind men and the elephant, the whole is always greater than the sum of the parts.

If properly understood and applied, the simple rite of passage of *B'nei Mitzvah* (and its parallel in other traditions) can serve as a powerful and remarkably cost-effective therapeutic antidote to this. This is particularly so if we are astute enough to sort out the therapeutic threads, reweaving them into new tapestries capable of embracing the broadest cross-section of tradition and belief, the widest spectrum of developmental challenges.

## ELEMENT 2: PRIDE OF ACHIEVEMENT

Because efforts at early intervention tend to focus so heavily on repairing deficiencies, they consistently reinforce feelings of brokenness and offer few opportunities for the children to demonstrate competence and potency outside of the narrowly defined parameters of success inherent to the therapies. Part and parcel of this are inherently lower or different expectations, and more often than not people tend to live up to those standards—be they high or low. Sort of like Goldilocks and the porridge, it is more of an art than a science determining what the appropriate level of achievement should be in terms of the Bar or Bat Mitzvah. Quite frequently, clergy who have minimal training or experience with ASD will suggest the most minimal of accomplishments, like touching the Torah, or saying "Amen" after someone else says the blessings before or after Torah. On the other hand, others will say that if a child can read Torah only from a transliteration (which for many children is in and of itself a huge accomplishment), they are not eligible for Bat/Bar Mitzvah. To me, the bigger question is how much effort is being invested to explore the individuality of the child, so that the requirements represent not some abstract standard but true growth and authentic accomplishment that can become significant building blocks for feelings of potency to be utilized in far broader real-life circumstances. Part of this entails creatively expanding our thinking beyond the tried-and-true tradition of chanting Torah and reciting blessings, to find ways to incorporate the particular skills and interests of the child into the ceremony. In the case of one of my ASD students, this meant investing enormous time and energy into his musical talents, something that had been grievously overlooked in his secular school settings. When he was allowed to sing and play instruments, he felt the inherent reward of doing something at which he could excel. Having this as part of his Jewish coming of age reinforced positive feelings toward Judaism, and as his grandfather said afterward, it "changed the way everyone in the family will look at him from this point forward." The grandfather also observed that the extraordinary accomplishment, well beyond everyone's expectations, was quickly followed by a demonstrable increase in his grandson's interest in and achievements at school. But again this success required sufficient investment in time to ascertain these skills, the resources and inclination to engage these skills, and the creativity to make them an inherent part of the ceremony.

Sometimes the skills are less obvious, less easily incorporated than musical ability, but nonetheless important or accessible. One of my students demonstrated consistent interest and ability in the area of technology. Because his service was not on the Sabbath, there were no concerns about the use of electronics. I decided to encourage this student to create a full multimedia presentation in PowerPoint, which he did with remarkable skill. To so do required his seeking help from other family members when he ran into some of his own limitations, most particularly in finding appropriate resources that would properly elucidate the key themes of his Parasha [Torah portion], which was Shoftim: "Justice, Justice shall you pursue." So while still maintaining creative control, he engaged with family members in ways that were more positive than had often been the case, most particularly with his older brother. The sense of accomplishment he felt was enormous and immediate, something that he had not previously had a platform to experience and demonstrate. The same creativity that allowed this to occur is another thread that can be distilled from this religious event and woven into a fabric of activities accessible to special-needs children of diverse backgrounds and ability.

## ELEMENT 3: MUSIC AND RITUAL

Inherent in virtually all religious and spiritual traditions is sacred music, which is the vehicle and conveyor of generational ethos that goes well beyond the cognitive. Music is certainly a key element of the Bar/Bat Mitzvah rite of passage. Coupled with this religious and spiritual tradition is extensive research demonstrating the musical abilities of ASD children as well as demonstrations of the power of music to calm, heal, and stimulate key neural pathways in children with autism.[2] In his bestselling book, *Musicophilia*, renowned neuroscientist Oliver Sacks further illustrates these points. So the blending of sacred music, text, ritual, and rites of passage into a seminal event presents an extraordinarily rich opportunity to touch and move the ASD child in truly transformational ways.

In one instance, I worked with a child who had little or no consistent speech. I did notice, however, that he joined in group singing, and frequently he could be heard singing the lyrics and melodies on his own. His mother had observed the same thing, but she doubted that he would be able to produce a result on cue or at appropriate times in the service. It turned out that this musical proclivity was sufficiently strong to enable him to master his prayers and Torah portion in a musical rather than verbal manner, as well as to focus him sufficiently to demonstrate that mastery even in the midst of the distractions inherent in being in front of hundreds of people, many of them strangers. Apparently, the part of his brain that manages music was far more intact than that which manages speech, and I have no doubt that ongoing stimulus of this healthier part could be used to stimulate, heal, and benefit the speech component as well.

The fact that his Torah portion was chanted from a transliteration rather than directly from the Torah in Hebrew was of absolutely no concern to me, considering the remarkable achievement that even this represented in this child's life and the manner in which it changed the perceptions of those around him (particularly since it is so frequently such limited and limiting perceptions that circumscribe such a child's existence). This is another clear example how all the elements work in concert. Deep relationship allows us to see the particulars of the child and adjust requirements and standards to those that are both achievable and beyond normal expectations, leading to pride of achievement, which provides ongoing benefit, particularly if built upon down the road. It is what in Hebrew is referred to as *Da Lifnei Mi Ata Omeid* [Know before whom one stands].

## ELEMENT 4: COMMUNITY

Several years ago, National Public Radio aired a show called "The Autism Chronicles," produced by Dan Collison and Elizabeth Meister for Long Haul Productions, in association with Chicago Public Radio. Perhaps the most poignant moment for me was when one single mother, a devout Catholic and active member of her church, sat alone in the waiting room of a renowned pediatric specialist, about to receive the news about her developmentally delayed son. The diagnosis, though not as bad as she feared, was nonetheless devastating, particularly considering her deteriorating financial circumstances and a second child at home that required her attention. Not surprisingly, she could not conceal her emotions and wept openly in the doctor's office. He did his best to comfort her, but without a doubt, the minute she left the office she was pretty much on her own. I thought about how many times a day that scenario is played out somewhere in this country and how little support such people receive from religious institutions, whether they are members or not.

I have also seen how this paralyzing sense of isolation is as destructive as the diagnosis itself, not only to the child but also to the entire family structure in which he or she exists. While there have been some excellent efforts to provide support systems that ameliorate this isolation, they are still few and far between, and for the most part they are secular in nature. Even as synagogues strive to provide more-inclusive opportunities for special-needs religious education, this rarely extends to the worship opportunities or specialized pastoral counseling so desperately needed by the families. Nor does it include opportunities for day school education. For many Jewish families, the special-needs Bar or Bat Mitzvah represents their very first contact with Jewish life, their first experience of being embraced by the Jewish community. If it is handled well, incorporating the entire family rather than just the student, and if it is followed up in comprehensive and substantive ways, this process can be a true win/win situation, dramatically improving lives while drawing in a significant demographic to Jewish life heretofore totally disconnected. But as said before, *Sof Maaseh B'machshava T'chila* [The end of the deed lives in the initial thought that creates it].

If the focus remains on the student only, on one venue, and on a one-time event, none of this progress is likely to happen. Moreover, if the inclusion rests almost exclusively on secularly oriented educators rather than clergy, the critical piece of pastoral counseling that typical families routinely rely upon and enjoy will not be available to these special-needs families who so desperately need it. Given the various obstacles that such families feel to participation in religious life, extra efforts, more creative experimentation, and more resources will be required to find the right mix that respects the congregational desire for decorum and solace, while not excluding those who might be less able to adapt to such demands. Thus, the catch phrase, sometimes we have to do extraordinary things so ordinary things can happen. For special-needs families, inclusion in religious life would be far from ordinary.

## NOTES

[1] See "'Invisible Disability' Kids Are Being Left Out," *The Jewish Week* (9 November 2009); http://www.thejewishweek.com.
[2] See http://www.coastmusictherapy.com/articles/diagnosisautism.

## FOR FURTHER READING

Shelly Christensen, *Jewish Community Guide to Inclusion of People with Disabilities* (Minneapolis: Jewish Family and Children's Services, 2007).
Zalman Meshullam Schachter-Shalomi, *Spiritual Intimacy: A Study of Counseling in Hasidism* (Lanham: Jason Aronson Publishing, 1990).
William Stillman, *The Soul of Autism: Looking beyond Labels to Unveil Spiritual Secrets of the Heart Savants* (Franklin Lakes: Career Press, 2008).